52 Churches in 52 Weeks

DAVE BOICE

52 Churches in 52 Weeks

Some names, personal details, and event sequences have been changed to protect the privacy of individuals.

Published by Fox River Ink, LLC

ISBN 978-0-692-18042-6

Printed in the United States of America

Cover design by Dave Provolo
Photography by Dave Boice
Copy editing by Elisabeth Chretien

CONTENTS

*Author's Note: This story is meant to inspire and be a positive outreach to you as the reader. While maintaining honesty, some churches were left unnamed if I felt that my lone visit may have been perceived as negative. There's great people within a church body, and just because I may not have had the best experience, that shouldn't reflect negatively on everyone associated that attends every week.

THE WAYFARING STRANGER

It all started with a bad date.

Based on her Christian Mingle profile, she was drop-dead gorgeous: brown Bambi eyes, feathery blonde '70s hair, and a 10,000-watt smile that was brighter than Thomas Edison's basement. After exchanging a few emails, we made plans for a fun-filled Saturday night at a bowling alley with a full-service bar and restaurant.

She pulled up in a neon-yellow car, her first name written on the license plate. When she stepped out and looked at me, my eyes lit up like disco balls in a John Travolta movie. My heart danced in time with the disco beat in my head, and as I confidently walked toward her, I imagined what it'd be like to have her as my girl. But first, I had to introduce myself.

"Hi, I'm Dave."

Intrigued, she flashed me a smile. With the wings of heaven at our feet, I took her by the arm, and we cha-cha-cha'd inside for our first social engagement together.

It was pulsing in there: the music was pumping, bowling pins were clattering, and everyone seemed to be in high spirits. However, when we got to the desk to stake out a lane, we discovered that there was a slight problem: all of the bowling lanes were reserved for a party.

No sweat.

I suggested we sit down in the restaurant, enjoy dinner, and get to know each other a little first. As we were seated, I made a well-timed dad joke, which made the waitress laugh, which made my date laugh, which gives social proof that you too can laugh at the horrible jokes in this book (I really don't want my mom to be the only one laughing at me). My joke must have been even more successful than I had hoped, because after it, she stared into my eyes just a few seconds longer than strictly necessary to give off that attractive vibe (cue the Barry White music). Twirling her curls, she said she wanted to know more about me (if only she were attracted to my apparent overuse of parentheses in this paragraph).

After an hour of dinner and some lighthearted back-and-forth chatter, my plan was to keep escalating the chemistry and have some laughs while bowling. We walked back over to the attendant who said the party was still going on and asked us to give it another 45 minutes.

Grr. Fine.

We sat down at the bar. Since our mutual attraction was founded on Christianity, our conversation soon moved to the subject of church. She loved her Foursquare church and told me how great everything was: the pastor, the music, even the friendships she had formed there. I didn't even know what a Foursquare church was, but I smiled and nodded approvingly, bobbing my head like Will Ferrell and Chris Kattan to Haddaway's "What Is Love" from that old Roxbury skit from *Saturday Night Live*. When she had finished her description, she smiled and looked down, searching for her next words.

"Would you like to go with me some time?"

I paused for a moment. Her question ricocheted off me like a bowling ball hitting a 7-10 split.

"Nah, that's okay," I responded, afraid of trying a different church even if it meant a great lead-in for a second date.

"Oh, okay. Well, tell me about your church."

"My church?"

"Yeah, what do you like about it?"

Nothing, I said to myself. "Everything," I said to her with a lying grin.

She was so passionate about her church, and I wanted a Christ-based relationship with a girl like her so badly, I felt the need to lie and be completely inauthentic about my true self. Instead of telling her the truth— instead of telling myself the truth—I spun elaborate stories about how great my pastors were, how inspiring the sermons were, and how much "fun" church could be.

I even made up a story about how powerful one of our pastor's illustrative sermons was, describing an imaginary scene where he brought in a sack of 30 pieces of silver and dumped them out onto the floor in front of the pulpit. As the spare change clattered to the floor, the pastor asked what price on earth would be worth betraying Christ and giving up eternal salvation.

"You just had to be there," I assured her. *That never happened*, I reminded myself, betraying my integrity in hopes of getting a kiss at the end of the night.

The truth was, it had been months since I had gone to the "One True Church," as my pastor lovingly called it. I had seen too much division, too much denial, and too much pain caused by the mighty fortress of my Wisconsin Evangelical Lutheran Synod (WELS) church. I recalled how, during my ushering days, the pastors denied communion to visiting believers, causing newcomers to leave in humiliation. When my brother developed his own reservations about the church, he told me about the threatening excommunication letter he received that not only made him throw in the towel on church in general, but the very idea of God altogether. And then there were the rumors about an associate pastor who allegedly became a bit flirtatious with an underage girl from his Bible study group, forcing a swift resignation that was quickly swept under the rug and never mentioned again. Over time, sermons stopped being about Christ and instead focused on everything wrong with other church denominations. Our sins would surely be forgiven, but members of those other "churches" who preached false teachings would go directly to hell. I was sick of the constant condemnation and double standards, and soon, I too found myself in the church's crosshairs, recently being questioned about my own lack of attendance. How soon would they excommunicate me too?

When I was finally out of fake material to puff myself up, I looked back at my date. She looked away bored. Our conversation had become stilted; our connection, shifted. Did she know I was lying? Suddenly, my hopes for a second date seemed to have more in common with the bowling pins crashing in the background than a rousing disco tune.

It was getting late, so after a third failed attempt to get a lane, I asked if she'd like to grab dessert across the street instead.

She yawned. "I actually need to head home."

Not this again, I thought. *Why didn't I take her up on the offer of visiting her church earlier? Stupid.*

I walked her back to her car, knowing a first kiss, first hug, first anything, was out of the question. In a desperate attempt to land a spare, I asked, "Do you—ya know—want to do this again sometime?"

"Maybe." She shrugged, quickly climbed into her car, and drove off.

Another promising first date had sunk straight into the gutter. This one had even given me a chance, and I had blown it.

Since getting dumped by the girl whom I had thought was The One, I had been tallying how bad my dating life was. My scorecard was rapidly closing in on 50 failed first dates with Christian women. Friends joked that I should write a book about it. The silver lining was that I had learned a great deal about women in the process, but something was still off. I wanted to find a Christian woman, but what kind of Christian man can't

3

stand to set foot in the only church he knows?

I drove home from the bowling alley in complete silence. I was stranded at a spiritual crossroads, trying not to blame God for my misfortunes. I still identified as a follower of Christ, but had too many reservations about organized religion. It felt too big, too political, too man-made, and too far from the basic premise of following Jesus. Considering that I had never met Jesus—or for that matter, seen His divine image in a three-cheese pizza—I wasn't sure what the basic premise of following Jesus even really, *truly* entailed. Still, it was something I needed to come to terms with and do something about.

Every Christian is faced with a spiritual identity crisis at some point, and their individual life experiences will ultimately dictate which direction the person will go. Based on relatively insignificant experiences, I found myself questioning the entire institution of the church. I had to do something. But what? How do you start over when you've invested your entire life, your entire identity, in one church? My concern—or my fear, if I wanted to be completely honest and vulnerable about it all——if I only followed Christ and dismissed the church entirely, what would I lose in the process?

So what came out of that drive home?

I made a decision that would start the very next morning. Left with no place to call my spiritual home, I would give church one final chance, a last-ditch effort to go all-in on my faith. Instead of writing a book about 50 failed first dates with Christian women from a variety of denominations, cities, and backgrounds, I would chronicle my experience of "dating" a new church each week.

Where will I go? Who will I see? How will this journey improve my faith? Who is inspiring others in their convictions?

As you'll begin to read, *52 Churches in 52 Weeks* is a wayfaring stranger's spiritual quest for something more. It's an exploration of what's being preached and practiced throughout the continental United States in the present day.

What started out as a crazy idea to find a new hometown church in wintry central Wisconsin ended up spanning from the streets of New York City to the beaches of Los Angeles. I sampled Catholic, Lutheran, Baptist, Presbyterian, Pentecostal, Quaker, Greek Orthodox, Christian Science, and many more denominations. From 20,000-seat megachurch stadiums to being the lone congregant at a Scientology service, no service was too big or too small. There were doll churches, heavy metal rock churches, even churches that staged professional wrestling events, all serving as niche entry points for new believers. You'll hear from some of today's most popular and well-known preachers, most intellectual speakers, and most controversial pastors. Along the way, we'll explore various issues that challenge what it means to be a Christian in today's increasingly secular age.

This book is for those who have found themselves teetering between faith and doubt. Maybe you were like me—contemplating abandoning God's grace and trashing faith altogether because traditional church is no longer helping—or you know someone who is.

This isn't your mother's devotional. Not every chapter will conclude with a warm-fuzzy, feel-good, Jesus-y type of verbal embrace. I'm not an esteemed pastor, priest, or theologian with a fancy-schmancy seminary degree that needs to appease a congregation. No, I'm a sinner—a single, lone sinner who sat in a different pew each Sunday morning for a year. I'm a sinner whose faith was tested, beaten down, and bloodied to the point that it made me question the entire institution.

Just like in the Biblical stories about Abraham, Jacob, Moses, David, and Jesus, it's our responsibility to go out into the wilderness to find our faith, face the wild unknown, and be tested through some level of suffering, all to find not only ourselves, but God. In essence, it's the traditional hero's journey in search of strength, wisdom, and knowledge who comes back beaten, yet victorious.

CHURCH 1:
CHURCH LADIES ENJOY MY WARM HANDS
MT. CALVARY LUTHERAN CHURCH • ROTHSCHILD, WISCONSIN

I t all happened so fast.

One minute, I was chanting the Apostles' Creed with about 50 other congregants at Mt. Calvary Lutheran Church. The next minute, every sweet elderly lady within my pew's proximity was shaking my hand during the traditional greeting, saying, "Peace be with you."

One of the ladies did a double take after shaking my hand, turned back to me, and complimented, "You have very nice, warm hands." She then turned to three of her friends, and they all nodded in agreement.

"Oh yes, he does have nice, warm hands," another said as her husband hmpf'd and turned away, facing forward in his pew.

"Thank you" was my socially awkward reply to this sudden turn of events. I was humbled by their warm welcome, but also suddenly self-conscious about my now-even-warmer hands. I actually thought the nice church ladies had really cold hands and that I was within a perfectly normal body temperature for my age. But I didn't tell them that.

Instead, I blushed.

I always blush.

Becoming the warm-blooded Fabio for a bunch of church ladies on Social Security was not how I envisioned starting my journey.

. . .

If you've ever watched *The Simpsons,* you've probably seen Ned Flanders's religiously devout son, Rod. In many ways, Rod was me growing up. I was raised in a staunch Christian household in a strict bubble of doctrine and morality. I automatically conformed to what our "One True Church" taught. Like any good Lutheran boy, I prayed first thing in the morning and right before bed at night, though my prayers were usually rather self-centered, expecting God to reward His faithful with more LEGOs and Teenage Mutant Ninja Turtles.

My parents attempted to shield me from the mischievous Bart Simpsons of the big bad world, which just resulted in ignorance and overdue questions to my parents like, "What does 'gay' mean?"

When I was old enough to put on my big-boy Christian underpants, I dutifully attended a Lutheran K-8 school during the week, took careful notes during the sermons at church on Sunday, and tithed 10 percent of my weekly allowance. During my later grade school years, I went to Catechism classes where we studied the Ten Commandments with Flanders-like reverence: "You shall not give false testimony against thy diddly-doodily neighbor" and "Remember the Sabbath by keeping it hi-diddily-holy."

All throughout high school and into college, I remained the model Christian. I was sure that if I didn't drink, smoke, or have sex until marriage—in short, all those sinful things that make baby Jesus cry—then lo and behold, God would bless me with the perfect girl, the perfect job, and reserve a jacuzzi suite in heaven for me, because *HEY!* I'm a Christian and I believe God exists. After all, I was baptized when I was three weeks old.

After college, I moved out of my parents' house, bought a home of my own, and had a terrific girlfriend who couldn't wait to get married. It was all coming together.

But just when everything seemed to be lining up, it all began to fall apart. The Great Recession of 2008 led to increased professional and financial stress, a Homer-like receding hairline, and more visits to McDonald's than the gym. I was stuck in a dead-end job that I frequently complained about, with a sense of entitlement that someone should hand me a high-paying job since I had graduated with a business degree. My church attendance became intermittent, since that one hour a week felt like an obstacle to my wide-open Sunday plans. And romantically, things felt off. We hurt each other and went down some dark paths, but tried to make it work out. To appease her, I agreed to start going to church on a consistent basis again. I wanted to try something other than the "One True Church" though, so I told her that I'd visit Mt. Calvary—a Lutheran church that was no farther than an Aaron Rodgers Hail Mary pass from my place.

That morning, I donned a black button-up polo shirt, brown khakis, and black Nunn Bush dress shoes. I was ready to step out the door when a sudden thought crossed my mind: I was too chicken to go.

Instead, I shrank away from the challenge, afraid to change my situation by showing up. I didn't want to start over in a new church, opting to remain in the same familiar place.

Later that night, my girlfriend called and was excited to hear how the church service had been. I described the service as vaguely as I could, detailing the similarities and differences between the two Lutheran churches. I discussed how different the pastor was, how boring the sermon was, even how the church seating was arranged. It was all a ruse to keep her happy. After that day, my lies kept growing taller than Marge Simpson's towering blue hairstyle, as I'd lie about Mt. Calvary for the next few weeks until finally going back sporadically to the only church I had known.

We broke up a year later, and for the next two years, I beat myself up over the number of lies I had told her.

I started taking walks around my neighborhood to visit two landmarks that seemed to symbolize my pain. The first was Mt. Calvary, and the second was a burned-down house just down the street.

I'll never forget the morning I looked out my window and saw a fog of smoke completely engulfing the neighborhood. Every fire truck in the village screamed past my place, blasting their sirens and doing everything possible to extinguish that house fire. To this day, you can still smell the charred debris when walking past it. The only remnants of that house include a pile of dirt, some melted lawn ornaments, and a private property sign to ward off trespassers.

Both landmarks reminded me of how beautiful things can be one minute, then be gone the next. They were a testament to how something small, whether it be a single spark or a stupid little white lie could set off something much bigger than it should have been, leaving nothing in its wake.

I always wondered what Mt. Calvary would have looked like if I had just gone in that day. What would have happened in my relationship if I had actually visited, instead of just lying about it?

So Sunday, instead of walking by, I marched straight into the unknown.

. . .

Mount Calvary Lutheran Church in Rothschild, Wisconsin
October 12, 2014 – 8:00 A.M. Sunday Traditional Service

7:55 A.M. Day 1. A very friendly man wearing a bronze blazer, beaming smile, and a tan that suggested he had just finished vacationing in Florida welcomed me at the door with an enthusiastic handshake. It was a great first impression, so great that when I turned to enter the sanctuary, he

9

stopped me, acknowledging that he had forgotten something.

"My apologies," he said with another smile, handing me the bulletin. "I better do my job."

I sat down in the pew closest to the doors, distancing myself from others due to my introversion bandwidth quickly reaching max capacity. Despite my antisocial stiffness, I was impressed with myself, unable to believe that I was really doing this. After years of doing the hokey-pokey when it came to church—putting my left foot in, taking my left foot out, putting my left foot in, and shaking it all about—I finally had hokey-pokey'd myself inside a new church.

Instinctively, my old habits as an usher kicked in, and I scanned the congregation to get a head count. There were 53 congregants, with an average age of about the same. The generation gap was alarming. Other than a married couple with a little boy, I was one of the youngest in attendance. I was paranoid people were whispering to each other, wondering who I was.

I started to get anxious, so I focused on my breathing. In and out. In and out. My goal for the day wasn't anything crazy—it was just to take one step away from the past and allow myself to be vulnerable to a new experience. Not "vulnerable" in the kind of way that makes most guys cringe by associating it with weakness. After all, guys are socially conditioned to do manly things like run through walls, eat bricks, and chop down trees with our bare hands. As a matter of fact, I'm doing 100 push-ups while typing this sentence since it needs to seep with more masculinity.

No, I was thinking about "vulnerability" in broader terms, both from an emotional, social, and spiritual perspective. If I was going to get anything out of this experience, I first needed to be vulnerable in my own beliefs and actions by putting myself in a position to accept that anything was possible. It's scary to stick your neck out spiritually. In a way though, this sense of vulnerability also reflected a kind of personal strength. I could be deep. Authentic. Honest. Real. If I could be open to this visit, what could come next?

After all. We sin. We screw up. We make mistakes. We make former grade-school teachers upset when they read our books as grown adults and see how poorly we applied their teachings when crafting sentences that only consist of two or three words and then follow them up with unnecessarily long run-on sentences just to make a point! It happens. It's okay to show some rough edges on occasion. I'm not Jesus, I'm just trying to follow Jesus. I need to stop trying to always be Christ-perfect.

"Hi, my name is Pastor Mike," said a man in white robes.

He startled me in my pew when he paused and looked at me, waiting for me to give a response. I was slow in responding to normal social cues. "Oh—hi," I stammered. "I'm Dave."

"Good to have you worship with us today, Dave."

"Great to be here," I said, feeling more out-of-place than a fish signing up for skydiving lessons.

Pastor Mike took a seat at the front of the room, and the service soon began. It opened with the gathering hymn, "At the Lamb's High Feast We Sing," followed by a congregational reading, which I had no idea how to even follow. I looked down at my bulletin completely perplexed, but it offered no clues. Then the organ started playing again for the next hymn, and instead of asking someone nearby where we were, I mumbled along in an attempt to sound like I knew what I was doing.

A lady in front of me turned around and said, "Yeah, I don't know where we are, either."

Glad I wasn't the only one.

When I found my place in the bulletin again, the service had shifted to the children's message. Pastor Mike invited the lone little boy in the congregation to come forward, but he was bookish shy and almost immediately retreated to his parents' pew to disassociate himself from the public eye.

Pastor Mike skipped to the sermon, asking the congregation, "Why do we read the Bible?"

The floor was apparently open.

"Comfort," said a lady near the front.

"Direction and instruction," said another.

"Inspiration."

"Peace."

"Because we're told we should."

The congregation chuckled at that. Pastor Mike acknowledged the response and quickly transitioned to his own understanding of why he reads the Bible, stating how God's very self is revealed when doing so. He talked about the importance of having a relationship with Him and how He is steadfast and forgiving.

While I enjoyed the open-forum sermon and the simplistic question, I had to admit that despite being a self-professed Christian and believing in the Bible, I had never actually read it. Oh sure, we're told we should, but for me, living in the contemporary social-media age where we want things now, it was much more convenient to be *told* the Bible at church rather than to sit down and actually read a 1,208-page NIV Bible for myself.

In general, reading 2,000-year-old literature from parts of the world I've never been has never been high on my priority list. More than 150 years ago, Abraham Lincoln delivered the Gettysburg Address with that iconic opening line: "Four score and seven years ago..." A little over 400 years ago, William Shakespeare opened *Romeo & Juliet* with:

Two households, both alike in dignity,
In fair Verona, where we lay our scene,
From ancient grudge break to new mutiny,
Where civil blood makes civil hands unclean.
From forth the fatal loins of these two foes
A pair of star-cross'd lovers take their life;
Whole misadventured piteous overthrows
Do with their death bury their parents' strife.

Both were written in modern English, and yet they still necessitate a Google search to understand their meanings. Nowadays, we've dumbed down the English language to LOL acronyms and Kermit the Frog memes. I mean, the Old Testament prophets didn't even include a single sad-face emoji to really drive their point home! :(

It was great to see Pastor Mike engage his congregation in his sermon. He had a gift for reaching out. As for me though, I was just sitting there, quietly listening and wasting away, just like every other time I'd ever been to church. Why couldn't I use my gifts to reach out to people? What would happen if I wrote about this experience and created something out of it, rather than sitting and consuming it? If I wanted to be vulnerable, maybe writing was the way.

At the end of the service, Pastor Mike took an extra moment to shake my hand and talk with me. He explained that this was the 8:00 A.M. "traditional" worship service, as opposed to the "praise service" at 10:00, essentially wink-wink, nudge-nudging me to let me know that the later service might be more up my alley after having read my body language during the service.

Before I left, the nice elderly lady who commented on my hands from earlier came over to shake my hand again before I could exit stage right.

"Thank you for visiting our church today," she said, and I thanked her for her kind words.

"He's so friendly," I overheard one of her friends say as I walked toward the door. I turned around briefly and saw that all four of them were huddled together in their pew, talking about me. When they saw me turn back, they all flashed Fixodent smiles my way.

"His hands were so warm."

LORD'S TABLE FOR WHO?

TRINITY EVANGELICAL LUTHERAN CHURCH • WAUSAU, WISCONSIN
MOUNT OLIVE LUTHERAN CHURCH • SCHOFIELD, WISCONSIN
TRINITY EVANGELICAL LUTHERAN CHURCH • STETTIN, WISCONSIN

The back of the my former church's weekly bulletin always included the rules for communion: "Our Lord Jesus has given us a holy supper in which we receive his true body and blood for the forgiveness of sins and bears witness to the fellowship we share. Therefore, we invite to communion those who share in our confession by virtue of their membership in [the "One True Church"]."

I'm still bothered by the memory of a moment that should have been insignificant and instantly forgotten. About five years earlier, I served as an usher at the "One True Church," handing out bulletins as parishioners walked in. One Sunday, I gave two to an older gentleman and his wife. They looked unfamiliar, and it didn't take long for our pastor to come over to their pew and welcome them.

The man had been reviewing the bulletin and pointed to the message on the back that detailed the rules for our church's closed communion. The pastor explained that visitors needed to meet with him earlier in the week and be active Synod members in order to receive the true sacrament.

It was a small, forgettable moment, and it should have just ended there. But it didn't. The image of the gentleman's reaction to my pastor's verdict latched onto my memory and never left. He was persistent in his belief that the church blocking them from Christ's body and blood was wrong. While our pastor preached policy, the visitor begged to receive the holy supper. They went back and forth in a quiet argument while I painted on a nothing-to-see-here smile as I handed out more bulletins to people coming in. Eventually, the husband threw his hands up in the air, grabbed his wife's hand, and sped past me in a huff. They never came back.

Good grief, I thought, loyally supporting my pastor's decision that day. I was upset at the man's audacity to challenge how we ran things in our church. But something didn't sit right with me, and over the next few years, that moment kept replaying and snowballing in my head. The more I replayed the man's reaction in my mind's eye, the more difficult it was to justify my church's teachings that so vehemently denied communion to believing non-members.

There seemed to be a rift between ideas and actions. We listened to sermons about Jesus promising paradise to the Penitent Thief, and then five minutes later, we calmly accepted the hoops and hurdles that told visitors, "Prove that you believe what we believe. Only then can you receive God's forgiveness with us." I started to question the entire machine of the church. We were supposed to bring others into the Kingdom, so what good was it to invite them into our church home and then refuse them at the dinner table?

Disturbed, I checked out the FAQ section on the Synod's website to see what they had to say about our communion practice. A man wrote in, saying that he had been confirmed in an WELS church 55 years ago, moved away to another state, and now, decades later, was returning to his old stomping grounds.

He asked if he could take communion at the same church he had grown up in. The website replied with a long-winded side-step, saying that the Synod remained faithful to the Bible's teachings about the Holy Supper and making a vague reference to 1 Corinthians, but never actually quoting the Son of God who started it. The website then jumped to the conclusion that other denominations follow false teachings and encouraged this man to re-establish his membership with the congregation, knowing how far-fetched that sounded by finishing the answer with, "I don't know."

I don't know?!

Apparently, not even our Synod had a clear-cut answer. Why did church membership feel like a glorified supermarket customer-loyalty program where communion was an add-on perk?

Frustrated, I went to the Bible and researched how Jesus had handled the very first Lord's Supper with Judas, the Benedict Arnold of the New Testament. The gospels indicate that he was there and that Jesus dipped a piece of bread for him, fulfilling the prophecy and outing him as the traitor. But did Judas actually take the bread? Some commentators interpret this scene in such a way to claim that Judas didn't receive it and left; others say he was there, so he must have partaken. No one seems to have a definite answer. Did he or didn't he? My mind felt even more tangled than Samson with 300 foxtails.

. . .

Trinity Evangelical Lutheran Church in Wausau, Wisconsin;
Mount Olive Lutheran Church in Schofield, Wisconsin;
Trinity Evangelical Lutheran Church in Stettin, Wisconsin;
October 19-November 2, 2014

The plan for the next three weeks was to play it safe, staying as close to the shore as possible and dipping my toe in to test the temperature. I still wasn't ready to dive head-first into the deeper waters of varied denominations. First, I needed to figure out how other Lutheran churches handled communion for visitors.

The adrenaline-infused cocktail of excitement and nervousness I had felt after Day 1 had already dissolved into dread, novelty reverting back to more anxiety and worry. I was afraid of being rejected at the Lord's Table by churches who took it upon themselves to judge people's hearts, rather than leaving that up to God, acting as self-appointed gatekeepers to His Holy Supper. Coincidentally, all three of these churches served communion during my visit, all with a different twist.

Up first was Trinity Evangelical Lutheran Church, a traditional Missouri Synod church that I had once visited before. I had been invited to a friend's wedding that stated it was at "Trinity Evangelical Lutheran Church," glossing over the address since I knew where it was. When I arrived however, the wedding was already in progress. Horrible, right? I slipped through the door and into the nave, receiving a wretched stare from an elderly lady who was handing out wedding bulletins and non-verbal judgments to tardy idiots. After seating myself at the pew farthest from the altar, the pastor was preparing for the "I Do's." As I scanned the wedding party, it became apparent that I was at the wrong wedding! Turned out, there were actually two Trinity Evangelical Lutheran Churches in the area. What better way for two of my first few stops then to check out both?

At Trinity in Wausau, I was welcomed by a lone usher with a typical "Good morning" and took a seat about halfway into the nave. When the service began, I noticed that the congregation was actually quite large, but the person closest to me was still three pews away. This was a stark contrast from the previous week's Mt. Calvary Lutheran Church, whose small congregation rolled out the welcome wagon for me. Here, everyone seemed somber and kept their distance. The liturgy was similar to that of my former church, and after the sermon, it was time for communion. I looked at the procedures on the back of the bulletin:

"We invite those who have been instructed in the teachings of the Evangelical Lutheran Church to receive the Sacrament of the Altar. Others are asked to speak with a pastor before receiving the Sacrament. Gluten-free wafers are available upon request."

Not "Christians." Not "Believers." Just "Others." I felt alienated being grouped like this, segregated from the church members. I had a chip on my shoulder and suddenly felt like I was in the shoes of the gentleman who had walked out of my old church years ago. As I watched the distribution from my seat, I got fed up and did something I had never done before during a service: I walked out.

It was weird getting all those pressing, glassy-eyed stares from the congregation as I did so, but I needed to do it. I was trying to be absolutely honest and accountable to myself in my pursuit of a more progressive spirituality, so I took a deliberate action compelled by my faith in Christ.

Was I right to walk out like that? Well, if I were to err in my interpretation of the Bible—which is quite likely, since I'm only human—I'd rather err on the side of what Jesus would have done.

My next two weeks were at Evangelical Lutheran Church in America (ELCA) churches. Both served communion, and unlike the closed communion I had learned from birth, both ELCA churches invited everyone to the Lord's Table, regardless of membership.

Mount Olive Lutheran Church invited the entire congregation to the table, but I hung back. I felt like one of those dogs in the depressing experiment done by Martin Seligman in the late '60s, where they placed dogs in cages with a mat that lightly shocked them. The researchers then changed the cages, still including the shock mats, but adding a space the dogs could walk over in order to avoid the shock. With this change, some dogs moved to the shock-less area, while others just gave up, passively lying down on the mats and whining at the shocks, despite there being a safe haven mere steps away. These dogs displayed learned helplessness—was that what I had been religiously conditioned to accept?

The third service at Trinity in Stettin started with someone shouting, "Bring up the kids," prompting a dozen Sunday School children to sprint to the front. The teachers popped in a DVD that flashed neon colors and the silhouettes of break dancers, and the kids sang along to Kidz Bop Christian songs as they bounced up and down. One young chap was unimpressed and decided to just stand there and pick his nose the entire time.

It happened to be Reformation Sunday, which commemorates Martin Luther's protest against the Catholic Church's use of indulgences, which was basically a shady fundraiser scheme to rebuild St. Peter's Basilica in Rome. It put salvation on sale, giving Catholics a papal guarantee of a reduced purgatory sentence after they died—for a price, of course. Calling it what it was, Luther threw down his B.S. card in the form of his contentious

95 Theses.

The Reformation probably would have stopped there if it weren't for the arrival of the printing press, which was the newest cutting-edge technology. Luther's *Theses* went "viral"—or at least as viral as something other than the Black Death could go in Germany in 1517—and headed straight to the top of the metaphorical *York Times* Best Sellers List. The document soon circulated all throughout Europe. It was the first crack that would eventually split the old church from the new, the Catholic from the Protestant.

In honor of this occasion, a traditional monologue sermon was replaced with a mock academic debate between two reverends. They both stood in front of the congregation, dressed up as reformers Martin Luther and Philipp Melanchthon (known among scholars as Luther's right hand man). The two went back-and-forth, mock arguing about the beginnings of the Protestant separation from the Catholic Church, reminding everyone what the Reformation meant and why it happened. They discussed the point that salvation isn't earned through works, but rather through faith alone in Christ's grace, an idea that the Catholic Church staunchly opposed.

The pastor playing Luther brought this point back to the present day with an interesting question: "Is the church today in need of reform?" Decked out in his German scholar cap, he turned to the congregation, looking for someone to answer his question.

Before anyone could say anything, the pastor playing Melanchthon rose his finger and shouted, "The church is always in need of reform and change!"

After the offering, both pastors changed back into their modern garb and started the Invitation to Communion with the following words: "All believers in Jesus Christ are welcome to feast at the Lord's Table."

Everyone came up. It didn't matter if they were nine months old or 90 years old. Everyone received either Communion or a blessing from the pastor. This was different from my former church, which instructed all children to sit back in their pews and wait while parents went up for Communion by themselves. Here, they made you feel like you belonged, no matter who you were.

Still, when the usher came over to my pew to dismiss my row as next to go up, I experienced a moment of raw fear as I stood and felt the full heaviness of stares behind me. I walked toward the Communion table, waiting my turn in line, my conscience condemning me despite the pastor's invitation.

When I reached the front of the line, the "Luther" reverend hesitated and leaned in to my ear, whispering, "What's your name?"

"My name is Dave," I replied, looking down at the carpet, fully prepared to be rejected by the church like I had been rejected by the majority of women I had dated.

"Dave," he replied, quietly taking a piece of bread in his right hand and handing it me, "The Body of Christ is given to you..."

I don't even recall the rest of what he said. I was completely taken back by having been accepted like this. After having seen so much division over this sacred ritual, I was shocked that this congregation had accepted me as a stranger. It wasn't the church that had decided that I was worthy of partaking with Christ; it was my decision.

I felt charged with energy—I felt changed—and for the first time in God knows how long, I felt pride in being a Christian.

SO A CHRISTIAN AND AN ATHEIST WALK INTO A BAR

A few years ago, I learned that mixing Christianity and atheism in conversation would result in being denied free nuts.

My best friend, Patrick, was back in town. We made plans to hit up the downtown Wausau bar scene in nostalgic fashion, starting at a new Irish pub. As we sipped our rail mixers, our conversation veered into one of our never-ending theological wrestling matches, seeing who could land the knockout blow to settle—once and for all, our opposing viewpoints. All we needed was a UFC-style video introduction with some *Gladiator*-inspired instrumental music and Michael Buffer providing the pre-fight introductions. It was just like old times.

I first met Patrick when we worked together at Walgreens. I immediately pegged him as a nerdy, hippie, emo stoner that had been fired from Hot Topic. As it turned out, he wasn't any of those things. Instead, he was a tall, gangly, street-smart liberal, the kind of person who would travel the globe for the best vegan restaurant. He was also kind of a jerk, but he did have a soft spot for kittens. He was the polar opposite of me: an introverted, conservative, Bible-following homebody who preferred the nearest McDonald's drive-thru over actually going out in public. When we got bored working our stations, we talked about everything from girls to baseball. We were both getting over our first major break-ups, and I was flip-flopping between the Big 'ol Book and a Big 'ol Bottle to help me figure

19

things out.

On the night of my 24th birthday, Patrick convinced me to hang out at a bar, luring me with a free Rolling Rock lager. *Why not*, I figured; it certainly beat my all-night plans of editing Wikipedia pages. A local band played, people danced, and it was actually a really good time. While waiting for Patrick to return from a longer-than-usual bathroom break, I decided to make a run for it and stumbled upon him outside making out with a hot girl way out of his league.

Impressed, I couldn't help but wonder, *how did he pull that off?*

After that, we started hanging out more. There should have been no way we'd get along—let alone become friends, but it worked with us. Despite being complete and polar opposites, girls and baseball became our common denominator. Over time, talk of broken hearts and broken bats led to real talk.

Over the course of our friendship, theology became a major discussion point between us. For a long time, I tried to demonstrate the power of my faith and how it could bring him peace in the face of his past troubles. But this never accomplished anything. Christianity was a been-there, done-that deal-breaker for him. Likewise, he brought up anti-Christian documentaries, like Bill Maher's *Religulous*, *The God Who Wasn't There*, and *Zeitgeist: The Movie* to sway my views, challenging me to understand why he thought the way he did. I watched them, but my faith in Christ remained solid. I was able to quickly denounce the films' claims, since they were obviously steeped with personal vendettas against the physical institution of the church, rather than the spiritual transcendence of Christ.

With all that behind us, with Patrick back in town, I decided *This is the night!* I was going to battle the Devil's schemes and heroically rescue the soul of my best friend. I metaphorically equipped myself with the helmet of Salvation and the breastplate of Righteousness and raised the Flag of Christianity.

Why was I doing this? Because I cared about him. And because my entire life, starting in my first Sunday School class when I was five years old, I've been conditioned to preach and convert someone—anyone—to Christianity. After all, Patrick must have been mentally, emotionally, and spiritually struggling ever since he left the Catholic Church during high school. My church was quite different from his, so I was sure that would make all the difference.

I told him about the power of believing in the Bible—a hypocritical statement on my part, considering the fact that I had never actually read the whole thing cover-to-cover myself. "Just believe," I insisted, "and you'll be saved."

That's when the bartender came over and offered free nuts to everyone, everyone except us, the obvious nut jobs.

Convincing Patrick to believe in Christ and the Bible never worked. How could I inspire real belief in what he considered a book of ancient Middle Eastern fairytales? Patrick always lobbed arguments back at me, pointing out the absurdity of laws found in Leviticus and challenging the literal context of the Old Testament in regards to marriage, purity, and agriculture. This would eventually morph into a discussion of Darwin's theory of evolution and then move on to the heavy-hitting subject of creation versus evolution. I would defend my stance that I believe in natural selection and evolution as scientific facts, but not the larger evolution of everything in our universe from the Big Bang. Over time, I'd adapted the philosophy of intelligent design to help explain the creation of the universe and everything in it.

If science is concerned with things that are observable and measurable, how could it assume that something came from nowhere, from nothing? I couldn't wrap my head around how an atheist could believe in the Big Bang Theory and the resultant chain-reaction sparking off all life in the universe, including us, yet that same atheist couldn't wrap his head around my believing in a 2,000-year-old book that claims a man once took an all-expense-paid vacation in a giant fish for three days before being regurgitated out.

To this day, Patrick's and my debates run in more circles than an ESPN Classic marathon of the Daytona 500, leaving both of us fed up and spending money on yet another round while staring at the unobtainable bowls of Planters behind the bar.

But what if Patrick was on to something? After all, I knew it sounded ridiculous to believe a talking snake duped Adam and Eve. Maybe I had been taking the Bible too literally. Had my sheltered Christian upbringing kept me infant-like to a modernizing world?

After my failed date with the blonde '70's girl, I called Patrick to talk about a baseball playoff game that night. But I didn't really want to talk about baseball. I wanted to talk about doing something with my life. He told me I had so much more to offer the world, but had sort of settled into an easy, predictable life. That hit hard. Despite not wanting to get into another theology debate, I told him about my crazy idea of going to 52 churches in 52 weeks then write a book about it.

"I'd read that," he said.

My eyes lit up. "Waa-wait, you would?!"

"Yeah, that's actually something I'd like to know more about. You should visit the old church I used to go to when I was a kid."

If this could be what intrigued my best friend enough to make him at least consider Christianity again and could help strengthen my own faith, then maybe this idea really was worth it. After all, a more progressive, thoughtful faith could be the answer to his skepticism, rather than the "just

21

believe" nonsense I had been pushing in the past.

. . .

"Patrick's Old Catholic Church" in Central Wisconsin
November 9, 2014 – 10:30 A.M. Sunday Mass

"At the end of this, you'll find wisdom and truth in conclusions you draw from your own experiences, the books you read, and the people you met along the way," Patrick texted the night before. "That's the beauty of being human and focusing on being human, not one of God's creatures who submits to His will."

Around this time, the media was having a field day misinterpreting Pope Francis's words during a recent speech, making it sound like he backed the Big Bang Theory over creation. Despite the misinformation—purposeful or not—Pope Francis made it in clear during that speech that he wasn't afraid to address the different views of the progressive scientific community and the forever-traditional Catholic Church. I wondered if a Catholic church would directly address this current issue, so I decided to visit Patrick's old church to find out.

I had long looked for answers to Patrick's spiritual dissension in what he had turned to: anti-Christian documentaries and books. I had long assumed they were what set him on his path of non-believing; I had never considered visiting the Catholic Church of his childhood that drove him away. Now finding myself in a similar boat, it seemed like the perfect time.

I couldn't have picked a better day for my first-ever visit to a Catholic Church. The sky was a clear blue, and there wasn't a cloud to be seen. Red and orange leaves decorated the grass like autumn's version of rose petals. Outside, the architecture of Patrick's old church reminded me of one of those triangle brainteasers you see on Facebook—with three triangles inside a fourth larger triangle—that asks how many triangles are in the picture.

No one greeted me when I walked through the front doors. Confused about where to go, I followed a trail of people like a worker ant, my antennae twitching, searching for the nearest worship colony. When I got there, a wall of glass separated the nave from the narthex. A single open doorway was the only way in. It was strange to note what was absent: there were no ushers, no bulletins, and no organ music. It was silent, the entire room engaged in quiet prayer. Suspended from the ceiling was a life-sized statue of Jesus attached to a giant cross, but instead of being nailed to it, both hands were outstretched like in images of the Ascension. It was an amazing piece of work, and combined with the sanctuary's morgue-like stillness, it communicated a respect for Christ I had never felt in a Lutheran church other than on Good Friday.

I took a seat near the middle of the church and looked around at the congregation, nearly all of whom were kneeling, their heads lowered and hands clenched together in prayer to Jesus, Mary, or the saints. With no bulletins, I was unsure of how the service would work.

I soon learned that a lady stationed to the side of the sanctuary would call out instructions for the next step in the liturgy with a microphone like it was bingo night. If the unseen liturgy said to sing hymn 252, she'd instruct us to turn to hymn 252 in our hymnals. If it was time to shake hands with everyone around us, she'd instruct us to do so.

The sermon was unlike anything I'd ever heard before. During his message, the priest announced that today marked the first service after The Commemoration of All the Faithful Departed. Then, rather than focusing on Christ, he talked about the necessary preparations for a funeral. He encouraged the congregation to take some time during the week to achieve peace within their families by pre-planning their funerals, especially for those over the age of 50. He went on to discuss some of the family conflicts he had witnessed after a loved one passed away and the negative effects such conflicts had on the families. He even provided a checklist that sounded like it had come from a wikiHow article, discussing the need for a proper will and the various practical preparations for a funeral. He went so far as to discuss music selection, cautioning his congregants that "I Walk the Line" by Johnny Cash might not be the most appropriate song for the church band at such an event.

The entire time, I impatiently waited to see how the priest would tie this to the headlines about the pope's comments about the Big Bang Theory or even to Christ Himself, but such a connection never came. Instead, the priest ended his message by informing his flock that the Dioceses' local bishop had called him and that he was being given a new assignment in another town. He would transfer within the next month. Another hush fell over the already silent congregation. The sermon apparently ended with that announcement.

The lady with the microphone awkwardly announced that the Eucharist was next. I had never even heard of a "Eucharist," but I quickly learned that it was Catholic for 'communion.' As everyone pulled out their kneelers again and bowed their heads in prayer, I continued to sit in my bench, bowing mine out of respect. When distribution started, different sections of the church went up to the altar together. When it was my section's turn, everyone went up except for me. I felt exposed and wide open in the exact center of the congregation. Nearly everyone who passed me to get in line looked at me, probably wondering who I was or what I had done to be expelled from the communion table. I stuck out like a sore King Kong-sized thumb.

After mass, very few people stayed to talk to each other, and most simply hurried to their cars and drove away, checking 'Church' off their

Sunday morning to-do list.

As a 33-year-old Protestant in a foreign Catholic world, I couldn't identify with the sermon's call to action regarding funeral arrangements. There was no message about Christ, little community outside of the service (that I could find), and nothing to uplift the heart. How could an outside visitor like me ever get connected unless you're "adopted in" by a significant other, friend, or relative? Utterly perplexed, I had to learn more.

I could now see why and how Patrick had developed such resentment toward Christianity. After mass, I finally realized that I would never be able to convince Patrick to have a relationship with God through conventional church. To believe is entirely dependent on him. I've grown to accept his atheism for what it is, and I hope that someday he will be able to accept my faith as a Christian in the same way. If he ever wants to seriously have a relationship with God, I'll do whatever I can to help. But until then, he's going to be my friend no matter what. That's the thing about friendship: you stick together through it all—the good and the bad.

The crazy thing is, I've had my own fair share of "Christian" friends, mentors, and dates—too many of them to count. All of them had no trouble dropping me from their circle if I didn't measure up to their unrealistic, holier-than-thou standards. And that's not to say that I'm not guilty of such a thing either; I'm just as bad! Yet no one has ever demonstrated the warm heart, loyalty, or values that Patrick regularly displays. The bottom line is that he cares just as much as I do. So why is it that my atheist friend has been a better example of true friendship than any of my Christian friends?

Nuts, isn't it?

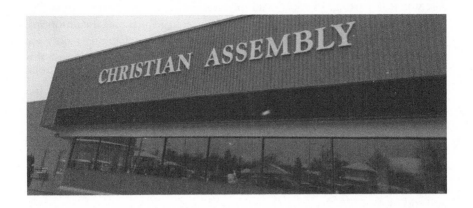

CHURCH 6:
SOME CHRISTIAN ASSEMBLY REQUIRED
CHRISTIAN ASSEMBLY • WAUSAU, WISCONSIN

I first met Tiff working at the local Walgreens.

It didn't take Sherlock Holmes-level skills to deduce that it was her first day, as she was nervously studying the basic training material while diligently maintaining her bubble of isolation away from everyone else. It was my goal to be the first to see her smile that day, so I equipped myself with a miniature Hershey's Kiss as a chocolate token and approached to introduce myself. Her eyes lifted from the material she was studying, and while I can't remember what was said, I do remember that I accomplished my goal: she gave me a small, bite-sized smile in exchange for the chocolate.

As we began working together, we discovered that we shared a lot of personality traits and a penchant for awkward humor. Over time, we started messaging each other outside of work, which usually involved plenty of oddball replies, ranging from bad fish jokes to Guitar Hero bragging rights. I eventually invited her out to see a horror flick that I nearly needed a second pair of pants for. Nevertheless, we had fun and ended the night sharing a chocolate shake.

Everything was going a little too well, so I knew what was coming next. Tiff looked over at me and asked a question that, based on all the dating books I had assimilated over the years, I knew hinted at possible attraction: "So are you dating anyone?"

I instinctively knew her question displayed romantic interest. She was attractive, but also a co-worker. I didn't want to go down that route.

Besides, we were at different ends of life: I was finishing up college, while she was just starting. I've lost track of the number of disgusting stories I've heard about college guys taking advantage of college girls and the emotional toll leftover as a consequence. I was trying to be a Christian do-good protector; I didn't want Tiff to fall into the same trap. I had meant this evening to be a practice date for her, helping her see what was positive and desirable so she'd be more selective in her dating life than many women her age were. I didn't want her to end up with someone who would wreck her college love life. At the same time, I thought I would also benefit from our excursion. I was going through a long string of bad first dates, so I could use the confidence boost. Nothing was meant to come out of it. In order to sidetrack her her question, I transitioned the conversation to the 1980s He-Man cartoons. I also threw a straw wrapper at her. That should have been the end of it.

It was around this time that my friendship with Patrick was becoming stronger thanks to the combination of baseball, beer, and Wii Sports. One night, Patrick played matchmaker and introduced me to a girl he knew from a church he had attended for a while before becoming a full-fledged atheist.

On paper, she was everything I'd been looking for: she was cute, ambitious, with a heart for God and a passion for serving Him. Our first date was a "church date" at the Christian Assembly church she attended, though we didn't actually sit together, as she was part of the worship team on-stage. The service was the complete opposite of what I was used to with the "One True Church": it was very animated compared to the serious, conservative services I was accustomed to. I didn't know what to make of it.

We dated for a while, but I eventually started nitpicking little things about her. She had trust issues from a past relationship. She wasn't a card-carrying Lutheran that my mom would approve of. She also got upset when I didn't answer her texts right away. As I grew frustrated, my mind started to slowly drift back to Tiff.

I went back-and-forth, trying to convince myself that it was a bad idea to ask Tiff out again. Eventually, 'Why not?' won out, and decided to pick up where Tiff and I had left off. We went on over a dozen dates as I tried to fend off my growing attraction, still unconvinced that a relationship between us could actually work.

On the 20th-something date, the subject of church came up while we were eating French fries at a fast food joint, and she told me that she was Lutheran. To most, this wouldn't be a big deal, but for me, it was the icing on the cake. Before the end of the night, I went in for a kiss. There was no looking back now. Instead of prepping her for Mr. Right, I was going to be him instead

That night, I removed my "Single" status from my Facebook profile, and the change popped up on all my friends' news feeds. I immediately received two reactions: one was a like from Tiff and the other was a comment from the church girl: "Why are you no longer listed as single???"

I didn't know what to say. I thought it was pretty self-explanatory since we hadn't dated for several weeks. It's not like the Bible has verses dedicated to how to handle dating drama, with descriptive step-by-step instructions for how to handle anxiety, heartbreak, and status-update confusion (trust me, I looked it up in 1 Corinthians 13). I didn't reply and ended up never talking with her again.

A few weeks later, Tiff and I made our relationship Facebook-official. I was ecstatic, but the cherry on top was what else she updated in her profile: she added "Lutheran" as her religious denomination and quoted her favorite Bible passage on her Facebook wall: "I tell you the truth, if you have faith as small as a mustard seed, you can say to this mountain, 'Move from here to there,' and it will move. Nothing will be impossible for you" (Matthew 17:20).

. . .

Christian Assembly in Wausau, Wisconsin
November 16, 2014 – 11:00 A.M. Worship Service

Sometimes it can be hard to pick up your cross and go to church. You walk through those doors dragging all your past burdens that are weighing you down. Once inside, you feel crowded, not only by those gathered, but also by what has been piling up inside your head. You look up and see the sun glaring down through those stained-glass windows like a divine interrogation light, examining the choices that led you to that precise moment.

That's how I felt as I walked through the doors for this visit. After seeing Patrick's childhood church the week before, I wanted to reacquaint myself with the rebound church he had tried before throwing Christianity away for good. Whereas the Catholic Church had been conservatively somber, the Christian Assembly church was animated and active, pulsing with sound to call upon the Holy Spirit. Although I had attended this church years before, this time, I was there to better understand why my best friend had left the faith for good. But that didn't happen. Instead, I found myself getting smacked into my own past.

There she was, on-stage as part of the worship team: the girl whose heart I had discarded. Last I heard, she had moved away and was trying to reconcile with her on-and-off-again husband. Apparently it was off, and she was back to square one—just like me.

The opening procession was different here than typical churches. After the opening worship song, the pastor invited everyone to join the "Coffee

Fellowship." Right on cue, an eight-minute countdown flashed on both sides of the stage and two large side doors swung open to reveal a small gym with a concession stand displaying signs for "Caffeine," "Decaf," and "Hot Chocolate." At first I stayed back, paranoid that she would see me and wonder what I was doing there.

"I don't think I've seen you before," said a woman with oversized eyeglasses and the personality of Edna Mode from *The Incredibles*. "Is this your first time at Christian Assembly?"

"Not quite," I replied.

Edna and her husband turned around in their seats in front of me and introduced themselves in the most sincere manner I'd ever encountered. I told them a little bit about my back-story, and they did their best to sell me on visiting the Christian Assembly again, especially giving a shot with their young adult group.

Later during the service, as the song "All Things New" began to slowly decrescendo, Edna started talking out of turn by herself: "Be free," she shouted, causing everyone to turn and look in our direction. "Be free, my children, from the bondages of sin!" She went on to say much more, but I was so taken aback to see someone in the congregation take the spotlight, I think my brain nearly short-circuited.

After Edna quieted down, the pastor tried to explain to visitors like me how the Holy Spirit could at times flow through us and encourage us to proclaim our faith. The explanation provided some context for Edna's behavior, but I was still taken aback by how someone could be so convicted in their own faith as to publicly demonstrate it in front of a huge assembly.

Preaching from an acrylic podium on a stage that could have been mistaken for an '80s Donahue talk-show set, the pastor transitioned to his sermon, called "believe" (with a lowercase "b" and bold "i" for some reason). It was based on Mark 9:23, "Everything is possible for him who believes." The passage was from the story of Jesus healing a boy possessed by a demon by rebuking the evil spirit within him. The pastor explained how the excited belief of the possessed boy's father helped Jesus perform the miracle, whereas the disciples were merely humbled and confused. Later, they asked Jesus why they couldn't drive out the demon, and He responded with a statement that smacked me in the face.

The PowerPoint slide flashed to a new passage that was all too familiar. "I tell you the truth, if you have faith as small as a mustard seed, you can say to this mountain, 'Move from here to there' and it will move. Nothing will be impossible for you" (Matthew 17:20).

As part of this series of sermons, the pastor was comparing stories in the different Gospels. Somehow, out of all the churches I could have gone to that Sunday morning, out of all the sermons I could have heard, *out of all the Bible passages that the pastor could have preached about*, I happened to go to the one church for the one sermon about the one Bible passage that was Tiff's favorite—and in the very church of the girl I passed over for Tiff.

I sat there stunned, as the girl I used to date was getting back on-stage to sing the final song of the service. The sermon had hit me over the head, my past creeping into my church experiment.

I couldn't help but think: did I make the right decision by picking Tiff?

CHURCH 7:
TOILET PAPER PUNS ARE TEAR-ABLE
FIRST UNITED METHODIST CHURCH • WAUSAU, WISCONSIN

First impressions, those split-second moments when two humans lay eyes on each other for the first time. Our minds race at lightning speed, zeroing in on the essence of the person's personality through things like eye contact, physical appearance, posture, body movement, or even if they have a booger dangling from their nose. This mental snapshot, based on mere seconds and snap preconceptions, can stay etched in someone's memory forever.

At the beginning of my spiritual reformation journey, I was cautious yet fascinated by these moments of first impressions. I was curious about the kinds of reactions I'd receive as a foreign worshiper. Who would greet me? What would they say? How would others perceive me?

Typically, the very *first* first impression was a generic "Good morning" from one of the greeters or ushers handing out bulletins by the door. In a few instances, a pastor picked me out from the assembled congregation before services started and ventured over to shake my hand as a first-time visitor. The best type of first impression though was when I'd settle into a pew and nearby congregants would strike up a friendly conversation, showing genuine interest in why I was a visiting stranger.

This week, on the other hand, a gentleman with gray hair styled like a lion's mane greeted me with "Good morning. Can you do me a favor? The kids will be collecting donations with a cart. Can you give them this?" He plopped a 12-pack of double-roll toilet paper beside me.

My initial thought was, *At least it's not one-ply*. My second thought was to reply with an adequate response, but all I could squeeze out was, "O...kay?" This was quite a contrast to the kinds of first impressions I'd experienced at other churches.

And so, this is the story of how I made my mark at First United Methodist Church, poop puns and all.

. . .

First United Methodist Church of Wausau, Wisconsin
November 23, 2014 – 10:00 A.M. Sunday Worship Service

Sitting on the pot earlier that week, I'd found myself contemplating my existence after watching *Cosmos: A Spacetime Odyssey*, hosted by astrophysicist Neil deGrasse Tyson. The show simplified science to make it a fun and educational experience, while also not being afraid to touch on the inevitable clash between religion and science.

I learned that our small city had a church called the Christian Science Society with services held every Sunday at 10:00 A.M. on 404 Franklin Street. Based on the name alone, I figured this was a newer denomination that merged Christianity and science together. I wanted to learn more about how Christian Scientists operated, so I decided to attend their services this week. There was a slight problem when I arrived though. It turned out that the church on 404 Franklin also had a '404 Not Found Error,' as the church was shut down and its doors nailed shut.

With only a few minutes remaining to find a replacement church, I noticed the stained-glass windows of a different church just a hop, skip, and a jump away down the street. People were still filing in, so I hustled over to the First United Methodist Church of Wausau without any idea of what the Methodists were all about. Inside, I promptly received a bulletin, found a corner in the back, and was greeted with the 12-pack of TP.

"My name is Wilb," an older fella with a sandpapery voice said. He had taken a seat in front of me and now reached out to shake my hand, which showed a certain level of respect and trust that I had washed my hands, given the toilet paper beside me.

"Webb?" I clarified, as it hadn't come out quite right in my head the first time.

He corrected me, "No—Wilb. Short for Wilbert. I was baptized at First United Methodist Church in 1924. It was in a different building back then." He pointed towards a wall in a direction where the church once stood.

I liked Wilb. The man was proud of his church. As a matter of fact, the entire congregation was proud of their church.

The service began with a welcome greeting, but this wasn't the typical, make-sure-to-greet-those-around-you type of forced handshakes that was a formality at the end of my former church's service just before everyone made a beeline for the exit to dust snow off their cars and get out of the parking lot before it became clogged with traffic. No, First United felt like a true church family. Everyone—and I mean everyone—got off of their keisters and floated around to shake each other's hands and have genuine conversations. Several of the congregants came over to greet Wilb, to whom he joked, "I lost my wisdom teeth last week, so now I don't have any more wisdom."

I figured the greeting would subside after 30 seconds or so, but it actually lasted for about five minutes. The church members were shaking hands, giving each other hugs, and some even wanted to tickle the toes of the newborn-baby members. Everyone seemed to know each other's name. It was like being in an episode of *Cheers*, except the happy hour beers were replaced with Holy Communion grape juice and Woody Harrelson's off-the-wall jokes were replaced by John Wesley's on-the-wall quotes.

This was a unique day, as not only was I given toilet paper to re-gift, but also, the pastor wasn't present—he was on a mission trip to Singapore. Instead, throughout the service, pre-selected members of the congregation came forward to speak from a lectern beneath a suspended bare cross. (Later, I did some research on Methodists and learned that their preference for the bare cross emphasizes Jesus's Resurrection, as opposed to the Catholic preference for depicting Jesus on the cross to emphasize His suffering for humankind.) Each speaker gave testimonials about their own lives and experiences within First United, an event they called "My Thanksgiving."

One gentleman in a suit ended his speech by saying First United "shows me the way of God." A magnificently bearded man said that it helped him "be a whole person." And a high school student who served as the church's pianist and resident high school heartthrob, as evidenced by the giggling teenage girls seated at the far end of my pew, thanked the church for providing an outlet for his musical talents.

The congregant speeches were a fresh change of pace for me and had much more effect than simply having a pastor rain down fire and brimstone from atop a pulpit. The talks were real, authentic, and very personable. Each individual made a well-thought-out speech and comfortably positioned their first-hand accounts for an audience who welcomed them.

During one of these speeches, I took a quick look at the church directory, which was located inside my pew. Paging through, I saw that they had a wide range of church activities, countless completed mission trips, and even a full church directory with every family's photograph. But the thing that stood out the most was the pastor's foreword. It opened with a question that had been bothering me for some time after witnessing some of the events at my former church that tested the integrity of my faith. I was so intrigued by this pastor's words that I jotted them down in a notepad:

> *What is the Church?*
>
> *That is a fair question, one that is being asked more and more often and more and more openly in our increasingly secular society. It is a question that everyone who is a part of the church ought to be able to answer. Who are we, anyway?*
>
> *Perhaps the best way to answer that question is through a book like this—a pictorial directory. What is the church? Just people. Single people, married people, divorced people. Old people, children, teenagers. Young families, multi-generational families, empty nesters. New people and people who have been here their whole lives.*
>
> *Look at us. In appearance and demographic description we are not different from the rest of our community or society or world, except for the one thing that brings all these disparate people together.*
>
> *We are people who have encountered God in Christ, who have discovered in that meeting that we are loved, and who are trying to figure out together how best to respond to that love. Look at us.*
>
> *We are the church.*

. . .

The revelation as to why I was safeguarding toilet paper came during the children's sermon. I always enjoy children's sermons because the pastor will often ask the kids a general question, and it quickly turns into an episode of *Kids Say the Darnedest Things*. This week though, instead of the kids saying something off the wall, it came from Karen, the adult giving the children's sermon this morning.

Karen was explaining how the Gathering of Gifts for Others would work later in the service, when the junior ushers would push several shopping carts down the aisle to collect canned goods and toiletries for the Wesley Food Pantry. However, her attempt at a simple explanation for where the donated goods would go didn't come out the right way: "Many could say we are a 'Toilet Paper Church,'" Karen said. "What do you think that toilet paper will be used for?"

It was at this moment that I could practically hear the entire congregation mentally reply, *After dropping a deuce.* The church erupted in hysterics as Karen retraced what she had said in her head. Instead of looking embarrassed though, she joined in on the joke and laughed it off, even giving a curtsy to the audience to top it off. She then reformulated her words to the kids about whom the toilet paper would be going to and the church's goal of helping others.

Out of all the churches I'd visited at this point, this one felt the most like going home to visit friends and relatives you can actually stand at Thanksgiving. Everyone had a sincere and gracious outlook and desire to really be there for each other, which was positively reinforced by the speeches that provided a fresh change-up from the usual sermon. In addition, I came away amused at how this church could poke fun of itself.

At the end of the day, I enjoyed dropping in at First United Methodist Church. For being a toilet paper church, they were truly "Charmin."

<u>CHURCH 8:</u>
ONCE UPON A TIME
CHRISTIAN SCIENCE SOCIETY • STEVENS POINT, WISCONSIN

Once upon a time, when I was still wrapped up in a mindset I'd had long, long ago, I wondered why I couldn't find "The One." I so often saw loving couples holding hands, hugging, and fencing each other with their tongues. Everyone seemed to be in love but me. Where was my One True Love?

I knew The One was out there somewhere, but where, oh where, could she be?

One fine day, I was galloping along in life and came across a lovely young maiden. Like a Knight in Shining Armor, I rode in on my magnificent white stallion and saved her from the evil trolls who wanted to date her in college. After the heroic rescue, our eyes locked and our hearts instantly melted. I jumped off my steed and swept her off her feet, and she then professed her undying love for me based on my charming personality, somewhat proportional nose, and overly exaggerated introductory paragraphs.

With passionate desire in her eyes, she looked into my soul and said, "Dave, I've been searching the depths of this unbounded world, hoping that one day, I would find you and have you hold me in your strong arms. I...I...I love you."

We then proceeded to sample each other's lips while softly whispering sweet nothings into each other's ears. I held her hand, and we pranced through a magical enchanted forest with lush green trees, bountiful flowers,

37

and gently flowing streams in slow motion. Little animated birdies flew around us, fluttering their wings in uncontrollable joy. One of the birdies even rested upon my shoulder and whispered into my ear, "You, my good sir, are the luckiest man on earth," to which I replied, "Thanks, bird!" As a matter of fact, every anthropomorphic animal we knew had to wipe their tears with ultra-soft Kleenex because the sight of our True Love was too emotional for dry eyes. Why? Because we were the perfect couple. Three words—three simple words—solidified it all.

It's amazing how, when uttered for the first time, "I love you" can cause all of life's emotions to culminate in a single moment. All the dreams, all the hopes, all the projected fascinations suddenly manifest into reality with just a trio of words. Feelings begin to dance, lungs join in rhythm, and heartbeats are shared.

This is how I recall the first six months of dating Tiff. I was convinced that she pooped cotton candy, sneezed glitter, and farted Glade lilac spring aerosol spray. She was perfect in every imaginable way. Our lives were like a fairytale dream headed toward a perfect Happily Ever After.

Then, one day, I got a text from her.

"My mom has cancer."

My heart dropped. Rainbows and unicorns suddenly evaporated into thin air and were replaced by doctor visits and chemotherapy. The girl I loved more than anything in the world was now making plans to go wig shopping with her mom. I tried my best to be supportive during these difficult times, to become Tiff's emotional shoulder so she could do the same for her mom. But the worst part was that I had no control over the situation. So I prayed.

I've never been a big prayer guy. One of the annoying things about prayer is that you can't just rub a magic lamp and expect God to jump out in a pair of parachute pants and snap His fingers to grant the wish you so desire. Sometimes it takes patience—a lot of patience—and by the time you see the end result, it's wedged so far inside a silver lining that it's not even recognizable from the original prayer.

Though I didn't share a last name with them, I became part of Tiff's family during its darkest, roughest times. I witnessed the breakdowns, the downtrodden moments, and questions that started with "Why, God?" I also got to see the family roll up their sleeves and forge on together, putting faith in God when nothing about it made sense. As one relative said, "We're going to shower heaven with prayers."

I watched this family climb out of its darkest valleys, and when it was time for me to politely exit their lives, they showed me the right way to live. In just a few short years, Tiff outgrew her insecurities and started to fight for a worthy ideal. Inspired by her mother's illness, she channeled her energy to become an activist for Susan G. Komen for the Cure to empower those battling cancer.

During one night of fundraising, I was with Tiff and her mom. Even though she was still going through treatments, she was high on life that night. I can never forget how she exuberantly reached for my hand, wanting to dance. At first, I was hesitant to venture so far outside my comfort zone by dancing in front of people I didn't know. But then I realized something: to live as if you're dying allows you to free yourself from everything.

Then I whipped out some really bad dance moves.

. . .

Christian Science Society in Stevens Point, Wisconsin
November 30, 2014 – 10:00 A.M. Sunday Service

The previous week, I had been disappointed to learn that the Christian Science Society in my hometown had shut down, though the "Toilet Paper Church" sure made up for it. Still curious about Christian Science though, I found the nearest church in the area was a half-hour away. Oddly, it was just a few blocks from the UW-Stevens Point Quandt Field House, where I had that dance with Tiff's mom all those years ago. As I drove by it, the scene replayed in my mind.

I had high expectations for my visit to the Christian Science Society. Granted, I wasn't expecting to find crucifixes combined with the periodic table or anything like that, but based on the name alone, I assumed the denomination would bridge Christian beliefs with those of today's understanding of science.

I was met at the front door by Phil, an older gentleman who wore flannel and was a tad on the heavier side. He apologized that the entrance was dirty and told me the tale of how, the previous week, the church had experienced a power outage. He lost me when he started discussing how many electric unit charges were involved.

"Do you have a bulletin?" I asked, interrupting Phil's story. At most worship services, that little paper pamphlet will give visitors a clue as to what to expect.

"No, we don't have any bulletins," he replied, "but we do have a bulletin board."

I was half-expecting Fozzie Bear to pop up and shout "Wocka, wocka, wocka!" at such a cheesy response. Instead, Phil raised his hand to point at the bulletin board like he was Vanna White and I'd just correctly solved a *Wheel of Fortune* puzzle. I found the moment socially awkward.

I escaped to the worship area, which felt doll-house small compared to other churches. There were only six pews on each side of the main aisle, each of which could only hold four people. Everything in the interior—the pews, the walls, the pulpit—was made of the same honey maple wood.

"Would you like a *Quarterly*?" asked a very sweet older lady who served as the usher. I said sure, and she quickly returned with a copy of the *Christian Science Quarterly* and a free copy of *Science and Health with Key to the Scriptures* by the 19th century founder of Christian Science, Mary Baker Eddy. I was a bit taken back. I hadn't been there for more than ten minutes, and the church had already gifted me a 700-page book. This was certainly better than the toilet paper I'd received at the church the previous week, which I didn't even get to keep!

There were seven people in attendance at this service, two of which were female congregants who co-piloted the pulpit throughout, since there is no pastor in Christian Science. Other than the sweet lady usher, Phil, and myself, there were only two others in the pews.

The Bible lesson for the day came from the *Quarterly* for November 24–30, 2014, on the subject of "Ancient and Modern Necromancy, alias Mesmerism and Hypnotism, Denounced." I reminded myself that I was trying to keep an open mind.

The sermon (if you can call it that) consisted of seesaw back-and-forth readings, in which the woman on the left side of the pulpit would read several Bible passages that were listed in the *Quarterly*, and then the other woman on the right side of the pulpit followed by reading selected passages from *Science and Health with Key to the Scriptures*. She prefaced these as being "correlative passages" that were "spiritually imported" and "divinely authorized" from the 19th century mindset of "our leader, Mary Baker Eddy."

When the readings started to get into "animal magnetism," how "matter is a mortal error," and how sickness is made-up and all in our heads, I began to get uncomfortable—and it wasn't just because of the Mary Baker Eddy readings. Those in the congregation looked bored and disinterested. Phil was seated up front and had clearly fallen asleep, which meant certain doom for him if he were accidentally hypnotized by the readings.

I wondered about the other congregants and how they had come to pick such a church, given the emotionless service structure that didn't offer parishioners any encouragement or inspiration—especially after the five-minute reading on how "animal magnetism exerts invisible evil matter." I couldn't wrap my mind around the dated scientific ideas, especially given that Mary Baker Eddy's words were considered to be on equal footing with the Bible. It didn't help that I later learned that modern science has debunked many of the 19th century theories that provided the basis for much of the *Science and Health* book. Plainly and simply, I couldn't fully comprehend what the worship leaders were saying, though I was starting to become more paranoid about what the squirrels in my front yard were now invisibly exerting.

The service concluded with a reading of the final hymn, since the CD player that contained the music wasn't working. The two female congregants' final words went in one ear and out the other, mostly because I was soon shocked to see them exit the sanctuary through trap doors behind the altar.

After the service, I did some research on Christian Science—okay, it was more of a Wikipedia search, so sue me—and the most glaring difference between Christian Science and more accepted forms of Christianity is their belief that disease is a mental error, rather than a physical ailment. Therefore, the sick are most effectively treated through prayer alone and should avoid medical care. Apparently, I was the only one in that congregation who'd signed up for work insurance that week.

Driving home from the Christian Science Society meeting, I thought back to when Tiff's mom was battling breast cancer. When she felt defeated and couldn't find the inner strength to go on, her family picked her up emotionally and spiritually to aid in the fight. While I disagree with the Christian Science philosophy toward medical care, I was reminded of the "showering heaven with prayers" line, which is something every Christian, regardless of denomination, can support and endorse. Before I politely took my last bow from their lives, I was privileged to see how the adversity the family faced had created stronger bonds between them.

Through the grapevine, I heard that Tiff's mom made a full recovery. To this day, she likely has better dance moves than I do. I like to think that those prayers contributed in some small way. For whatever it's worth, the threat of dying showed me the art of living.

CHURCH 9:
PARA-ABNORMAL ACTIVITY
DOWNTOWN MISSION CHURCH • WAUSAU, WISCONSIN

"C'mon, Dave, just answer the phone."

Tiff's Facebook message popped up on my computer screen. I responded by clicking the 'X' to close it. My phone starting buzzing again, and I ignored it for the third time. I wasn't ready to talk. Not after what I'd learned. My head felt so scrambled, you could have served it with bacon and toast.

Just a few hours earlier, I had been watching the Packers battle the Seahawks in a NFL preseason game. With football on TV, it was an excuse to pig out on Totino's, my lips becoming smothered in a greasy mess from the pizza rolls that had just slid down my esophagus. While my digestive system was playing air traffic controller to figure out where to store all the pepperoni and Italian sausage coming in for landing, I noticed that Tiff hadn't logged out of her Facebook account on my computer. After two years into our relationship, we trusted each other enough to share everything—that is, until she suddenly changed her password after attending a friend's party earlier that week. It wasn't the end of the world—maybe she had to reset it due to a security issue—but something seemed off, and it wasn't just my increasingly bloated stomach. So now, seeing that she'd failed to log-out, I decided to look at her messages. She allowed it in the past, usually it consisted of her gloating to her friends about how sweet and caring I was for her. But not that day. What I found rocked me harder than a Clay Matthews blindside sack: she had messaged her closest friends, explaining to them about how she'd made out with another guy at a party.

After finding out, I texted her that I knew what happened. Whether it was a response of rage or trying to relieve her of guilt, I didn't fully know. My emotional state was too raw, too confused to know either way, so I just sat back and watched the next text, Facebook, and voice messages roll in.

Another text came through: "I'm coming over. Please answer my call otherwise ill be driving in a state i shouldn be in, please dave i need to explain i know you hate me but i love you so much n this needs to be explained."

Despite the shock, I didn't want to see her go. As a matter of fact, it wasn't even a deal-breaker for me. Based on the various messages she'd sent her friends, I rationalized that her remorse was real, and she'd placed a great deal of emphasis on how much she loved me. She was simply seeking their advice on whether or not she should tell me about her mistake. This reassured me that we were going to make it through this rough patch. I could live with a one-time spit swap that she regretted.

But the thing that really bothered me though was what else she messaged. For the past year, she'd thought about breaking up with me to see what else was out there. I got it: she was a good-looking college girl who had never dated anyone besides me, and didn't want the two words she said at the altar to be "What if?" instead of "I do."

I finally answered the phone and let her come over to talk.

Tiff came over with a waterfall of tears gushing from her eyes like a rainstorm in Niagara Falls. I studied her face through the eroded mascara that now contoured her features, my eyes interrogating her heart, and using my love for her as a compassionate jury. She confessed everything that had happened with the guy at the party, which lined up with what she'd told her friends.

I wanted to use the experience to enhance our relationship, which is more or less what happened. After everything had been swept under the rug of my intuition though, one question she'd asked still stood out and never receded from my memory: "What else did you expect?"

What did I expect? I expected loyalty. I expected trust. I expected encouragement and personal growth and for us to admit our weaknesses to each other so we could work together to fix them as a team. I expected laughter during the good times and support during the bad. I expected bumps in the road, which would be cushioned with forgiveness. But I didn't say any of that. I couldn't answer her question. Instead, I forgave her without a second thought, pretending that everything was all right. I applied a Band-Aid to a deep laceration.

Because in the deepest, darkest shadows of my "perfect Christian boyfriend" persona, I had no idea how I could expect all that from her when I couldn't expect the same from my hypocritical self. I forgave her so

I wouldn't need to forgive myself, to face my own shame, which was hanging over our relationship. I was too weak to admit to the sexual brothel that haunted the darkest corners of my mind. I was in denial.

I was cheating on her in a much worse way.

. . .

Downtown Mission Church of Wausau, Wisconsin
December 11, 2014 – 7:00 P.M. Café Night

Sunday morning didn't go as planned that week. My first attempt to visit a megachurch stalled in my garage when my old beaten-up Pontiac Sunfire , failed to start. With Sunday morning shot, the next best thing was postponing church for a few days for a Thursday night service. The top Google search for my area was "Café Night" at the Downtown Mission Church at The Fillmore.

When I was growing up, The Fillmore had a reputation for being haunted. Rumor had it that a woman was murdered in one of the upstairs apartments in the early 1920s. A few years after the murder, the building became a funeral home, where it was the first in Wausau to practice embalming. When the funeral home closed, the Fillmore was reportedly used as a brothel during World War II before transforming into a movie theater. It remained that way for decades, and I can recall singing along to "Hakuna Matata" when *The Lion King* hit its silver screen when I turned 11 years old. Paranormal activity was often reported over the years, with tales of a ghost nicknamed "Bob" who would dress up in a black suit and frighten theater employees. A few workers confirmed reports of rows of seats violently bouncing, lights turning on and off, and unexplained whispers.

After 50 years, the theater closed as well, and the building was vacant for nearly a decade until the property was renovated and turned into a nightclub. The new owners reportedly found a knife hidden in one of the upstairs apartments during renovation, and they eventually displayed the supposed murder weapon over the bar. The paranormal activity continued, with one employee freaking over a ghostly woman seen in the basement, dressed like a cross between a Roaring Twenties flapper and a *Game of Thrones* White Walker.

I had a few drinks there with Patrick when it first opened as a bar, but the crowd was lame, so we never bothered going back. Eventually, it did attract bigger crowds and better bands. As its popularity increased, more girls started coming out, then more guys. Fights broke out, followed by police citations, medical bills, and lawsuits. Rumor has it that one night, a bartender tried to dissuade a handful of drunks from harassing some girls, which ended with the drunks jumping the counter and breaking his arm.

Fed up, the property owner changed his business plan, having realized that he could make a better return on investment by renting it out as a church than dealing with the financial liabilities of nightlife. Now, several years later, The Fillmore is home to the Downtown Mission Church (DMC). A stream of flashing light bulbs on its marquee proclaiming, "Come as you are!"

Initially, I thought this tagline alluded to a more casual dress code, so I dressed down with a plain black baseball cap and some torn-up designer jeans, bringing along a chocolate mocha as my companion. However, I soon discovered that "come as you are" had much more depth than merely making a clothing suggestion.

When I walked in, it was like a crossover between the nursery in *Rugrats* and the Island of Misfit Toys. Three kids were literally crawling across the front entrance door like they were auditioning for the next *Spider-Man* reboot. Over a dozen kids were bouncing off the walls in their very own mini parkour league, several of whom had no problem cutting me off in their pursuit of running around. The adult congregants were much more subdued, probably because their numbers included a handful of elderly men in wheelchairs lined up side-by-side. They all had obvious mental disabilities or physical handicaps, and one even had a wooden pirate leg. I was accustomed to "normal," healthy people in church and had never seen this many rampaging children and suffering adults in one place. I immediately felt out-of-place and judgmental.

"Hi, my name is Billy," said a man in a black hoodie that had come over from the bar counter, introducing himself with a handshake. "I'm the pastor."

He certainly wasn't like any stereotypical pastor I'd ever met before. Billy was laid back and super chill, and he looked like a shorter, albeit more sophisticated, Ashton Kutcher with his patchy beard and shaggy hair. He encouraged me to enjoy some complimentary nachos. He was very open, and we talked a bit about our spiritual histories—my past at the "One True Church" and his childhood of growing up in a Universalist Unitarian church. He became a critic of Christianity before later finding truth in His Word.

Before he walked away to start the service, Billy warned me, "You picked an odd night to visit. Tonight's sermon might sound a little controversial."

Controversial? I was preparing for an Advent service by eating nachos inside a haunted building that used to be a brothel. How much more controversial could it get?

"We live in a Catholic community," Billy said to start his sermon, taking me by surprise. Once again, this was not what I was expecting.

He went on to emphasize that he wanted to be respectful, but clear. He had studied Catholic doctrine a great deal over the past week and found much of it to be "grossly unbiblical," leading him to consider several practices to be idolatrous, particularly the worship of Mary. If he had to give his sermon a title for the Sunday service, it would be "Mary was a special person, but let's not get weird about it."

"I forgot my pills," an older lady sitting on a bar stool announced. She was seated next to a hyper man wearing a hot-pink fleece bathrobe who immediately got up and speed-walked toward the nachos to fill his Styrofoam plate.

"Ethel, we love ya, but we're in the middle of a sermon," Billy said. "Maybe we should get one of those signs that say, 'No talking while the sermon is playing.'"

There was an awkward silence for a few moments. Billy resumed his sermon until he was interrupted by Ethel again: "I just thought about it now!"

"Only at DMC," Billy joked, a catchphrase that he used throughout the night.

Apparently, DMC's Café Night essentially served as a practice sermon before the Sunday morning service, giving Billy a chance to get through and find ways around the various interruptions he experienced.

Billy's sermon was scatterbrained at times, mostly due to the number of interruptions strewn throughout, and while I was cautious about the theme, it did shine a light on some inconsistencies that influenced several of my now-atheist friends in their decision to leave not just Catholicism, but Christianity in general.

Although "Bob" didn't descend from the rafters to haunt the church, the sermon felt like a Catholic version of *A Christmas Carol* tour, with the congregation being taken on a ride by the Holy Ghosts of Past, Present, and Yet To Come. While Billy explained various Catholic practices like the Assumption of Mary, the Immaculate Conception, and papal infallibility, several congregants interrupted by sharing their own haunting memories of being a practicing Catholic. A lady my age in plaid pajama pants recalled how she was told to pray the Rosary 50 times a day or else she wouldn't be considered a good woman. A man who also grew up Catholic said he felt like a "blind follower," walking out of church "like a barn animal."

While I agreed with these criticisms, one of my pet peeves from the "One True Church" was actively teaching "my religion is better than your religion" arguments. I didn't understand the Catholic practices either, but if we're to follow His example, it's a slippery slope to get trapped in a contest where we pick up Christ's cross only to use it as a sword against other denominations.

So where was this all going? Eventually, Billy got back on track and said that Mary knew she needed a Savior just as much as anybody. "We are created to worship God. Everyone worships something. Everyone lives for something. It can be religion, drugs, sex, whatever."

As I thought about my own sins and about the history of The Fillmore itself, this line resonated with me, speaking to all the different types of idolatry that exists.

Billy then referenced several passages from the Gospel of Luke to support his argument as to why Mary shouldn't be worshiped and that only Jesus is the mediator for forgiveness and salvation. He finished with 1 Timothy 2:5, "For there is one God and one mediator between God and men, the man Christ Jesus."

The Downtown Mission Church was abnormal in its own way. From the site of a 1920s murder to 1940s prostitution, from playing graphic movies to playing host to drunken bar fights, The Fillmore itself is an unconventional structure. But here it still stands, carrying a sinful reputation, yet redeemed with a marquee lit up for Christ.

While I didn't particularly jump on the bandwagon for this sermon, as I looked around at the people gathered to hear it, I had to commend Billy for being a leader who had emptied himself to become a servant. He transformed a former brothel whose doors hid all kinds of indecent secrets into a symbol of hope for the upside-down kingdom that Christ talked about.

Jesus never said, "Don't let the children come up to me," or "Keep away those who are sick." No, he talked about a new kingdom where the poor would become rich, the suffering would be relieved, and the children would come to Him. He would give eternal housing to those who believed, looking past social status and reaching out to the weak, humble, or damaged.

Downtown Mission Church was reaching out to people I never would have, and if I was to follow in Christ's footsteps, this trip was a wake-up call. I had to do some serious soul-searching for what it means to serve.

WHERE DID THE MILLENNIAL CHRISTIANS GO?
CHIPPEWA VALLEY BIBLE CHURCH • CHIPPEWA FALLS, WISCONSIN

I'd always thought of myself as being a member of the Generation X camp. After buying a house, I was annoyed to see Millennial high school kids park their cars in front of my property to hang out with the other neighborhood teens. With 2 Chainz blasting from their stereos, they would crawl out of their cars like crabs escaping a shell and scuttle sideways to avoid having their saggy pants drop. I never could understand the teenage angst of their rebellion against the common sense of using a belt. Seeing this, my generational discrimination would instinctively kick in.

To be fair, I possess the innate ability to channel the mindset of a hunchbacked old man perched in a rocking chair on his front porch, wearing nothing more than a white tank top, Depends, and knee-high black socks. Whenever my made-up Lawrence Welk vintage spoon collection began rattling due to the house-quaking noise pollution, my elder alter-ego would violently start shaking his cane and shout, "Turn that darn music down, ya hear?!" When the ghetto wannabes would take a shortcut to their friends' houses by trespassing through my yard, I would conjure fantasies of building a fence made of pesticide warning signs and of filling their gas tanks with Metamucil before ultimately going to the doctor for my thoughts on the latest designs of Rorschach inkblots.

After turning the Big 3-0 though, I discovered it was Wikipedia-official that the Millennial generation actually starts with those born in 1981.

Having been born in 1983, I no longer felt compelled to drink from the nectar of Gen-X prune juice. All of a sudden, I felt younger, hipper, more Ryan Gosling-like. I celebrated this discovery at my computer keyboard with a mini Tiger Woods fist pump, hoping the generational realignment would also magically replenish my receding hairline. Unfortunately, this news did nothing for follicle restoration, so instead, I resorted to practicing "Hey girl" poses in front of my bathroom mirror while beatboxing out to a remix of that "#SELFIE" tune by The Chainsmokers.

After nine straight weeks of visiting different worship institutions and sailing through the high seas of religious complacency, I would have thought to hit land by now, finding somewhere to stake a flag for my progressive Christian beliefs, shouting "I claim this church in the name of my Millennial self-identification!" Alas, this has happened as many times as people use the word "alas" in everyday language. While many churches had been far more progressive than my former church, I still hadn't experienced that "A-ha!" light bulb moment. Part of that was probably due to the fact that I'd only run across a small handful of Christians my own age, and they all had children. Plus, I had yet to hear a sermon that spoke to the challenges I was facing in a rapidly changing world.

So before I took a selfie, I was left asking myself, *Where did all the Millennial Christians go?*

. . .

Chippewa Valley Bible Church in Chippewa Falls, Wisconsin
December 14, 2014 – 9:00 A.M. Sunday School Christmas Service

While searching through YouTube sermons, I was excited to find sermons that were courageous enough to not shy away from everyday issues that Millennials are confused about and that are often neglected at church, such as the need to bridge Christianity and science or the increase in at-home porn consumption. How do you address these topics without riling up people who don't want to hear about them?

One local church that popped up was Chippewa Valley Bible Church (CVBC). After watching a handful of the lead pastor's sermons, I was impressed that his convictions were transparent and grounded. He wasn't afraid to tackle such heavy-hitting issues, while also being graceful enough to forewarn parents in advance. I assumed that this church housed other Millennial Christians who were searching for the same practical advice. I needed to see this church in action.

CVBC was packed when I got there, and the only seating available was along the back wall. I was eager to see what the pastor would cover this week, but I cringed like the Grinch watching a Rudolph the Red-Nosed Reindeer marathon when I found out this was their Sunday School

Christmas program.

Everyone and their grandmother loves these types of services. Except me. Don't get me wrong, it's fun for the whole family to see Little Johnny onstage, covering timeless Christmas songs that have been passed down through the generations with blood-curdling, off-key yowling. But if you're single and have no personal ties with anyone in the church, then you're at the mercy of what's to come.

My only saving grace was reflecting on childhood memories of when I'd been forced to participate in Christmas services like this. I can still see the teachers swabbing their sweaty foreheads during rehearsals, praying that the entire 1st grade class wouldn't make a break for the nativity and take a nap in the manger with baby Jesus. We'd practice everything: from walking into church, sitting down in church, how to turn toward the aisle in church, how to apprehend the 2nd graders who tried to escape from church, etc. Eventually, we'd have all of ten minutes to actually practice our lines. Every year, we would recite the same old Luke 2:1–20 passage with about as much enthusiasm as we'd have for watching Cheez Whiz dry on a cracker. I wouldn't be surprised if, after rehearsal, the teachers downed a Three Wise Men, and I don't mean the Biblical Magi.

Now, as the Sunday School children screamed "Happy Birthday, Jesus," I began to daydream, thinking about what had become of my classmates since leaving parochial grade school 15 years earlier. It was strange looking back to our confirmation in church, when our pastor forewarned that half of us would leave the church. I remember thinking that was crazy at that time. But as I reviewed who was in my class, it turned out he was right. Half of my class still maintained Synod membership, while the other half stopped being religious. Matter of fact, I'd be the last one to get hitched. All but one had kids in their 20's, and even that person had a few cats—didn't that count? In the past, I would have been pretty distraught at these thoughts, as my number one priority in my 20's was to get married. Now, I had accepted my singleness for what it was, and could appreciate the advantages of freedom while being single (though cycling through different women on different dates was getting old).

The kids moved on to a song called "Christmas in Reverse"—at least the teachers actually made these programs fun for the kids. This stuff seemed miles better than the recycled material I grew up with. As the kids shouted their song, my mind drifted to the congregation, where I noticed that the Millennial population was smaller than expected. It was mostly adults in their 40's and 50's, with a strong grandparent presence for their grandkids. I found this shocking, as I had assumed that with the genuine passion of this church's pastor, the age demographics would be younger. Other than some Millennial parents in the back pews with small children and the occasional baby bump, there weren't many present within my age range.

After the service, the narthex was packed with kids, parents, and grandparents all talking, laughing, hugging, and embracing. It was a family affair, whereas I was all by myself. I got a few glancing stares, but overall, I was an unobserved outsider in the mass chaos of people. All I had were my thoughts.

When I walked out, I had no idea what to write about this visit. Surely, I could conjure some great Gandalf-worthy analogy for it? But, in all honestly, nothing about this visit spoke to me. My mind was a blank slate. Most people say that the hardest part about faith is feeling isolated from God, but I disagree. In my experience, the hardest part is finding a community where you feel like you belong.

It looked like I would have to keep on wandering, searching, and hoping that such a place was out there.

CHURCH 11:
CTRL+ALT+DELETE
FIRST UNIVERSALIST UNITARIAN CHURCH • WAUSAU, WISCONSIN

I had to have her.

I still remember the night I first saw her at Best Buy. My heart leapt higher than a kangaroo on a trampoline. She had the perfect dimensions, exactly what I was looking for back then. One guy strolled up to her and sized her up, but I had a feeling that he couldn't close the deal, much less afford her. She was gonna be mine that night. So I played it cool—waiting and biding my time until the opportune moment. Finally, when no one else was looking and she was all by her lonesome, I warped in faster than the starship *Enterprise*.

There was no small talk; we both knew what was going to happen next. I scanned her up and down, then placed my hands around her sides. It was so wrong, but felt oh-so right. When I finished checking her out, I knew she was officially mine. One thing led to another, and we went back to my place. I was firmly in control at this point, placing her upright on my desk, where I wasted no time plugging it in. Things went really well during the initial hook-up, and just when she got turned on, that's when things really took off.

I don't say this often, but the two of us really clicked. I had met all different types of women, but no one could compare to what she could do. She would do anything I wanted, when I wanted it, and all I had to do was press her buttons from time to time. If I needed space, all I needed to do was make a simple command, and she would give it to me. She would never ask for anything in return. She was simply irresistible. And best of all, Tiff complimented me on having walked away with a steal that night: my new computer was $100 off the original retail price!

If that isn't a great deal, I don't know what is.

. . .

I knew something was wrong one Saturday afternoon. A few months after the forbidden kiss, Tiff crept to my bedroom quieter than a mouse, not so much as a peep after checking Facebook on my computer. Playing the part of the "perfect Christian boyfriend," I instinctively could read her feelings like the text in this book. I asked if everything was okay, but for the first time in our relationship, she wasn't "there." It felt like she was translating her emotions into Braille.

We had overcome a number of obstacles that had actually strengthened our relationship, but I couldn't get a read on this. Maybe the semester was getting to her. Maybe she had received some bad news about her mom having a relapse. Maybe—nah, it couldn't be that.

Impatient with the guessing game, I asked again what was wrong. "Nothing," she said, refusing my attempted embrace in favor of a pillow, which she suffocated her tears into. I couldn't make any progress, so I decided to give her some time and went into the other room. A cold sweat enveloped my quickly paling body, and my tongue dried with cottonmouth. I looked over at my computer and the worst possible thought crossed my mind: *Did I delete my browsing history from last night?*

I had known for awhile that if I couldn't CTRL myself, didn't ALT my willpower, and failed to DELETE the increasing .addiction that hid in the darkest corners of my mind, it would only be a matter of time before I'd slip up and she'd discover the eBathsheba hiding in the broad daylight of my living room.

That Saturday afternoon turned out to be the day.

She eventually got up to retreat to her car, refusing our customary goodbye kiss to hint that I was the one responsible for her sadness. An hour later, after she was home, she texted me with the findings of her undercover investigation, shining a light on a fleshy website I had tried to conceal from her notice. I was caught. I couldn't hide this anymore. I had been cheating on her with my computer.

I couldn't go to TASK MANAGER and click END TASK. It was too late to hit RESTART on the wrong choices that I'd clicked ENTER on. My irresponsibility and selfishness had installed a virus that infected the bandwidth of her trust. My Gateway computer was a Trojan horse, maliciously tricking the feelings she'd acquired from Cupid's arrow into spearing her heart when she least expected it. Not even the Geek Squad could pile into their Volkswagen Beetles to make a home visit and repair this. I had abused her love for me. I had failed the one person I loved and trusted more than anyone I'd ever known.

Now, because of my failure to firewall my own sinful temptations, our relationship was on the verge of getting the Blue Screen of Death.

. . .

First Universalist Unitarian Church of Wausau, Wisconsin
December 21, 2014 – 7:00 P.M. Solstice Service

I was lost. To those waiting in the narthex, I probably looked more confused than a chameleon in a tie-dye warehouse. I had no clue where the worship service was held inside the First Universalist Unitarian (UU) Church of Wausau.

My goal this evening was to challenge my preconceptions and remain unbiased in observing different theologies. UUism is an entirely different cup of tea from Christianity and is probably most famous for tasting the rainbow and raising the LGBT flag alongside many others. From what their brochures in the narthex said, all were welcome: Christians, Jews, pantheists, atheists, agnostics, gays, lesbians, interfaith families, guys with really bad direction, you name it. It's a self-described liberal religion that appeals to freethinkers and humanists by incorporating and deriving inspiration from all major world religions. An online article I came across described UUism with an anonymous quote: "If you've got questions, we've got answers. No, that's not right. If you've got questions, we've got more questions."

Applying this logic to my current predicament, I walked up to a female greeter with a supremely intellectual question of my own: "Um, where's the church service at?"

The greeter stared at me blankly with gray eyes, looking at me like it was my first day in kindergarten and I had just taste-tested a glue stick. "Tonight is our Winter Solstice service," she said. "Do you know what the solstice is?"

"Yeah-yeah-yeah," I triple-replied, knowing full well that we were observing the longest night of the year and all that jazz. "So where's the service located?"

Instead of answering, the greeter shrugged and said, "This is our first Solstice service, so we really don't know what's going to happen tonight."

Great.

Now more confused than ever, I was going to have to find it myself, which resulted in my awkwardly mistaking a doorway to the worship area for a locked restroom. Eventually, I bumped into a familiar face. Being in a church, I figured I would have seen an image of Jesus Christ somewhere,

55

but not here. Instead, there was a framed poster of "100 Unitarians and Universalists who made a difference..." I had to do a triple-take. The first face I recognized was none other than Charles Darwin's.

"Diiiiiiiiiiiiiiinnggggggg!"

A bell chime sounded, interrupting my thoughts. It echoed throughout the gathering hall to signal that the service was about to start. Everyone formed a line and entered a narrow, cave-like entryway that looked like it had been borrowed from The Shire.

Still perplexed, I left the poster and was greeted by two ushers handing out small LED candles and bulletins made from black construction paper, with a carefully crafted cut of yellow paper in the top corner edge to illustrate a light coming out. This foreshadowed some of the theatrical creativity that was about to come.

Walking in, I noticed that the church had a rustic smell. Red and white poinsettias dotted the front stage, and a talented musician played a cello solo as a relaxing pre-worship mediation to relieve any stress. A female reverend presided as the night's host, attired in all-black clothing. She rang a second chime to start the solstice service and then addressed the congregation with the words of an unnamed "famous theologian" (I was later told it was from *Telling Your Own Story* by Sam Keen and Anne Valley Fox):

"So long as human beings change and make history, so long as children are born and old people die, there will be tales to explain why sorrow darkens the day and stars fill the night. We invent stories about the origin and conclusion of life because we are exiles in the middle of time. The void surrounds us. We live within a parenthesis surrounded by question marks. Our stories and myths don't dispel ignorance, but they help us find our way, our place at the heart of the mystery. In the end, as in the beginning, there will be a vast silence, broken by the sound of one person telling a story to another."

Next, a number of children wearing cut-out animal masks huddled around the front of the church to act out a Native American folktale called the "Fire Race." The kids then pantomimed the narrative of a local storyteller, starting with a girl wearing a Yellowjacket mask protecting a glowing orange prop torch. The eldest child, wearing a Coyote mask, devised a plan and enlisted all of the other "Animals" to help seize the burning torch. The Coyote then stole the stick and escaped through the church's aisle with the Yellowjacket in hot pursuit. At the narrator's instruction, the eyes of the congregation followed the Animal children maze through the aisles as they passed off the prop torch like a relay baton, chasing each other until the Yellowjacket finally gave up. Eventually, the Frog "swallowed" the burning stick and spit it out into a piece of coal. The Coyote then taught the Animals how to rub sticks together to create fire, thus showing the importance of the need to live cooperatively.

After a round of applause, the reverend made preparations for the Invocation to the Darkness, leading with a Wendell Berry poem:

"To go in the dark with a light is to know the light. To know the dark, go dark. Go without sight, and find that the dark, too, blooms and sings, and is traveled by dark feet and dark wings."

The church lights were then turned off, and the congregation was left to its own thoughts in the dark. A lone light was centered on the cello musician for a mediation solo, before that light ultimately went out as well, leaving the entire church in pitch darkness. After a few moments, guitars started to play, and an unseen lady sang "A Lullaby for the Darkness." Then, a ferocious drumbeat echoed through the shadows for several moments until a figure darted in front of the stage. It used multiple fluorescent glow sticks to highlight an artistic fluidity of motion.

With the church bathed in darkness, the first glimmers of the LED lights started lighting up in the front row. The congregation had been advised earlier to "pass the light," so a nearby congregant turned on my LED light, and I did the same for a nearby child in my pew. After the candles were all lit, illuminating the church like fireflies, a light-up "sun" rose behind the stage to signify the return of the light.

. . .

In life, we can take a lot of different paths based on the choices we make. It's part of being human, and if we're going to experience life in its purest form, we have to experience the lows with the highs, the losses with the wins, the darkness with the light.

In the past, I made a series of wrong choices that ultimately led me down a murky path that hurt someone I had sworn to love. It was quite the juxtaposition: I promised to protect her from the douchebags of the world, and yet I was the one who betrayed her most of all.

That night, when everything had finally been exposed and my relationship hung by a thread, I tossed and turned in darkness. My companion that night was guilt, and I eventually found myself thinking, *I will not be defined by my mistakes.*

While on this church odyssey, I've become intrigued by the different paths and directions people take as they search for God—however they perceive Him. That's one thing I came away with after visiting First Universalist Unitarian Church, where the only mention of anything that could be described as "God" was the reverend slipping in a remark about "the Divine" and the "spark of life," leaving the interpretation entirely up to the individual. In a way, this was strangely refreshing, as it didn't comply with the rigid rules most religions abide by. Still, I couldn't get over my disapproval of depicting Charles Darwin as a religious hero in a church. I doubt that will ever change.

We must all travel a lot of dark paths, and we will end up hurting people as a result of our human failures. But if this church service taught me anything, it's that even when we're lost in the deepest darkness of our own personal solstice in life, there is always a light. It's just up to us whether or not we light the candle.

CHURCH 12:
ONE NATION UNDER GOD
FORT SNELLING MEMORIAL CHAPEL • MINNEAPOLIS, MINNESOTA

My hidden addiction was under the interrogation light of a woman's scorn. The red-light district of my perverted psyche was on full display. Tiff peeked into the peep show of my thoughts, my mind completely disrobed to reveal its barest essentials. It didn't take long for her to realize that I'd been favoring a hard drive over her. The backlash couldn't be wiped away with a tissue. I had nothing left to cover myself with except a scantily clad apology.

"I'm sorry."

My regret failed to dislodge the knife I had used to stab her in the back. Instead, her wounded feelings started to bleed even more resentment. She called for a recess by hanging up on me and wouldn't answer my calls or texts. The wait to hear back from her felt longer than waiting for a snail try to figure out dial-up connection.

Finally, a few hours later, a text came in to reestablish the prosecution's line of questioning: "What r u doing right now, watching those WHORES on ur computer again?"

In vengeful retaliation, her scorned emotions had hopped into the operator's seat of a giant industrial crane, ready to go full-blown Miley Cyrus and swing a wrecking ball at the facade of my face, which was suddenly misplaced atop her fantasy Mount Rushmore alongside the likes of David Beckham, Ryan Gosling, and what's his face from *Twilight* with the chiseled six-pack abs. As I prepared for our relationship to be demolished to cinders, I was wracked with guilt for my disastrous decision to place graphic twerking over my relationship with Tiff.

I used internet porn as a therapeutic agent to deal with stress. In reality, that was merely a sad excuse for my lack of willpower and for pathetically allowing my body to have control over my mind. Porn made me soft, pun intended. I lost my fire and drive, my ambition vanished, and I settled into mere complacency, only interested in being able to get my fix, which didn't really require me to be much of a man.

Worst of all, I had to admit that I had failed Tiff. I had no alibi, no excuse. I had to come clean, choosing truth over lies and facing accountability for my crimes against her feelings.

Tiff finally brought her prosecution to a rest when I confessed to my crime and then tried to understand where I was coming from in her cross-examination. After addressing a number of small, specific things in our relationship she eventually slammed down her gavel, declaring my sentence to repair the damage I had caused: "You need to start going to church again."

After being sentenced to church, I made up white lies about the services I didn't actually attend while we patched things up. Rather than repair our relationship by constructing new lies, I soon retreated to my old religious stomping grounds to obtain proof of attendance in the form of bulletins and to re-adapt to church doctrine in a half-assed attempt to find God. I didn't mind going but I could never get excited about it and I couldn't put my finger on why.

Church felt like it was slowly neutering my Christian masculinity. I would sit. I would stand. I would bark hymns and roll over to the correct page in the bulletin. Like a good boy, I obediently conformed to the religious views presented and consumed the messages like they were a bowl of Purina Puppy Chow, nodding my head in agreement and trying to believe that I was on the right side, because my church said so. With my lack of Christian self-identity, I couldn't even imagine how Jesus would go about reaching out to others who were different. I chose to domesticate my faith for the purpose of behavioral modification that was on par with training a dog at your nearest PetSmart.

When I witnessed my church refusing Holy Communion to visiting believers, it set a number of things in motion, including my questioning of man-made religion. Too afraid to challenge the Almighty WELS Steeple or to seek a different church that better aligned with my beliefs, I remained complacent and continued to come back every Sunday, like a game of spiritual fetch. Sometimes, I half-expected a pat on the head from a pastor, accompanied by a "That's a good boooooy."

Is this how most Millennial Christians feel about church today as well?

These days, the stereotypical Christian male is seen as dull and boring, choosing to seek security by blindly conforming to church doctrine rather than seeking God for himself. Would Moses have passively read about the modern-day Egyptian Revolution by scrolling through the news on his tablet? Would Jonah go to Red Lobster for seafood every Friday night? Would David be content with a 9-to-5 job alongside his sheep? No. The Bible tells tall tales of how these men became leaders, embarking on spiritual adventures to discover not just God, but also who they truly were as men.

This is why it was difficult to respect my father as a spiritual leader. Sure, he served the church as an usher once a month and would raise his hand at church meetings where male members—and yes, only male members—vote. He conformed to what the church preached and got in line with religion, likely because he started a family.

It wasn't until I met Tiff's father that I got my first glimpse into how a spiritual leader should actually lead his family. He was proud of God and his country. Christ flowed through his veins with his blood mixed with camouflage. He never said much, but he knew how to preach the gospel when necessary.

After Tiff discovered my deep, dark, internet porn secret, I resolved to mirror my character after his, the greatest Christian role model I'd ever encountered.

He was a military man, proud of his nation and proud of those who served. When I first met him at a family party—which I prepared for by getting buzzed on Mike's Hard Lemonade—he didn't pull the standard overly protective father shtick by sitting on the porch with a loaded shotgun. Instead, he shook my hand, looked me in the eye, and introduced himself man-to-man. More importantly, he made a point of saying that he worked hard to ensure that his children would have a better life than the dirty jobs he had. My initial reaction was to think he was odd for saying that and maybe to hand him a Mike's as well. Still, I immediately respected him for his transparency. He gave me his blessing to court his daughter, the greatest gift that God had ever given him.

When his wife was diagnosed with cancer, he was like Samson with a crew cut, staying strong and holding his family together through its darkest and roughest times.

He served as an elder in his church, and once, when I visited, I stayed back while the Lutheran Missouri Synod members received Holy Communion. After the service, he was perturbed by my exclusion and challenged the doctrine in a respectful, yet pointed manner to the pastor, saying, "We need to fix that."

. . .

Fort Snelling Veterans Memorial Chapel in Minneapolis, Minnesota
December 28, 2014 – 11:00 A.M. Worship Service

As I pondered the craziness of making a six-hour drive to Minneapolis simply to go to church, the term "spiritual adventure" sprang to mind. After searching for Minneapolis churches online, I decided to go with Fort Snelling Veterans Memorial Chapel to see how a church treats its veterans. Built in 1927, it originated by request from a group of Sunday School children who wanted to worship on base. The church was decommissioned a few years after World War II ended, and it sat unused until the 1960s, when it was scheduled to be demolished to make way for President Eisenhower's highway system. It narrowly escaped the wrecking ball thanks to some last-minute efforts to preserve and restore the chapel.

My car navigated the roads of historic Fort Snelling like it was a Plinko board, my GPS telling me to zigzag with a number of turns to finally reach the base. Upon arrival, the chapel was unique with its protruding turret that extended vertically from the chapel's fortifications. It overlooked a parking lot with more Buicks, Oldsmobiles, and handicapped-parking signs than I'd ever seen in one place.

When I was about to enter the sanctuary, the usher stopped me to inform that communion would be held later. Because the majority of the congregation was elder veterans, he advised I should sit on the left side if I'd want to walk up to the altar, or sit on the right side if I had a handicap, where communion would be served in the aisle.

As I walked to a pew on the left side, a prelude was already in progress as a veteran musician exhibited his harmonica talents to the delight of the entire congregation. When he was done, he received a much-deserved round of applause, which was likely followed by a fair share of arthritis flare-ups.

Despite the majority of the congregation being able to collect Social Security, the church's energy was amazing. It also smelled like potpourri. My nose spent the entire service curious about where the scent originated.

Aesthetically, the chapel was steeped in military history. Colorful military flags hung overhead, proudly representing various Minnesotan units. Stained-glass windows honored pioneer military leaders. Memorial plaques in remembrance of those who had served gleamed throughout the interior.

The service began with the two chaplains lighting two candles: one for the altar and a second in honor of prisoners of war and those missing in action (POW/MIA). From the lectern, one of the chaplains, who was outfitted in a black gown, greeted everyone with a charming, "Welcome to the beautiful and historic Fort Snelling." His was a voice made for afternoon baseball. He then inaugurated the service by ringing the ship's bell that stood beside the lectern.

The second chaplain was the polar opposite of the first. He looked like the long-lost twin of Rod Roddy from *The Price Is Right*. He was energetic and animated, wearing a brightly colored doctoral gown with a pair of eyeglasses, shouting "Come on doooooown!" when he summoned the children for their special message. I half expected Bob Barker to pop out of the pulpit to begin the bidding on the mysterious potpourri.

Roddy's sermon was titled, "The Praise of the Wise," and it examined the mindset of the Three Wise Men. These were prominent, influential men; so why did they bother going on a journey to worship a baby, a journey that contemporary scholars estimate would have taken two years? The pastor reasoned that the Magi were students of the Old Testament prophecies and had read the prophecies so much that they had fallen in love with the promised Savior like a young couple hopelessly in love. "It's nauseating," he joked about couples that read and re-read their letters (or texts nowadays) who couldn't wait to see each other in person. Yet the Three Wise Men were in a similar state of mind in their pursuit to see Jesus in person.

Roddy summed it up with a question that really resonated with me: "I have a question for you: have you heard of King Jesus? How many of you have come to seek Him here today? How many of you are doing more than just showing up? The Three Wise Men didn't see Him and then just go on their merry way and neither should you. Yet there are some who show up, see Him, and leave, checking it off their to-do list. Others just want to *feel* religious."

In the past, my religious mentality—and especially my mentality regarding the meaning of Christian masculinity—would have had me shying away from such a question. But on this particular day, my faith felt alive.

As I drove home, I realized that my conception of Christian masculinity was beginning to break away from the conformity and restrictions of religion. Going on a crazy trek to a church service at a historic military fort reminded me that I could forge a new path for my beliefs and myself. After all, I was in the midst of a spiritual quest. I had a story to tell, one that went beyond the same old religious routine that most people follow on autopilot. As I toured different churches in my pursuit of Christ, I was becoming something more within myself.

This congregation of military veterans had all proudly worn squadron jackets, many with patches decorating their sleeves. Those jackets and patches symbolized their pride for the adventures they'd had while defending our freedom and, thus, upholding their own Christian values.

When the chaplain had lit the POW/MIA candle at the beginning of the service, it reminded me of Tiff's dad, the wise man who had earned my respect and who was brave enough to challenge complacency and put his faith into action. Though I most likely will never speak with him again, he is still my model for what Christian masculinity should look like in a household.

In living out his own American Dream, he raised two flags in his front yard. The top flag displayed the proud colors of Old Glory; the second was the black POW/MIA flag. He did this every day. It was his way of paying respect to those who made a difference, those who sacrificed to make all our lives better, and those we may never meet again. The flag features a motto: "You are not forgotten."

ALL'S FAIR IN LOVE AND WAR

THE EPISCOPAL CHURCH OF ST. JOHN THE BAPTIST • WAUSAU,
WISCONSIN

"We need to take a break."

Her mouth was like an M60 automatic machine gun. Every word was a bullet blowing holes through our fairytale dreams like water balloons in the middle of a war zone. I was completely out in the open, defenseless, and under heavy fire while sitting next to her on my living room loveseat with matching pillows. I tried to radio in empty "I love you's" to call off the verbal airstrikes, but her affection had transformed her into a cold-blooded turncoat that would have made Benedict Arnold proud.

I was in shock: dropped-jaw, utter disbelief shock. Just three months earlier at McDonald's, we had discussed getting promise rings after I secretly swiped some of her French fries when she got up to use the restroom. Now my mind was scrambling for a medic to provide CPR to my wounded fantasies of wedding bells, clever Facebook announcements, and making babies.

Any kind of Happily Ever After dreams that had miraculously survived the first salvo were then sniped off one-by-one with headshot statements like, "The timing isn't right," "You're not who you used to be," and "I need to date other guys." I tried to salvage anything that resembled the feelings we'd had for each other, but she countered with the same stone-cold words, which she repeated over and over again, both tormenting and motivating me to this day: "You've settled."

My mind was in shambles, frantically trying to process what was happening. Just hours earlier, everyone—including me—had thought we were destined to be together until death do us part. We were an iconic couple, like Adam and Eve or Romeo and Juliet. Despite some bumps in the road, we were always militantly by each other's sides, supporting each other through thick and thin. I had never expected to get the "We need to talk" text message. Being optimistic, I had assumed that she'd forgotten to tack on "...to decide which Mexican restaurant will serve us free samples of RumChata tonight."

Unfortunately, I had missed all the warning signs. Our last goodnight kiss possessed as much romantic passion as watching your grandparents making out in a nursing home. The last time we'd held each other, she talked about how she wished we hadn't moved so fast, counting off the dozen or more dates it took for us to even have a first kiss. On our last phone call, she grasped at straws with trap questions, trying to find a reason to get into an argument. When that didn't worked, she'd switched topics, going on about the novelty of finally being 21 in a college town. At the end of the day, she just wanted something...someone...different. And now, she had the freedom to find it.

After our "talk," she escaped to her getaway vehicle with a barely concealed smile, discreetly celebrating her liberation from the repression of our three-year relationship. Mission accomplished. I was left to assess the wreckage of false dreams heaped in a mess of lies.

At first, I was in denial.

The worst part was, if I were completely honest with myself, I knew her criticism of me was dead-on.: I had settled.

Loss often leads to confusion and identity crisis, as the mind twists and bends to deal with what has happened. Seemingly out of nowhere, my favorite person in the entire world had left me alone to my thoughts. *What's wrong with me?* was the question that haunted my mind in the following hours.

After spending 24 hours in a depressive state, I decided to refuse to let the situation control my attitude and live in mental purgatory. I was going to take back control of my life.

. . .

The Episcopal Church of St. John the Baptist in Wausau, Wisconsin
January 4, 2015 – 9:00 A.M. Eucharist

Overnight, the roads were blanketed with a fresh coat of two or three inches of snow, and the wind chill made it colder than an Iditarod husky's Kibbles 'n Bits. As I hustled to the church's front doors to avoid losing feeling in my toes, the rector was standing outside, braving the elements to welcome everyone as they came in. He was a friendly fellow with a jolly face, a tonsure-like haircut, and a smile that made you feel like you belonged.

There was a lot of history inside this church. It had been founded in 1854 as St. John's in the Wilderness. The city that would become Wausau was younger than a toddler then. It was founded by loggers harvesting the surrounding pine forests and then transporting the fallen lumber on the nearby Wisconsin River. St. John's was one of the first churches established in the area, but it was destroyed by a windstorm just three years later. After the Civil War, the locals built a new church at the same site, and it was finally consecrated in 1887. Seeing as how the church was no longer in the wilderness, it was renamed The Church of St. John the Baptist, eventually adding the Episcopal label and insignia.

The cold, snow, and holidays had an impact on travel this morning. The congregation was small and intimate, only 26 adults and two small children in attendance.

My first impression to describe the Episcopal Church service is to term it "Catholic Light," with the congregation being a mix of Catholics and Protestants. This was very apparent during prayers, when 13 of the adult congregants pulled out the kneelers to pray in the Catholic style, while the other 13 adults, myself included, chose to remain standing and bow our heads per the Protestant tradition.

The service whizzed by, the rector finishing the sermon just 20 minutes after the service started. While the sermon was exceedingly short compared to what I'm accustomed to, the rector spoke with genuine clarity and guided his listeners through his message with precision, emphasizing God's love for us.

He began the sermon by mentioning that he had just watched *Into the Woods,* a Broadway musical that intertwined the plots of several Brothers Grimm fairy tales. "But what happens after the 'happily ever after'?" he asked, quickly getting to the point. Everyone knows about the birth of Jesus, but what about the story that comes after it? This lesser-known story still serves an important purpose, as the focus suddenly shifts to Joseph. It's now his responsibility to protect his new family from Herod's forces. The rector moved on to talk about parenting and the joyful discoveries two parents experience again and again while raising and protecting a child, never taking the child or marriage for granted.

The most powerful motivational statement I ever heard came from Tiff the night she called off our own Happily Ever After.

"You've settled."

Now, with time and distance, I can see that her decision to discard everything we had built together took a great deal of courage. I find that I can now respect her choice to pursue something better. She was right, and she was brave to tell me the uncomfortable truth that I had settled. I had taken our relationship for granted and allowed my life to be affected by the various poor choices I'd made, which further sabotaged any efforts to find a higher purpose in life. In the long-run, her words lit a fire under me. I wanted to prove to myself that I could get out of this slump and never let myself settle again, whether it be physically, mentally, or spiritually.

When I left The Episcopal Church of St. John the Baptist, I felt like this was a church service that I'd quickly forget compared to some of the others I'd attended. With a 50/50 split between Catholic and Protestant prayer styles, I was confused about how others could get dialed into such a church. But as I considered the emotions and experiences that I brought into this church, I found myself being more drawn to it than I had originally thought. While it may not have been the most extroverted denomination, with all the bells and whistles, I'm not the most extroverted guy, either. As a protector whose natural impulse is to shield those I care about, I appreciated how the Episcopal Church's traditional symbol—a shield—symbolized protection.

To a certain extent, the end of my three-year relationship with Tiff paralleled the very church's early history, having been destroyed just three years after it was built. The next day, when there was nothing left, we were both faced with two options: to give up or to start over with a better foundation. No matter what may have huffed and puffed to slow you down, we can eventually build ourselves back up again to create something even better that wouldn't have existed before the fall.

FINDING THE JOHN AT A CATHOLIC BASILICA
THE BASILICA OF ST. JOSAPHAT • MILWAUKEE, WISCONSIN

When I arrived at the Basilica of St. Josaphat, I needed to find the men's room.

I don't mean to be disrespectful to the 1.2 billion Catholics in the world, but after you drink 96 fluid ounces of Powerade Zero while driving for three straight hours while drumming your steering wheel to Taylor Swift's sick beats, ya gotta go when ya gotta go.

When I reached my destination and found an empty space in the parking lot, I could finally look up and take in the building. I couldn't believe the grandiose scale of the Basilica. My eyeballs were larger than they were the first time I accidentally walked into my parents' unlocked bedroom and saw my mom changing. To borrow a phrase from T-Swift, my traumatized five-year-old self had to "Shake it off, shake it off."

Located along the Milwaukee skyline, this grand masterpiece of architecture was modeled after the famed St. Peter's Basilica in Vatican City. Six Corinthian pillars nearly 100 hundred feet high supported the outer portico, and twin bell towers marked the very top. But the building's most noticeable attribute was its copper dome roof, which towers more than 250 feet overhead and is rumored to be larger than the Taj Mahal.

It's majestic.

It's opulent.

It's magnificent.

And I couldn't find a single men's restroom.

The original church caught fire in 1889 and burned to the ground. (I was starting to notice that churches in the 1800s had a knack for falling apart in their formative years.) Due to the rapid growth of the Polish immigrant community in southern Milwaukee, in 1897, the founding reverend enlisted a prominent architect to construct a new church home. The reverend pinched pennies at every corner, going so far as to purchase a shutdown federal building in Chicago and shipping the salvaged materials to Milwaukee on 500 flat railcars. The Polish immigrants worked at their trades by day, and then at night, they worked on the basilica into the wee hours until its completion in 1901.

In 1929, St. Josaphat was officially deemed the third basilica in the United States, meaning it needs to be ready for a surprise papal visit at all times. As a result, there is a giant throne near the front of the altar, with a scepter on-hand in the unlikely event that the Pope actually visits Wisconsin and has the papal tiara converted into a cheesehead.

Strolling through the front doors, I wasn't met by human ushers, but rather by two four-foot-tall angelic statues with golden wings. They were encircled by red poinsettias and holding holy water fonts for parishioners to make the Sign of the Cross upon entrance. Given how the light was illuminating everything with a golden glow, I half-expected those *Game of Thrones* dragons to serve as acolytes, flying out of the balcony to breathe fire at the altar candles. As I continued to the front, I was literally dizzy from staring up at the *Stargate*-like portal into heaven, a breathtaking oil painting of angels, prophets, and saints that adorned the domed ceiling. As you can probably guess, there were no restrooms signs up there.

I still had a few minutes before mass started, so I trudged off down a long corridor that branched off into the Pope John Paul II Pavilion. This corridor featured intricate stained-glass windows beside numerous framed murals of what I recognized to be late Catholic popes.

It was here that I came across a portrait of Pope Sixtus V, who's mural gave bypassers the heebie jeebies with such an uncomfortable staring stink eye, it looked to have been conjured from a Stephen King novel. Before that day, I hadn't even known there was a Pope Sixtus V. After some internet research, I learned that he served as pope from 1585 to 1590 and unsuccessfully attempted to instate a law that made adultery punishable by death. He was considered impulsive, obstinate, and severe—also words that could be used to describe my bloated bladder as I pressed on in my pursuit of the lavatory.

. . .

The Basilica of Saint Josaphat in Milwaukee, Wisconsin
January 10, 2015 – 4:30 P.M. Mass

After failing to find Tinkle Town—or asking for help since I'm a man with a horrible sense of direction—-I returned to the nave just minutes before mass started. I encountered several parish members kneeling on padded, foldout kneelers, their hands tented. I assumed they were praying to the saints for something important, like to feed the homeless.

I wanted to interrupt: *Excuse me, can we discuss my personal issues for a second? Who does a guy need to pray to in here to find the loo?*

As I contemplated the john's location, mass began. The sermon was about John the Baptist and the significance of Holy H2O. *Oh great! I managed to attend the one sermon involving river streams,* I thought as I contemplated Lamaze.

The rector's voice was muffled throughout the service, making him sound like the cast of Winnie the Pooh. He had the glum cadence of Eeyore, the aged wisdom of Owl, an odd whistling articulation at the ends of his words like Gopher, and the inflection of the titular bear himself. I couldn't tell if it was him, his mic, or me, slowly becoming deranged as my eyeballs starting to turn yellow. Either way, I couldn't understand much of the message, and all I caught was something about discussing our faith with our godparents and how Jesus was baptized to make the water holy through His Spirit. He finished the sermon with the Renewal of Baptismal Promises, which involved scooping and subsequently flicking holy water at the congregation. For those in the front pews, it was like the Jordan River's version of Sea World.

After mass, I figured that a prayer to Jesus for a well-placed restroom sign would help work things out for me. Fortunately, my prayer was answered when I realized that the basement of the Pope John Paul II Pavilion wasn't closed. I explored it further and eventually found what must have been the only restroom in the entire place.

I finished my business and washed my hands.

They were low on paper towels.

SOUNDTRACK TO A SOUL
AXIS AT FIRST BAPTIST CHURCH • HENDERSONVILLE, TENNESSEE

It was Facebook official: Tiff went from being "In a relationship" to "Single."

Just an hour earlier, she had ripped up the script, leaving our fairy tale in the dust as she drove off into the sunset with her new future riding shotgun. The necklace I had gifted her to symbolize our three-year relationship had been traded in for a newly minted "Single" status that she proudly wore on social media like a "For Sale" sign to any interested suitors with high testosterone.

I had missed all the warning signs, and now that she was 21, her ID was suddenly a Golden Ticket to the alcoholic retelling of *Willy Wonka and the Chocolate Factory*. She was now free to mix and mingle at bars and clubs as she pleased, and she was taking advantage of that fact. No longer was she bound to the repressions of our relationship and was free to be wooed by the Oompa-Loompa doo-ba-dee-douchebags who wanted to hit on her with their orange tanning-bed complexions.

I was left in the position of having to put the pieces together from clues on her Facebook wall, as I tried to understand just what had caused the break-up. I knew it wasn't emotionally healthy, but I needed to know. I scrolled through tagged photos at college parties, newly accepted friend requests, and those ridiculous Marilyn Monroe quotes. The worst was when a random guy posted an ominous message on her wall that gained her instant 'Like': "Proud of you."

Proud of what? In the blink of an eye, the girl who had been my sweetest sunshine now felt like she was a million miles away. She had mutated into someone I no longer knew.

She claimed that she wanted to maintain our friendship, requesting that I be demoted from "The One" to just one more of her 400-plus Facebook friends. She sent me a few texts in an attempt to dump her feelings when she wasn't numbing them at the nightclubs with UV mixers and LMFAO remixes. Despite every fiber of my being wanting to maintain contact, I couldn't settle for mere friendship when she meant so much more than that to me. I hopelessly scoured the internet for answers or ways to truly reconcile with her. In reality, I was doing everything I could to ignore the situation.

Then one night, Tiff's Chamber of Secrets was revealed when a new Muggle friend posted a picture of her on Facebook. She looked gorgeous, had bouncy curled hair, and was outfitted in a nightlife dress. What really drew my attention though was the fact that she was wrapped in a lustful embrace with a guy that looked like Lord Voldemort to me. It was the first romantic photograph she had ever taken with a guy who wasn't me. The guy she had previously deemed "just a friend" from her college courses had slithered between us and was constricting her waist with his elongated arms.

The picture didn't look real; it was like one of those magically animated portraits from Hogwarts. Her smile seemed painted on, while her ice-blue eyes were alive, her gaze appearing to shift between He Who Shall Not Be Named beside her and me on the other side of the computer screen. His snake eyes remained still, taunting me through the screen.

Searching for answers, I researched his timeline and noticed that the very same weekend Tiff had made plans with a former roommate to celebrate her birthday out of town, He Who Shall Not Be Named and his best pal had coincidentally befriended the same roommate. It didn't take Dumbledore-like intellect to figure out what must have happened. She must have developed feelings for this guy and had been seeing him behind my back. I had no idea. And what made it even worse was that despite her betrayal, I was still in love with her.

This photo served as a eulogy for any hope I'd had for reconciliation in the near future. I pulled the trigger by deleting all our photos together, blocking her on social media, and then trashing our physical mementos.

Questions started to flood my mind: *For how long had my dream relationship been a lie? Why didn't I keep Christ as the focus? What have I become?*

With my sunshine having been taken away, outdated 500-year-old Protestant hymns and sermons with themes that were designed for a general congregation were no longer cutting it for me at church. The Bible—written 2,000 years ago—wasn't giving me the spiritual guidance I needed in the wake of a sudden break-up that was suffocating my identity. I still believed in Christ, but I needed something more, something different, given the gray skies shadowing me. I needed something that would speak directly to my pain.

Then I listened to Johnny Cash's version of "Hurt" (originally written and recorded by Nine Inch Nails).

"Hurt" wasn't just Johnny Cash's chosen epitaph shortly before his death. To me, it was a song of salvation that quickly became the soundtrack for my soul, a New Age testament that I could relate to when I felt imprisoned by emotional isolation. Every word felt like a counselor helping me catalog the deepest parts of my wounds so that I could derive inspiration from them. The song spoke to feelings that had been collected throughout my lifetime.

It captured the essence of anyone's break-up, contrasting the highs of the now-black-and-white memories and the somber cruelty of the in-living-color present. The reference to Jesus' crucifixion—which Cash added in his cover of the song—was like an epiphany for me, reminding me that even through the betrayal and enduring pain I was feeling, I had power through Christ to resurrect my future and to rise again. Even after his death, Johnny Cash was a sinner-turned-saint whose music helped rebirth my soul.

Discovering Johnny's dark Christian spin on other covers, like "Ain't No Grave" and "The Man Comes Around," was exactly what I needed during this period. These songs were gospel to my ears, speaking to my Christian roots even as I allowed myself to feel the full range of emotions caused by the betrayal of someone I loved.

If I was going to be hurt, I was determined to channel my pain into something positive. I used my grieving time for self-reflection and healing that focused on my growing to be a better man in Christ—physically, professionally, and spiritually. Ultimately, it served as a crucial lesson for me, allowing me to access the deepest parts of myself and learn who I really am.

A week after the photo was posted online, Tiff came over for the last time so we could exchange belongings. I realized that I essentially had to disappear for a while, so she could live out her new life. I prophesied that her rebound relationship—along with the short-term friendships she was forming on a daily basis—were going to be her downfall. Still, I had hope that the experience would lead her to become something even better and greater than she had been before. She needed to experience the lows in order to really appreciate the highs in life, to feel the pain with the pleasure, to experience sadness in order to fully know happiness. But what absolutely killed me was knowing that if she was going to become the amazing person I knew she would, I had to make the hardest sacrifice of my life.

If I truly loved her, I needed to let her go.

. . .

First Baptist Church of Hendersonville, Tennessee
January 22, 2015 – 8:00 P.M. AXIS College-Age Ministry Gathering
(Hearthside Room)

Johnny Cash passed away in 2003, shortly after recording "Hurt." His death was officially due to complications from diabetes, but several say he died of a broken heart after the death of his wife, June Carter, who was laid to rest just four months earlier.

After receiving some last-minute vacation time, I decided to take *52 Churches in 52 Weeks* on a mini-road trip through the Bible Belt. My first stop was Nashville, Tennessee. I've never been a country music fan, so the only things I really wanted to do there was see the new Johnny Cash Museum and attend a service at the church where his funeral was held. I was excited to learn that I'd be in town for First Baptist's inaugural AXIS, an event targeted at college-age Millennials seeking a faith-based community. It was a perfect fit.

Being 33, I had already worshiped at a few churches where I was the youngest person in attendance, so this was a strange role-reversal, as I was the oldest person there. It was like being in a Abercrombie & Fitch ad. All the guys who greeted me at the check-in desk looked like they'd just finished an appointment with Zac Efron's hairstylist. I momentarily regretted not bringing a surfboard or spraying on some Hollister cologne that smelled like the beach.

AXIS was held in the church's Hearthside Room, which was designed to be a relaxing setting for young-adult Christians to mingle. Low-lit lamps gave off a peaceful glow, with a few rows of a dozen chairs lined up. The front of the room featured a flat-screen TV surrounded by speakers and microphones. A crackling fireplace and wood-mounted decor of the state of Tennessee completed the ambiance.

A young lady outfitted in a camouflage jacket and a plaid-shirted male with a neatly groomed Rollie Fingers handlebar mustache kicked things off with their musical stylings. They both played guitar and passionately performed some praise songs, while the lyrics were displayed on the TV screen behind them, allowing everyone to sing along. It was like karaoke for Christians.

Matt, who previously served as an assistant for a state senator before finding his calling to become a minister, led AXIS. Despite being only 23, Matt was superbly articulate, explaining AXIS's genesis as the result of First Baptist's desire to facilitate a faith-based gathering that focused on the unique circumstances that young-adult Christians face. In the same vein, the message that night was about community, taking the New Testament theme of encouraging one another in Christ.

When Matt asked everyone to follow along in a reading from Hebrews, I was rather surprised to see the majority of the attendees pull out their smartphones and open a Bible app. Even after attending over a dozen different Midwest churches, this was the first time I'd seen today's technology replace a hardcover Bible.

Matt read a passage from Hebrews 10:18: "Where there is forgiveness of these, there is no longer any sacrifice for sin." He went on to explain that sacrifice implies giving up something that has a lot of worth to us. Christ died so that we could have access to heaven. In the Old Testament, having such access would have entailed sacrificing something valuable—such as a lamb, which may have been a household's only source of food, demonstrating that they put their trust in God to provide for them. With Jesus having been the sacrificial lamb for our sins, we could move forward in confidence and faith in Christ.

When I contemplated this, I never realized how much the sacrifice of losing the one I loved had strengthened my faith. My pain helped erode the weaknesses within me and then deepened my relationship with Christ.

What I really appreciated about First Baptist was its decision to be proactive in its relationship with Millennial believers. In most churches, after congregants leave high school, the approach is much more hands-off. After the church invests numerous years of Sunday School lessons and confirmation classes to teach young people the ways of Christ, the church community seems to simply forget them. Even worse, this occurs right when young adults face difficult choices with very real consequences. In my experience, this has led to countless young Christians seeking out fun with a Big 'Ol Bottle, rather than seeking out a community of like-minded individuals holding the Big 'Ol Book. In this, AXIS felt like a sanctuary, and despite living thousands of miles away, I was glad to be a part of its first of many gatherings.

While I still had regrets about not being a better Christian boyfriend, I was starting to realize that the breakup was for the best. The only thing that had been holding me back from doing something truly amazing...was me. I truly believe that one of the greatest challenges in life is being yourself in a world that is trying to make you just like everyone else. There will always be someone with better hair, someone who's funnier, someone who's younger, but they will never be me. My life improved tremendously when I took the time to reflect on who I really am and what I want. I just needed to take that one step off my comfortable little ledge and explore the amazing possibilities all around me.

"CAN I GET AN 'AMEN'?"
LAKEWOOD CHURCH • HOUSTON, TEXAS

I f you've ever watched oldies songs on YouTube, there's times when you can't help but scratch your head. Take for instance, Neil Sedaka's 1962 signature hit, "Breaking Up is Hard to Do." It's a timeless classic that narrates the emotional disaster of an imminent break-up. Yet despite the heartfelt misery in the lyrics, he sang it with a smile that made him look like the happiest man alive.

Despite my frustrations with how the breakup with Tiff came about, as bizarre as it sounds, I wanted her to be happy. At the same time, I needed to be happy too and that meant learning from my mistakes, taking full responsibility for what I had control over, and moving on. Before I did, I had one final request before gracefully bowing out of her life: "I need to say goodbye to your parents."

I had to. I was a part of the family through its roughest times, doing what I could to be supportive while her mom showed me the art of living despite cancer trying to destroy her body, dad having the strength of the Hulk on Red Bull to pull the family together with a modern-day Christian masculinity. The family was an inspiration and had grown for the better through the hardships faced.

With Tiff out of the picture that night, I came over to say goodbye to her parents by myself. I genuinely thanked them for showing me the blueprint for how a Christian household should look, one that I hope to create someday for my future family. When I asked what type of resources helped power their faith during such a horrible time, they both turned to each other and smiled.

"Joel Osteen," they said.

When it was time for me to make my exit, we hugged, shook hands, and the final goodbyes were said. The door closed on a significant chapter of my life. I turned around and took one final stare at the closed door, looking from the outside knowing I'd never go back in.

That... that was a tough day.

. . .

Lakewood Church in Houston, Texas
January 24, 2015 – 7:00 P.M. Worship Service

If overused idioms have taught me anything, it's that when everything is bigger in Texas, you either go big or go home. What better way to test that theory than by going straight to the top by visiting the largest megachurch in the United States to witness Joel Osteen preach live and in-person?

After my last conversation with Tiff's parents, I had subscribed to the daily Osteen email messages and watched numerous sermons on Sunday morning. I won't say that his messages changed my life, but what he preached could resonate and I became a fan.

But America seems to have a love-hate relationship with the world's most famous televangelist of our time. You either love him and his divinely starched white chompers, or you spit him out for being the prosperity gospel golden boy. Instead of focusing on negative things like sin, Osteen's messages focus on hope and the goodness of God, simplifying the gospel with inspirational ideas.

Going into this visit, I didn't understand the negative views about Osteen and this so-called "megachurch." If it brought people closer to God, what was so bad about it?

After all, everyone loves the story of the underdog, the little startup that could, the companies that started in a home garage or dorm room and eventually grew to become world-famous entities that changed the world. Just think of Steve Jobs with Apple, Bill Gates with Microsoft, or Mark Zuckerberg with Facebook. Lakewood Church was cut from the same cloth. It traces its origins to 1959, when it started in the back of an abandoned feed store. Founded by Joel's father, John Osteen, the church boasted an attendance of about 90 people a week. Despite the church's struggles, John's talents improved and he remained faithful to spreading the Word even through adverse times. Transitioning from being a Southern Baptist to a charismatic independent church and introducing television broadcasts, weekly attendance eventually boosted to over 5,000.

After dropping out of college, Joel came back home to work at his father's church and founded the church's television program. John saw potential in his son, but Joel was content to remain behind the scenes, which he did for 17 years. Still, his father never gave up on asking Joel to preach, and he finally gave in, preaching his first sermon at Lakewood in 1999. Six days later, John passed away from a sudden heart attack. Joel stepped up to carry Lakewood Church's mantle and was soon installed as the senior pastor, despite never having attended seminary. It's never been the same since.

With Joel Osteen as the new face of Lakewood, attendance skyrocketed faster than a NASA space shuttle. His messages span the globe, with televised sermons that, as of 2018, reach 100 countries with an estimated seven million views each week. His first book, *Your Best Life Now*, sold four million copies and remained on *The New York Times* Best Seller list for more than 200 weeks.

Lakewood was light-years ahead of the megachurch curve, becoming the largest congregation in the United States with an average gathering of more than 43,000 worshipers per week. Attendance grew so much that in 2003, Lakewood Church purchased the NBA's Houston Rockets' former arena to house its growing congregation. Lakewood Church became a spiritual universe of its own.

I arrived two hours early for a Saturday night service, giving myself ample time to scope things out. Tucked underneath a scenic metal forest of high-rise skyscrapers on the banks of a flowing highway stream, Lakewood's gargantuan stadium certainly doesn't resemble a "church" from the outside. Coming from the frozen tundra of Wisconsin, it was the first time in my life to experience January in a 70-degree climate. After the 17-hour drive, I decided to walk all around and enjoy the weather, finding garden beds of various colorful flowers right next to carefully landscaped bushes, even 14 American flags waving in the wind.

When I walked inside from the west side, a giant poster promoted Osteen's newest book, *You Can, You Will.* At the opposite entranceway was an escalator that would take you to up the next level, where statues of Joel's parents are immortalized as the church's founders. The walls of the corridor were filled with aquariums featuring a variety of fish, possibly a reference to Jesus being fisher of men. Next to the aquariums was a bookstore selling a huge selection of Christian literature and gifts, with one table featuring stacks upon stacks of Osteen's latest book arranged in every conceivable way: towering upward, twisting around, even bookended with more copies of the book.

I continued to tour the facility until about 45 minutes before the service started, when a pair of volunteers invited me to partake in Holy Communion. I jumped at the chance, and they ushered me into the New Beginnings room, which featured several framed posters of scenic views paired with inspirational Bible passages, a white podium, and a table covered by a blue tablecloth with silver Communion tray. As more people flowed in, the room took on a quiet, everyone-here-is-a-stranger-so-I'm-afraid-to-talk-to-those-around-me vibe.

Once the room had reached capacity, a pastor who looked like a clone of Steve Forbes walked in with an escort of three others, presumably to assist him in serving communion. He presided over the podium wearing (what looked like) a combed-over toupee, ending nearly everything he said with "Can I get an 'Amen'?" which typically got an "Amen!" from a handful of people.

Pastor "Forbes" opened by saying that it was a pleasure to be heading Lakewood Church's third-ever Communion. I was shocked at that statement; surely, there had to have been more. The ushers promptly handed out a white piece of paper to everyone that contained Forbes's "Food for Thought," which included three Bible verses (John 3:16, Romans 5:8, and Romans 8:38-39).

Things were going fine until his sermon ended with him parading out front his adorable 10-year-old daughter—complete with fawn eyes, pigtails, and a flowery pink dress—prompting an "Aww" reaction from several of the ladies. With both hands on his daughter's shoulders, Forbes spoke about the depths of God's John 3:16 love for us that He would sacrifice His only son. He then finished with—and I quote—"I wouldn't sacrifice my own daughter for any one of you. Can I get an 'Amen'?" No one responded.

The pastor blessed "the elements," as he called them, then an usher passed the Communion tray around. When it came, everyone pulled out a discount-wholesale double-peel cup. Everyone, including me, looked around confused, unsure where the wafer was located in these dinky cups. Fortunately, someone figured out that we had to peel away the top layer. The first peel revealed a wafer that was about the size of a dime, while the second peel gave access to the grape juice.

In front of me was a woman with three young boys, all of whom wore blue hoodies. When the Communion tray came to them, two of the boys grappled over it like they were in a mixed martial arts clinch, while the third began swiping multiple cups and stuffing them into his pockets. The woman sternly barked his name, causing the boy to hesitate with a mischievous smirk and enter into a momentary staring contest until he finally surrendered the pilfered cups back onto the tray. The kids dug into the elements like they were Lunchables, then got on their marks to Usain Bolt out the room while the Communion tray was still being passed around.

With my views on how Communion is often used to segregate visitors and church members, I was initially thrilled to be invited to partake. However, seeing Communion used as blessed Juicy Juice for kids who lacked the proper education to know what they were participating in was a sacred letdown. This was the first time in my journey that I found myself drawing a line in how Communion should be distributed. For me—and the others present—the lack of importance attached to this Holy Sacrament resulted in a watered-down experience.

Can I get an 'Amen'?

Please?

Anyone?

. . .

After Communion, I hustled to the arena, which was rapidly filling up. I was afraid I would have to settle for a nosebleed seat. *I've come so far to be here though. Why settle now?* I thought and decided to gamble with my five minutes before the worship service started to find a better view.

On my way past the TV production area on the main floor, I snapped a picture of their camera layout to document my trip. This caught the attention of an usher. "Hi there," he said, "is this your first time at Lakewood?"

I figured that my odd picture selection was a sign of unconventional behavior, so I explained that I had driven down from Wisconsin and that this was indeed my first time at Lakewood.

His eyes lit up. "If it's your first time here, let's get you a seat up near the front. Follow me."

My usher got on his walkie-talkie and began securing a seat for me as he escorted me toward the front, where I was inserted in a row that had a single vacant seat. I shook hands with those around me, which included a couple from Maryland and a couple from New Jersey. As a matter of fact, it seemed like everyone around me was vacationing from out-of-state, married, and—based on the number of Dockers khakis and Macy's floral blouses—were baby boomers.

In the very front row, the congregants were markedly different from the congregation's niche demographic. Up there, they all appeared to be in their early 20's and dressed like supermodels. In fact, they looked more like they were at a Black Eyed Peas audition than a church service.

When the worship service started—which felt more like a rock concert—these too-cool-for-school congregants busted a move like none other, jumping up and down like Tigger on a trampoline and waving their hands in the air. Everyone quickly joined in. The atmosphere was dynamic, and each powerful drumbeat felt like God's hands clapping along, the musical notes in sync with the Holy Spirit. Lakewood's giant rotating golden globe was erected in the middle of the stage, flanked on the sides by choirs of about 40 singers each. Each side clapped in unison to help synchronize the congregation into a steady beat. The worship music was so uplifting, I wouldn't have been surprised if the entire handicapped section had suddenly risen from their wheelchairs and started to perform the Harlem Shake.

Maybe I'm sounding overdramatic, but the moment when Joel Osteen hit the stage, everyone in the audience looked at him like he had just fed the thousands in attendance with two of the aquarium fish. He opened his mouth to speak, and his glistening teeth were whiter than the transfiguration. His curly black hair glimmered in the spotlights like a halo. He raised his hands to lead a prayer, and Lakewood's water fountains started pouring forth wine instead of water.

As everyone gazed at him in astonishment, the Maryland woman seated to my left leaned over to me and whispered, "He looks much shorter than on television." Okay, so maybe not everyone was impressed.

What you don't see on TV is what happens when the Osteens take a seat in the front row after coming onstage to welcome its congregation. A flurry of crying worshipers rushed forward to meet him. This must be a common occurrence, as Osteen's bodyguards were prepared to block the aisle and turn the horde back. I couldn't hear what was said, but a few minutes later, there was something called "Prayer Partners," where the service allowed worshipers to the front and pray with a church volunteer. A select few who had been turned down earlier by the bodyguards were now granted a chance to pray with Osteen. I lost count of how many Kleenex boxes were passed out to those who had come up to pray.

After Victoria Osteen gave a mini-sermon on the many blessings that tithing will bring, Joel came onstage again, radiating grace and charm. He smiled to the thousands in attendance, as well as the millions more watching on their media devices, opening with the customary Lakewood invocation you see on TV: "This is my Bible. I am what it says I am. I can do what it says I can do. Today, I will be taught the Word of God. I boldly confess. My mind is alert. My heart is receptive. I will never be the same. I am about to receive the incorruptible, indestructible, ever-living seed of the Word of God. I will never be the same. Never, never, never. I will never be the same. In Jesus's name. Amen."

He opened his message by saying that if we're being completely honest with ourselves, we all have secret frustrations. God could remove the obstacles we face, but that rarely happens. Sometimes God takes a long time to take action, "But with the right attitude, it won't work against you. It will work for you."

Osteen talked about how God used Paul in amazing ways, basically writing half of the New Testament by himself. Paul witnessed the power of God's healing, yet he had a secret frustration: his "thorn in the flesh." Despite Paul imploring God to remove his thorn, He never did.

What I appreciated about Osteen's sermon is that he didn't just say, "God will make everything better." Instead, he preached with practicality, encouraging listeners to not focus on the thorn and the "why"s of life. Instead, he explained that our secret frustrations serve as a reminder of how much we need God—even Osteen himself. If Paul had focused only on his thorn during his ministry, he never would have accomplished what he did. Such frustrations may just be a test, where you have to prove to God that you're going to be content and do your best, even when things aren't going your way; to keep giving, even when you're not receiving; to keep trying, even though the doors are closing; and to keep doing the right thing, even though you're not getting the right results. God could be using that to help you grow up and to develop your character. There are some things that you can only learn through the trial of your faith. You can't learn them from reading a book or listening to a message; you learn them through experience.

Osteen quoted 1 Peter 1:17, saying "Our faith is tried in the fire of affliction." He explained that our spiritual muscles are developed only when they're put under pressure, worked out, and exercised. It can be uncomfortable, but if you stick with it, you will be prepared for new levels in your life. It's easy to trust God during the good times. But if you have a secret frustration, the question should not be "Can I trust God to help me?" The question should be, "Can God trust me?"

By the time the service had ended, I loved Lakewood: the music, the lights, the atmosphere, everything! Even the volunteers, every single one of them, seemed to have a genuine smile on their face. They were glad to be there! After the service, I made sure to get as many pictures of the stage and selfies with the rotating golden globe in the background as I could.

Back in the corridor, throngs of people were standing in a roped-off section, having been handpicked by the ushers for a chance to pray with Osteen. When he appeared, everyone started clicking their camera phones like the paparazzi. Osteen was smiling—as he always seemed to be—surrounded by four well-dressed bodyguards with earpieces.

I made my exit shortly after that, amazed that the journey I had started in my hometown had expanded to witnessing Joel Osteen preach live and just a few rows in front of me. Never before had I been so quick to throw money in a collection bucket. As I left, I was so excited, I could have tap danced on water.

And yet, when I was done for the night, I felt something similar to what I had felt after thinking about the Communion issue at my former church. Sure, there were Communion issues here, but it was something else as well. Something was off, and I couldn't put my finger on it.

What was it?

CHURCH 17:

STRANGER DANGER

"FIFTY SHADES MEGACHURCH" • GRAPEVINE, TEXAS

I am fascinated by the various ways people seek answers to life's biggest questions. How did we get here? What is the meaning of life? What happens when we die? These are all philosophical questions that have an infinite scope for potential answers, and I'm interested in understanding how people seek God's face—or reject the idea of a universal Creator entirely.

After hitting the reset button on my spirituality and peeling myself away from my earlier religious indoctrination, my quest to follow Christ led to an interesting discovery: the people who were most interested in my *52 Churches in 52 Weeks* project were my ex-Christian atheist friends and co-workers. This led to a revelation that I'm sure would cause most ultra-conservative Christians to throw a flaming pitchfork at me: I can be a devout follower of Christ and still warmly accept atheists. Strangely, it was my discussions with ex-believers that strengthened my faith the most, forcing me to better educate myself and become a more well-rounded Christian. These theological discussions actually forced me to think—really think—and gave me new information to consider.

I wasn't always like that. Growing up in an ultra-conservative Evangelical family, I was often warned about the atheists of the world and how they would plague my mind. I was taught that they rejected the Bible entirely, wanting to live and breathe in their blind sin. If I wanted to be really nice, I could pray for them in the hope that God could drop the scales from their eyes so they could see the light. In reality though, I judged the lifestyles of non-believers from the perch on my celestial throne. After all, I was a believer who learned at a young age that "Jesus loves me—this I know, for the Bible tells me so."

Because of this religious programming, I allowed my faith to become stale and automatic. I didn't need to think, and I allowed myself to merrily sin away, since I had a "Get Out of Hell Free" card. After all, the church said I just needed to believe and, like all Christians, I would own a piece of real estate in heaven. This created a slippery slope that I unwittingly fell down until my faith was softer than the Pillsbury Doughboy rocking a Snuggie.

In the past, when I learned that many of my most treasured friends were atheists, I instantly wanted to convert them to my spiritual way of thinking. I wanted to save them and to rescue their souls. But I ended up being surprised: nearly all of my atheist friends told me that they had read the Bible cover-to-cover, ultimately becoming more skeptical and eventually discarding it for good. What was most interesting to me was how atheists were the ones asking questions to understand the roots of my belief system, whereas my Christian friends never engaged in such philosophical discussion. "That's what the Bible says, so that's what I believe," was the answer I had been spoon-fed since birth, and it's what I initially turned to, often paired with some random, out-of-context Bible passage to validate this reasoning.

If I were to communicate my ever-evolving beliefs regarding theology and philosophy to my atheist friends, "Because the Bible said so," was an uneducated, blind response that didn't cut it. I needed a more fundamental understanding of my own beliefs if I wanted to show the value of faith.

I wasn't just trying to prove this to my atheist friends though; I was also trying to prove it to myself.

. . .

North Texas Church of Freethought at the Hilton DFW Lakes Executive Conference Center in Grapevine, Texas
January 25, 2015 – 10:30 A.M. Freethought Salon

Several of my ex-Christian friends encouraged me to visit an "atheist church," which, according to a handful of media outlets, was growing in popularity. So, by popular request, the plan for my 17th church voyage was to visit a nontheist church in Texas. There were three between Houston and Dallas that looked intriguing. In the end, I decided to go with the North Texas Church of Freethought (founded in 1994), which is considered to be one of, if not, the first nontheistic churches in the United States.

Going into this, I assumed that my passive understanding of the atheist stance would aid me, despite my philosophical disagreement with it. Still, I called the Big Guy Upstairs for a quote on some faith insurance that morning.

After researching their Meetup page, I arrived at the Hilton DFW Lakes Executive Conference Center five minutes early for a three-hour "Freethought Salon" to be held inside The Vineyard restaurant. My understanding was that many atheist churches only formally meet one Sunday a month, and the other Sundays are typically reserved for smaller get-togethers to discuss whatever is on your mind. Surprisingly, there were no greeters, no signs, no indication of any kind that the church was hosting an event there. Other than a few families, the only group in the restaurant was an enclosed table of six elderly men who, based on the amount of argyle they were sporting, looked like they were pre-gaming for a golf outing. The table was secluded with no open seats, so rather than bump in and ask, "Pardon me gentlemen, is this where the atheism happens?", I decided to wait five minutes for the 10:30 A.M. start time to see if anyone else joined them.

What am I doing? I thought. As I waited wondering if this church actually existed, I couldn't come to terms with myself. What if I was wrong and that table was the Freethought Salon? I could hear the rooster crow three times in my head, thinking to myself, *why would you spend three hours faking your faith with a bunch of strangers?*

So I left and walked out of The Vineyard perturbed at myself for wasting my own time. What was more upsetting to me was that I had missed out on other Texas churches that I could have visited that morning, fallen for the mainstream media's claims that atheist churches were gaining widespread popularity, and I hadn't eaten anything. I was moody, and the scrambled eggs being served looked downright delicious.

I was 1,500 miles from home and my Sunday morning church plans were in shambles, so I pulled up Google Maps to search for the nearest church to see if I could find another service before the eleventh hour.

Surprisingly, there was a church just two miles away that started at 11:30 that morning. I assumed it would be some kind of cowboy church out in the middle of nowhere, but as it turned out, calling an audible resulted in a visit to a prosperity gospel megachurch where its senior pastor was doing a sermon series to promote his newest book, which was based on a wordplay from *Fifty Shades of Grey*.

. . .

"Fifty Shades Megachurch" in Grapevine, Texas
January 25, 2015 – 11:30 A.M. "The Experience"

"There's no cameras allowed in here," shouted a lady fiercely marching up to me. I hadn't been at this megachurch for more than five minutes. I was amazed at what was inside and wandered across the gift shop to take a picture of a pillar that was decorated like the Tree of Life. It didn't even turn out.

I can't remember what she looked like, except that she was shorter than me and had a crooked front tooth that looked just like my crooked front tooth.

I wanted to joke, *I'm visiting, and we don't have pillars that look like this in Wisconsin,* but all I got to say was, "I'm visiting—" before she cut me off, hypnotizing me with her crooked tooth. It was like the scene where Austin Powers couldn't stop staring at Fred Savage's mole in *Goldmember,* close-up camera effects and all.

"We have children around here," she proclaimed, earning the attention of those walking by. I'm sure they were parents walking hand-in-hand with their tooooooth... er, youth, who were excitedly jumping up and down as they talked about the gospel tooooooth... er, truth, that they had learned in Sunday School. But I couldn't look at them; I was spellbound by her lone pearly white. As I tried to pull out of my tooth-induced trance, it slowly dawned on me that I was a man... alone... taking pictures... and there were children everywhere.

Oooh noo, she thinks I'm a Stranger Danger!

"No-no-no-no-no-no..." I rapid-fired back, my eyeballs spiking out of my skull like overhand-served volleyballs at the misunderstanding. I suddenly noticed two teachers behind a desk to my right, one of whom I suspected was equipping herself with pepper spray. I made eye contact with the second teacher, who was likely about to call 911 and ask them to dispatch the on-duty police officer from the Grapevine Police Department, who was conveniently perched a few hundred feet away for the big crowds. You'd be amazed at how quickly you can become paranoid after such an implication in a church. I was convinced that I was one bad comment away from being asked to turn around with my hands above my head, read my Miranda rights, and patted down for Tootsie Rolls.

"If you like, you can go online for a virtual tour of the entire church," she said, pointing her finger toward the main hall like she was Babe tooooooth...er, Ruth, calling his shot. She followed me out of the area to get the final word: "You're not allowed back here. May God have mercy on your soul, sick-o."

I may or may not have made up that last sentence. Either way, due to my talent for being oblivious to where I'm going, I ended up giving off a creeper vibe and reenacting the end of Genesis 3 by being banished from the Sunday School of Eden. I can only imagine that Crooked Tooth Lady requested a few cherubim and a flaming sword to guard the Tree of Life pillar in case I should ever come back.

Up until the moment I was profiled as a suspect for Texas's next Amber Alert, this megachurch made a strong positive first impression. Signs in the parking lot pointed first-time visitors to reserved front-row parking. When I strolled past the giant welcome sign beneath an equally giant iron cross, a friendly associate pastor who was stationed at a welcome booth quickly greeted me. We made some small talk, and he asked where I was from.

"Wisconsin," I said. "About an hour outside of Green Bay. I've been traveling around to visit different churches."

He didn't believe this, much less believe that I had just randomly decided to attend their church.

"What really brought you out here?" he asked, suspiciously raising his eyebrow like The Rock. I sidestepped the question, uncomfortable that I tipped him off that I was some kind of secret church shopper. *I was actually planning to attend an atheist church down the street, but figured I'd settle on yours instead,* didn't seem like an appropriate response.

In exchange for my name and address, the associate pastor gifted me a blue Gap-like swag bag, which included a Starbucks gift card, a coupon for a complimentary beverage at their church cafe, and numerous glossy brochures in various shapes and sizes that led to an unexpected amount of reading.

Less is more, and this megachurch understood this perfectly when it came to their marketing material. I looked through the contents of my VIP swag bag and found the reading material was Twitter-short, with everything consolidated and explained in 140 characters or less. For more information, a CD with a message from the pastor was included, along with music by the church's talented student musicians to pop in for the drive home.

On the downside—and it's a steep downside—other than in the "Next Steps" brochure, the swag bag brochures didn't include a single mention of "Jesus" or "Christ." Three separate brochures focused on money. The largest envelope in my bag gave various payment options for tithing, and a "Top Five" index card counted down the five things one needed to do to join the church, with number one being to pre-order the pastor's upcoming book. Last, but certainly not least, there was a brochure about a 90-day tithing challenge. It read: "If you're not tithing already, a great way to start is with the 90-day tithing challenge. We commit to you that if you tithe for 90 days and God doesn't hold true to his promises of blessings, we will refund 100 percent of your tithe."

Tithing with a money-back guarantee? No wonder the prosperity gospel gets a bad rap, I thought.

As I walked around, I could have sworn I was in a mall that catered to teenagers. Instead of conventional religious symbols, the church took full advantage of the color wheel, ornamenting the building with eye-grabbing designs and snazzy furnishings. Everywhere I looked, there were advertisements encouraging churchgoers to pre-order the pastor's upcoming *Fifty Shades* book. Several churchgoers were wearing t-shirts with the book's release date, and by the main entrance, there was a photo booth that encouraged the church's younger members to post a picture of themselves on their Instagram and Twitter accounts with a hashtag of the book's title.

. . .

The doors opened up about 20 minutes before service started, and I was still super embarrassed after my altercation in the Sunday School area. I took a seat in the fourth row from the front and grew increasingly paranoid by several stagehands who watched the incoming foot traffic like hawks, continually talking on their walkie talkies. Eventually, one woman came over to my seat and looked straight at me.

"Move up here," she told me.

Oh great, I'm getting kicked out of church, I thought at first. *I should have stayed at the atheist church.*

She started asking others behind me to do the same. Eventually, those sitting behind me and myself were herded up and moved to the front row, completely oblivious as to why.

I eventually started to calm down and immediately noticed the church's high production values. A Siri voice-a-like counted down the time until the service—dubbed "The Experience"—started. "The Experience" kicked off with the church's student group running onstage to cutting-edge music that blended hip hop with Pentecostal gospel.

Despite the bizarreness of the shameless self-promotion in the hallways, I was fascinated by how expertly the church utilized its youth to contribute to the service, rather than expecting them to be silent spectators. The church's youth movement was designed with popular culture in mind, serving as a launch pad from which aspiring and talented go-getters could pursue their dreams. Choir robes had been replaced with cutoff-sleeved hoodies, Converse sneakers, and AXE body spray. The young people performing onstage were not only singing praise to God; they were also seemingly practicing for the next *American Idol* every Sunday morning.

And it wasn't just young people performing onstage. Multiple students assisted behind-the-scenes with the production, the cameras, the lighting, and the sound system. Several had even put together a video package featuring a popular contestant from the most recent season of *The Bachelor*, encouraging young people to get involved with the church.

As someone who had struggled to find a church that was geared toward a younger generation of Christians, this was refreshing. Not only was it giving them the necessary resources to develop skills for a future career, but it also served as a creative model for how to connect a new generation to church and to God, using advances in technology as a conduit.

After the teens' performance, the senior pastor came out for the message. This was the third part of his *Fifty Shades* sermon series, and before he started, a video package promoted the new book by touting its celebrity pastor as a *New York Times* bestselling author. It highlighted his Twitter and Instagram handles, along with a Twitter hashtag to help congregants search for the book online.

The pastor's message was the only time in my life when I had to constantly switch between a Bible app and urbandictionary.com to understand what he was trying to say. Between mixing passages from Ecclesiastes with slang phrases like "the par-tay," "that's whack," and "The HL" (short for Holy Land), I found myself thinking, *DAWG, dat iz ridiculous*. Despite his unconventional approach, he had a commanding stage presence that demanded attention. Outfitted in skinny jeans and a fair amount of makeup for the camera, the pastor exuded a cavalier charisma with a significant amount of firepower behind each word.

He asked the congregation to consider who we bring into our lives, as they often determine who we become. God wrote the owner's manual on relationships: the Bible. As an example, the pastor talked about a friend he used to play basketball with, who was later imprisoned for killing a man. During a visitation, he asked his friend what went wrong, and the friend said that he had fallen into the wrong crowd.

He was trying to pull at the heartstrings, but he also couldn't resist using controversial language. He argued that believers need to "yoke up" with other believers to plow straight lines in life, comparing it to how Jewish farmers would always yoke two oxen together. A farmer would never yoke a clean ox with a dirty donkey. "So what are you doing being yoked up with a *jackass*?!" he demanded.

At that, the pastor stopped and stared out at the crowd with a George Carlin expression beneath his George Hamilton makeup, waiting for a few cheap laughs.

He continued, using this analogy to warn against pairing opposite beliefs in friendships, dating, and marriages—defending his use of the word "jackass," since the Bible references it.

If that didn't cause some parents' eyelids to twitch, he next tried a comedic take on the sex life of King "SOOO-low-MAaAaAaaN," who wrote the book on marriage and intimacy in Song of Songs. Solomon was so rich that he had 700 wives and 300 concubines, many of them foreigners with different beliefs and different gods. "The guy had more sex than a porn star," the pastor said, transitioning to scripture for a CliffsNotes version: "King Solomon made alliances with foreign kings... and loved many foreign women" (1 Kings 11:1–10). But ultimately, if you mix with the wrong people, it can lead to defiance of God, as it did for Solomon.

The pastor finished by going for a feel-good ending, saying that we need to invite the right people and un-invite the wrong people to the "par-tay" in our lives. At the end of the day, when Jesus died for our sins, we gained an intimate friendship with Christ, allowing us to yoke up and plow a life that will be truly "off the chain."

I get where the pastor was going with wanting to be yoked with other believers, despite the pressures of the secular world. But removing oneself from the company of non-believers completely? No. How does one represent God's kingdom by shying away from non-believers? What kind of confidence do you have in God to flee from non-believers? That's not the answer, and that's not why I'm writing this book.

When thoughtful people come to Christianity, atheists and agnostics are going to come to the table asking heavy questions, like "How do you know God exists?" and "How could a good God allow evil and suffering?" Christians need to wrestle with such questions. Many believers, myself included, were raised in churches where those questions are never posed; they inherited a faith that they still haven't made their own. Both doubters and believers have a moral and intellectual responsibility to examine their doubts and beliefs. Being stuck in the middle was an eye-opener.

Having started the day by attempting to visit an atheist church, then being labeled a stranger danger, and then listening to a celebrity pastor try to look cool in a marketing sermon to sell books named after a BDSM bestseller, this day was just weird. Even though both visits ended on a sour note, the experience helped me understand the massive segregation that currently exists between the two camps.

Later during the week, I looked up the mega-pastor's Twitter account. Somehow, he had amassed 500,000 followers, though there couldn't have been more than 400 people in the service I attended. I also found the sermon on YouTube and was quick to learn how important *Lights! Camera! Action!* was to charismatic Texas megachurches. During the sermon, the camera would cut to those sitting in the front row and for a brief second, showed me squished-in with those who also were told to move. It upset me to an extent. I had visited as a Christ follower, but found myself as a pawn to help sell more book pre-orders. Using the congregation, we were part of an elaborate staging to fake social proof that this mega-pastor's following was bigger than it actually was.

CHURCH 18:

MAY THE ODDS BE EVER IN OUR SAVIOR

CENTERSHOT MINISTRIES AT HIGHLAND COMMUNITY CHURCH •
WESTON, WISCONSIN

When friends learn that I've only ever read the first six pages of *The Hunger Games*, they look at me like I'm more full of it than a constipated bull on a year's supply of ex-lax.

Now, I have nothing against Jennifer Lawrence; she could host a PBS marathon on the history of goulash, and I would watch every minute with my jaw on the floor. I enjoyed the first movie, but when it came to the book and its opening description of the hideous Grumpy Cat, the next page felt like it had come with a scratch-and-sniff sticker with the aroma of a litter box. I couldn't go any further with this book set in a barbaric dystopia marked by poverty and hunger. Ever since, the paperback has resided in my car's glove compartment on the off chance that I'll crash my Pontiac Sunfire into a ditch where no one can locate me, and while I'm trapped and unable to get out, I'll pick up from page seven. I remain hopeful that I'll never have to test that scenario. To borrow a phrase, "May the odds be ever in your favor."

The fictional homeland of Katniss Everdeen's District 12 was like a reflection of the mindset I set out to destroy with my new spiritual quest. In the movie, the dastardly President Snow required all citizens to own a TV, using it to feed propaganda in order to control the country's emotions. I did it voluntarily in real life, waking up each morning to fill-up my mind with TV stories about shootings, stabbings, beatings, kidnappings, gangs, riots, wars, terrorists, robberies, recessions, layoffs, protests, taxes, politics,

95

scandals, prostitutes, rapes, diseases, drugs, suicides, accidents, droughts, house fires, wildfires, heat waves, hurricanes, tsunamis, tornadoes, blizzards, and other catastrophes. Then I'd go to work, and start my day wondering what was wrong in the world. Why bother trying to become someone better in a world that was falling apart?

Before my breakup with Tiff, I had been content to mindlessly float along in the currents of conformity, settling for what others told me to do and avoid doing something worthwhile. I had allowed outside forces to pollute my mind, allowing myself to take my bow and aim low, shooting for the bare minimum in life. But after the break-up and my American Dream fell apart faster than the Tower of Babel if the makers of Jenga constructed it, that created the spark to catch fire. Instead of nervously looking at the odds, it was time for me to reap what could be sown.

So I turned off the TV and decided to do something with my life.

. . .

Centershot Ministries at Highland Community Church in Weston, Wisconsin
February 8, 2015 – 6:00 P.M. Young Adults Gathering
After the previous week's celebrity pastor preaching about yoking up with believers, I was ready to finally visit my hometown's most talked-about church. I hadn't gone right away, as I'd assumed that Highland Community Church would be the top runner for my new church home. After all, it planted churches at three different locations throughout the area. I had high expectations that it'd be so good, that I would settle and never sample other local churches.

I attended their Sunday morning service, and while I could have stopped there, I was more curious about Highland's young adult group which met at its Weston campus. As I've struggled to find a place of worship that I could identify with, I had great hopes for this group. Because of the expectations, for some reason I was more hesitant to visit this hometown church than getting the nerve to walk into the atheist church from the week prior, sitting in my car an extra five minutes before gaining the courage to go in. At least with the atheist church in Texas, they'd never see me again.

When I arrived, I took a deep breath and opened the door. Whatever I had been expecting, it wasn't this.

The room itself was nothing I hadn't seen before: there was a stage with a wooden cross fixed to the wall, flanked by a pair of blank projector screens. A central podium on the stage held two white flowers to symbolize new members who had joined during the week.

It was on the main floor that things seemed really strange. Specifically, all of the folding chairs for the congregation had been rearranged to form a shooting gallery with banners promoting Centershot Ministries. As I soon found out, Centershot was an outreach ministry that uses archery as a tool to assist church communities.

I was a few minutes late when I walked, so the archery instructor had already begun his presentation by asking what comes to mind when we hear the word "archery."

"Robin Hood," shouted one guy.

"Safety," said a younger woman.

A third person yelled out my first thought: "*The Hunger Games.*"

After that, the archer got right down to business, instructing everyone to lift an arm straight out and extend their index finger in the air. Within seconds, he was able to assess each individual's eye dominance to determine what hand they'd be shooting from. Even if you're right-handed, you might be left-eye dominant, so you'd be shooting with your left hand.

The instructor called up the different groups of Tributes when it was their turn to shoot. The first group was all guys, and when they were called, it was like the start of the 74th Hunger Games, with every guy speed-walking to the archery stations to avoid being last and thus getting stuck with the Barbie-pink bow.

We were shooting with what's called a Genesis Bow, which was engineered for young beginners. It features composite limbs, cabled drawstrings, and an aluminum idler wheel to enforce accuracy. Everyone got two rounds, with three arrows each.

When it was my turn, rather than looking at the "11 Steps for Archery Success" poster, I focused on one step: don't make a bad first impression by killing someone with an arrow at church.

As my mind was littered with images of my mug shot leading off the five o'clock news, my draw was toddler-weak, and my first arrow fell pathetically limp to the tile floor. Recalibrating my mindset, I decided to actually listen to the instructor this time and pulled off two decent shots, although neither ended up anywhere near the target.

The targets for the second round were a bunch of balloons. Going in with a better mindset this time, I grabbed the feathered cut of my first arrow, set it on the rest with the end perfectly placed on the drawstring, applied the advice of my instructor, confidently pulled back the arrow the proper length, and let it fly.

Bullseye.

After successfully keeping everyone alive, the instructor gathered everyone around and talked about archery being the most popular sport mentioned in the Bible. The bow and arrow was humankind's greatest discovery at that time, second only to fire, due to its ability to help provide food for many people.

The most intriguing part of his presentation though was when he mentioned that the term "sin" originated from archery. The best archers were often determined by a long-range archery competition using a shield as a target. When the archer hit the target, it was called a "mark," and when the archer missed the mark, it was called a "sin."

The archer described how Paul, when speaking to the Roman Empire—home to the world's greatest archers—said, "For all have sinned and fallen short of the glory of God" (Romans 3:23), it hit a mark for that culture.

This analogy resonated not only with my first puny shot, but also my own personal development when it comes to targets and goals. A target is a mark to shoot at to obtain the desired result (a bullseye). Goals are the actions we take or the behaviors we perform to help us hit the mark (i.e., "Eleven Steps of Archery Success"). To quote Earl Nightingale, "Success is the progressive realization (goals) of a worthy ideal (target)."

For the moment, forget about the Biblical ramifications of sin and whether we go to heaven and hell. What would happen if we re-imagined sin as "missing the mark" in our everyday lives? It takes a lot of personal insight to find a worthy ideal in life, and I can attest that when I lacked a target, my quiver was equipped with excuses. I shot excuses off like arrows toward the things to blame in life.

But when I started setting targets, creating goals to help me hit those targets, and actually going for them with obsessive perseverance, that's when things began to change. Taking shots in life practically requires failure, which is something we're typically taught to avoid. But when I started going for it, I also started confronting my self-imposed fears of failure. Instead of filling my mind with negativity that kept me trapped in unhealthy thought patterns, I began pouring healthy mental ingredients into my outlook. That's when things started happening.

As you begin to learn, you begin to change. When you begin to change, you begin to grow. And when you begin to grow, you begin to become. Through perseverance and determination, you can take your personal failures in life, let it motivate you, and spring into successes. You begin to have a new respect for failure, since you're continually striving to hit the target. You don't need to fear, since you have God on your side to give strength.

Instead of "May the odds be ever in your favor," I learned to say, "May the odds be ever in your failures."

Or better yet, through the aid of Christ, "May the odds be ever in Our Savior."

NEVER PULL A LION OUT OF YOUR PANTS AT BIBLE STUDY

IMMANUEL BAPTIST CHURCH • WAUSAU, WISCONSIN

A word to the wise. It's never a good idea to pull a stuffed lion out of your pants while shouting Spanish at ultra-conservative Christians during Bible study. I would know. And I still have the lion...

When I was 21, I had a crush on a girl that I worked with. The problem was, when it came to dating, I was greener than Oscar the Grouch learning about recycling on Earth Day. One night, I mustered the courage to ask this unfortunate girl out for a cup of coffee after work. She took me up on the offer, and I brought her to a restaurant, which turned out to be closed. Rattled and with no alternative in mind, I wished her a good night, giving her the impression that I was definitely not from the Rico Suave genepool.

She soon got a job elsewhere, but we bumped into each other again a year later. I asked her out again, and for some unknown reason, she agreed to redeem that rain check date!

Things started off well—so well, in fact, that she invited me to her young adult Bible study. Unfortunately, after that, the date fell apart when a number of my buddies from high school showed up drunk and decided to crash our date. They were shocked that I was dating someone and tried to convince her to keep dating me. It didn't help. Her beet-red face resembled Elmo after participating in a Blazin' Wing Challenge at Buffalo Wild Wings.

Still thinking I had a chance, I took her up on the Bible study invitation, also seeing it as a way to befriend fellow Christians my age.

Three things stood out on the first night of Bible study: 1) I made a poor fashion choice by wearing a blue turtleneck made of the same material as Cookie Monster; 2) the group leader mentioned how an "eye for an eye will leave the world blind" as he looked at my turtleneck, almost certainly pondering where the googly eyes were located; and 3) someone brought cookies, and I definitely ate more than one (nom nom nom).

My attempts to ask this girl on a third date weren't exactly inspired. I lacked the emotional maturity to woo her properly, and my sure-fire pick-up lines morphed into comments like, "Hi, those are some nice white socks you're wearing. What type of laundry detergent do you use to make them so white?"

One night at Bible study, she apparently became fed up with my latest advance of asking her what type of dish soap she preferred. She made a daring jailbreak-like escape by weaving through living room furniture as I followed in hot pursuit. Eventually, she reached the safety of the door and unintentionally slammed it in my face, fleeing to her getaway car. The door was made of high-quality, sturdy wood, in case you were wondering.

While I had no clue how flirting worked, I had found my niche in the group by using improv comedy to add a new dimension to our Bible studies. I made use of props in the room to dramatize the sins of others, such as comparing the fall of man to a pen (don't ask) or combining a Tonka truck with a fog light to illustrate how David's adultery with Bathsheba drove him further from the light. Everyone loved it, even my crush when she wasn't praying for a restraining order. It was a neat little twist in our otherwise literalistic Bible studies. At one point, the group leader asked whether I could do something creative for the story of Daniel and the lion's den the following week. He soon came to regret that request.

That night, the turnout was double its usual, since the study was just a few blocks from the nearby Immanuel Baptist Church, where many within the group called their church home. Those who had seen my previous improv skits couldn't wait to see what I had prepared for that evening. When it was my turn, I pushed back my natural introversion, pulled a stuffed lion from my khakis, and declared that I had voices in my head, all of which spoke Spanish. I maniacally shouted my favorite Martin Lawrence one-liner from the movie *Blue Streak*: "¡Tengo un gato en mis pantalones!" I shouted this Spanish phrase over and over and over. I don't even know if I translated it for the benefit of the non-Spanish speakers in the room. (It's "I have a cat in my pants," for the record).

No one found it funny. Sensing that this was a really bad idea mid-act, I decided to make things worse by grabbing a nearby potted plant and pranced around with it while pointing out the sins of those who do pot (since I was holding a pot, get it?). It looked exactly as stupid as it sounds. Several attendees started tsk-tsking my erratic behavior, and I saved myself from further embarrassment by planting myself in my chair.

I screwed up, feeling like fresh Mr. Snuffleupagus meat if he was swapped for Daniel in the lion's den. Frankly, I can't even remember how I had been planning on connecting my crazy rant to Daniel, but I do remember the mortifying feeling of condemning stares on my back. I looked back, offering an eye for an eye. Then I hung my head. I knew I was never going to get that third date.

. . .

Immanuel Baptist Church in Wausau, Wisconsin
February 15, 2015 – 10:15 A.M. Worship Service

Sometimes my decision-making process for selecting a new church resembles that of a squirrel crossing the street. This was even more true than usual for visit number 19, as I alternated between four different churches before finally settling on The Shepherd's House for a Seventh-Day Adventist service. When I looked at their website, their choice of Bible passage as a mission statement caught my eye: "We believe that God has given The Shepherd's House congregation a ministry of hope, of grace, of salvation—not a message of condemnation. John 3:17 states: 'God did not send his Son into the world to condemn the world, but to save the world through him.'"

Everyone knows John 3:16 by heart, yet almost no one knows the passage that comes right after. I was intrigued. Why use John 3:17?

The website said worship service started at 10:00 A.M., but no day was listed. When I arrived at The Shepherd's House on Sunday morning, I discovered that no one was there. As I later found out, Seventh-Day Adventists hold their services on Saturday.

Fortunately, I knew that Immanuel Baptist Church was both nearby and that their service would be starting soon. Walking in felt like crossing into enemy lines. My idiotic stunt with the stuffed lion had happened just a few blocks from Immanuel, and several young adult members of the church had witnessed it. This time, I made sure there were no stuffed animals in my pants.

Before service started, I had taken a front row seat in hopes of avoiding anyone that recognized me from that day. While waiting for the service to start, two children wearing matching neon-yellow t-shirts started playing patty-cake in front of me. Soon, it became four children, then eight, and pretty soon, 20 children wearing the same highlighter-yellow shirts were surrounding me in this patty party. The teacher eventually came over and instructed them to climb up onto their chairs for the service, their little chicken legs dangling from their seats. Being in the middle seat, I stuck out like Big Bird in an Easter basket of Peeps. After being implicated as the

101

potential source of Stranger Danger a few weeks earlier at the church in Texas, I knew enough not to take a picture of the scene here.

Moments later, service started and the kids went onstage to recite their memorized Bible passages. At the end, two girls remained. One recited the softball verse of John 3:16, but the final passage was, strangely, the very same verse that had spiked my interest in the Seventh-Day Adventist church down the street.

"John 3:17," the little girl said before trailing off. She was more frozen than Elsa, forgetting her memorized Bible passage as her blue eyes took on a deer-in-the-headlights expression. The teacher quickly went into action, softly reading the words so the girl could repeat them: "For God... for God did not send His son into der world to condemn da world, but in order that da world might be saved for Him."

The congregation applauded the girl for being able to get through it, but my thoughts were on the passage's irony for me, as I'd felt extremely condemned by members of this very church after my stunt years ago. Every Christian can rattle off John 3:16 with no problem, yet why don't we remember and practice the very next passage?

Later in the service, the pastor took the stage for his sermon, which was part of a series titled, "This Means War." This Sunday's message was based on five words from Ephesians 6:17, "Take the helmet of salvation." The series was very militant, focusing on one piece of armor each week and weaponizing the Bible through allegories, so that we would be prepared to battle the forces of evil in the war for our souls.

The pastor first talked about the helmet of salvation by describing a 1st century battle helmet and how it was designed. He pointed out that the helmet surrounds the head to protect it from the enemy: "It's a head game. The battle is won or lost in the mind."

He explained how several Biblical characters lost ground in the battle for their minds, pointing out the sins of Adam and Eve as well as David's lust for Bathsheba. (If he needed props for those examples, I was all over it.) The pastor finished by stating that the Gospel has saved us. "Deliver us from the one we are battling against," the pastor said to end his sermon. "Deliver us from the evil one."

At first, I'd found the sermon rather uncomfortable, given how combative it felt. I'd been on the receiving end of judgments from fellow Christians who felt I didn't measure up to their Holier Than Thou standards. After all, how often do Christians take the steeple above their churches and use them as spears—sometimes even against other Christians?

But when the service ended, I turned around to see if there was anyone I recognized burning a hole into the back of my head with laser-pointer eyes. To my surprise, not a single person from that Bible study was in attendance. The little girl's recitation of John 3:17 seemed like an important counterpoint. It reminded me that Christ's purpose is not to condemn—not even those who make fools of themselves while trying to be funny.

P.S. No stuffed animals were harmed in the writing of this chapter.

CHURCH 20:
LGBT. WWJD?
REVOLUTION CHURCH • MINNEAPOLIS, MINNESOTA

One May Day when I was going through a peanut butter Cheerios phase, I came across an image of a Minneapolis church distributing Communion. This wouldn't normally be a big deal, except the blessed bread to represent the body of Christ was rainbow-colored to celebrate Minnesota's legalizing same-sex marriage.

"Blasphemy!" I decried from my laptop, a volcano of whole-grain oats erupting from my bowl as I shook my fist, substituting it for the right hand of God. *How dare these false prophets vandalize a traditional religious sacrament to forgive the sin of those who sin,* I thought from the moral high ground that was my love seat. I thought the world was going to hell in a Communion breadbasket.

My feeling of persecution was justified by years of conservative Evangelical indoctrination against the LGBT community. I was actually proud to be homophobic and professed this to my friends. I weaponized my Bible by arming it with Post-it notes and camouflaging the pages with neon highlighter. I was able to read-off Bible verses like Battleship coordinates, raining down Sodom and Gomorrah to morally obliterate those living in sexual sin. Homosexuality was an easy target, and I would lock-and-load Scripture with heavy clips of Biblical ammunition to launch an all-out religious assault on those whose lifestyles offended God.

Long story short, I was a self-righteous dick.

Then I pulled a stuffed lion out of my pants during Bible study to be funny. No one laughed. I got a front-row seat to see just how cutthroat religious persecution can be, even in cases of friendly fire. My Christian "friends" stoned me with stares for my bad humor. The group's second-in-command called me the next day, probably to make sure I didn't have plans to sacrifice a live lamb on someone's coffee table for the following week's lesson on Abraham.

"I should really apologize," I told him.

"I think it would be best to never bring it up again," he replied.

The group's attendance nose-dived. Several members unfriended me on Facebook. Some just stopped talking to me altogether. I was shunned to the point where I was expecting to be tossed 30 pieces of silver and exiled to the wilderness for 40 days and 40 nights. *How can Christians treat me like this?* I thought, unable to comprehend the hypocrisy of the group's reaction to my blunder. I felt like they were actually questioning my faith. I stopped going.

Throughout my 20's, I held a similar judgmental stance regarding same-sex relationships. As more and more of my friends came out of the closest as gay or lesbian, I sensed the cultural consciousness changing. My generation had grown up on history lessons about Rosa Parks and Martin Luther King, Jr., courageously confronting racial injustice. I started to see a similar tone with sexual discrimination, and I realized that, in this case, religious doctrine was the oppressor. When I began to actually look in others' eyes, I slowly started to realize that they weren't choosing to live in sin. They were gay because they were gay, just as I get morning wood from dreams of Kate Upton.

So after 33 years of judgment, my time as a spiritual wayfaring stranger forced me to take a step back and take a fresh look at such a controversial social issue in the church. I was left asking the question: LGBT. WWJD?

. . .

Revolution Church at Bryant-Lake Bowl in Minneapolis, Minnesota February 22, 2015 – 3:30 P.M. Talk

Visit number 20 was a road trip to the urban wilderness of downtown Minneapolis to check out Revolution Church, which is located inside a funky bowling alley. It's the same venue that prompted me to cry "Blasphemy!" when I saw images of the church breaking rainbow-colored Communion bread to celebrate same-sex marriage.

Bryant-Lake Bowl is not a typical setting for a church. The glass windows display times for Happy Hour and Cheap Date Night, and a chalkboard above the bar lists specials for drinks called the Madhatter, Loon Rise, and Gramma's Candy Dish. The bathrooms are populated with graffiti, the porcelain tiles providing thought-provoking questions like,

"How many midgets does it take to !@#k a waitress?" Beneath it, someone had answered "12" with a permanent black marker.

By the bowling alley itself, an overhead sign pointed me toward a door to a small theater, which could easily be mistaken for an emergency exit. After passing a framed picture of a bowling ball with a middle finger sticking out of it, I walked into the theater to see Revolution's pastor, Jay Bakker, warming his hands up from the sub-zero windchill outside.

Jay Bakker isn't your typical pastor. His arms are sleeved with tattoos; his face, a connect-the-dots of silver piercings scaffolded with black-rimmed glasses and a no-shave November beard that had gone a few months too long. A self-proclaimed Christian agnostic, Bakker is a punk preacher who openly supports gay marriage. As a result, gatekeeper Christians have called him many radical things over the years, such as "heretic," "apostate pastor," and even "emerging false prophet." The list goes on.

Despite this criticism from the conservative right, Bakker's personal background and social stance have earned him interviews on *Larry King Live*, CNN, and MSNBC, where he is always introduced as "the son of former televangelists Jim and Tammy Faye Bakker." His parents were a big deal in the Evangelical scene in the 1970s and '80s, hosting a popular religious talk show and even creating a Christian theme park. Eventually, his father was implicated in several scandals and was shipped off to prison, leaving the Bakker empire to collapse in a hostile takeover. The resultant media circus and corrupt betrayal of his religious community left Jay in a downward spiral during his teen years that led him to question his faith. After recovering from several years of substance abuse, Jay Bakker emerged preaching grace and God's love.

Few were as accepting.

Bakker had recently completed an interview with Barbara Walters earlier in the week, yet now here he was, sipping from a Starbucks cup in front of five introverts keeping to themselves and the recording apparatus for his podcast, which reaches over 13,000 people each week through his Facebook page.

With bowling pins crashing in the background, Bakker's talk was titled "Galatians Again, Part Seven," referencing Galatians 2:17–21. Never before have I heard a sermon that mixed the ethos of Christianity with Comic-Con references. Bakker was like a verbal bartender, mixing Paul's message to the Galatians while stirring in pop culture references to *Star Wars*, *The Dark Knight*, and *The Walking Dead*.

The transformation of Saul into Paul reminded him of Darth Vader at the very end of *Return of the Jedi*. Darth Vader had destroyed planets and killed Jedi babies—yet after he died, the Force showed him grace by allowing his spirit to still hang out with his former BFFs and mentors, Obi-

Wan Kenobi and Yoda. Likewise, Paul had done heinous things as Saul, yet God showed him grace and gave him new life. Most people would look at both examples and say, "Hey, that's not fair. Why do they get a free pass after doing such terrible things?" Although there are consequences for both Vader's and Saul's past sins, the past is the past. That's the power of God's grace and forgiveness, as we are made new by Christ.

Bakker called out the church's "rigid rules and regulations" that ostracize many Christians into becoming post-Christians. He quoted Harvey Dent, who would go on to become the villain Two-Face in *The Dark Knight*: "You either die a hero, or you live long enough to see yourself become the villain." His argument was that many post-Christians retaliate against Christians with the same judgmental attitude the Christians showed them. He referenced a saying he had often heard when he was little: "The church is the only army that shoots its wounded." Bakker took this one step further by describing the wounded post-Christians as being like zombies who get back up and start attacking the very Christians they had once stood side-by-side with.

Bakker admitted that it was difficult, even for him, to practice grace in the face of those who openly persecute both him and the friends he cares about. The church's persecution, especially of those Christians who live alternative lifestyles, has led to a lot of doubt for many. In Bakker's case, it even resulted in a kind of agnosticism:

"There's times I have a lot of doubt... My faith kinda comes and goes. I always tell people I'm kind of like a Christian agnostic, constantly wrestling and struggling with my faith... And it's not often [caused by] my studies as much as it is the church and other people. 'Oh Jay, you're so angry at the church,' [they say]. I'm not really angry at the church; I'm more disappointed. I'm not angry for everything that happened to my parents—I think it was a bad thing, but I moved on. But I'm disappointed that I see the same shit happening 30 years later. We [feel] justified kicking and destroying the wounded... And we still [feel] justified not marrying people because they lived with each other or [because] they're gay or lesbian. The church still does a lot crappy things... So I wondered: if I ever lost my faith, what would I take with me? I'm taking grace with me."

For Bakker, grace is about forgiveness. He wants to see grace actively working in people's lives. He wants to see his enemies transform through grace. He wants to see the world become a better place for everyone. "To me," Bakker concluded, "that's what my faith is about."

Jay Bakker preached with brutal honesty. He made himself transparent, admitting his struggles with the lack of social progress in the church, which is largely due to outdated thinking.

Two years earlier, I had drawn a line in the sand when Revolution Church used Communion bread to celebrate same-sex marriage equality. I was narcissistic in my prejudices against the LGBT community and hostile toward their inclusion of sacred rituals like marriage and Communion. Now, as I progress through my own spiritual transformation, I wonder, *Why would a true Christian want to keep someone out of heaven over the color of their Communion bread?*

I'm still wrestling with this issue. On one hand, anything that doesn't preach, "God is love," is missing the point to Christianity entirely. On the other hand, procreation was designed to be accomplished by a man and a woman. But regardless, I'm saying grace as a LGBT apologist. I was wrong in how I viewed, talked about, and even treated others who didn't live my own lifestyle.

As I continue to conceptualize Jesus and separate myself from the religious doctrine that was spoon-fed to me since Gerber was prepared as my dinner, I'm trying to rid myself of the dysfunctional hate that can stem from man-made churches. I don't have a clear-cut answer on how Jesus would address the debate about the place of the LGBT community within church, but I see now that the problem isn't about sexuality. The problem is that we're human.

Jesus set the bar in terms of showing grace in the face of persecution. Jesus didn't spend all his time in temples. He was the most revolutionary figure in history, warmly embracing people and accepting them for who they were. Prostitutes, Pharisees, tax collectors—you name them, He loved them. To me, grace says, "I love you, I value you, and I care for your welfare. I'm not going to leave you to waste." That's what Jesus exemplified, and I sense that Bakker understands that.

So while many will continue to cast stones at Bakker and call him a heretic, a false prophet, a blasphemer, and countless other names, I came away from his sermon with the impression that Bakker is courageous enough in his faith to stand up to hateful religious persecution in order to support the people he cares about. No matter the sexual orientation of his congregation, every Sunday, he extends his hand to reach people who have been pushed far from God.

There's not many who would do the same.

CHURCH 21:
WHEN THE WALLS BURN DOWN
WILLOW CREEK COMMUNITY CHURCH • SOUTH BARRINGTON,
ILLINOIS

"Some of you veteran Willow Creekers might recall that during the eight years that President Clinton was in office, I went to Washington, D.C. nearly every single month to meet privately with him. He asked me to be his spiritual adviser. This was at his request. Now I know what some of you are thinking: I didn't do a very good job."

With a tongue-in-cheek grin and a chorus of chuckles from the congregation, this was how Bill Hybels kicked off his five-part sermon series, "Unwavering," at Willow Creek Community Church on March 1, 2015.

Back in 2015, Hybels was to Christian leadership what Luke Skywalker was to *Star Wars* spaceships. Inspired by a college lecturer who possessed a Yoda-like wisdom, Hybels gave up his humble business aspirations as a young man to instead seek adventure by modernizing an Empire of boring churches. Applying the lessons bestowed by his mentor, Hybels co-piloted a new generation of churchgoers to form Willow Creek Community Church in 1975. The inaugural turnout at the rented Willow Creek Theater—the source of its name—was 125. By the time *Star Wars* came out in 1977, regular attendance had grown to 2,000. Not since the unknown farm boy Luke Skywalker rose from utter obscurity to blow up the Death Star had the galaxy seen such a cosmic rise.

Combining modern music, dramatic skits, and Christian messages, the church laid the groundwork for the style of contemporary worship service that has since revolutionized churches across the country. 40 years later and after various expansions, Willow Creek Community Church continues to serve a Christian community of about 24,000 per week, making it the largest megachurch in the Midwest.

Throughout his four decades in the ministry, Hybels has penned approximately 50 books, served as the chaplain for the Chicago Bears during their Super Bowl heyday, and launched the Willow Creek Association (WCA), linking 14,000 churches through leadership conferences. During a roundtable luncheon to discuss the spiritual condition of the country in 1992, his insights caught the attention of then-President Elect Bill Clinton. Later, during a private meeting, Clinton asked Hybels to serve as his behind-the-scenes spiritual adviser, a position he held from 1993 until 2001. Just imagine being in Bill Hybels's shoes. What would you say if you had the ear of the President of the United States, and he looked to you to discuss his faith while he went through one of the biggest sexual scandals in history?

Strangely, Hybels would find himself in a similar situation three years later.

. . .

Willow Creek Community Church in South Barrington, Illinois
March 1, 2015 – 11:15 A.M. Sunday Worship Service

My first thought as I drove through the sprawling panorama of white snow, brown brick, and endless architecture was, *Willow Creek Community Church should have its own zip code.* In truth, it resembled a corporate office building more than a church. At first, I was surprised at the lack of religious symbols both inside and out, but after some thought, I realized that the church's success was built on its ability to attract the average non-churchgoer. It made sense that the building itself reflected this approach.

"What do you think so far?" a smiling lady asked.

She must have noticed my astonishment as I stepped through the doors. She introduced herself as Sarah, and upon learning that this was my first visit, she offered to get me a seat up front and invited me to join her for refreshments after the service. With that, she passed me off to an usher who guided me to a vacant seat near the front.

I will confess that I went into this journey with a rather negative preconception about the Walmartization of today's megachurches. From online articles, TV reports, and the large-and-in-charge stadiums that they were housed in, megachurches seemed more about showboating than about personal connections. But after 21 weeks, I had to admit that the churches that made the best first impressions were actually the megachurches. Their members and volunteers knew how to recognize newcomers and talk to them. They always showed genuine interest in me and my story, which was something I hadn't experienced as much at smaller, hometown churches.

When I arrived, the worship service was already in full swing inside the impressive three-tiered auditorium. According to the church's website, the auditorium is double the size of the Dolby Theater, which hosts the Oscars. The stage looked like the size of an NBA basketball court, with neon light fixtures hanging above like chandeliers made of lightsabers. On either side of the stage were giant LED screens, like those you'd see at a professional sports game.

The "Unwavering" sermon series kicked off that morning with a trailer that had better production values than most Hollywood movie trailers. After his tongue-in-cheek intro, Hybels told a story about how close he had become with several senior Secret Service agents during the eight years he served President Clinton. Yet despite the relationships he formed with them, never once did an agent wave him through when he went to the White House. Every time, he was asked for identification, was patted down, and had his briefcase checked. The president's life is important enough that they cannot make any exceptions, no matter who you are or how well you are known.

Hybels transitioned this modern-day tale to the story of Nehemiah, who served as a sort of Persian senior Secret Service agent for King Artaxerxes in the 5th century B.C. During those times, the easiest way to kill a king was to poison his food or drink—which I was shocked to learn, having always imagined it required Gerald Butler-esque six-pack abs, like in 300. As a result, kings had their most trusted advisers taste-test their food. In this case, King Artaxerxes passed over his own people for this position in favor of Nehemiah, who must have had a stellar track record to be chosen despite his Jewish heritage.

One day, Nehemiah's brother arrived in the Persian capital and informed him that the holy city of Jerusalem had been burned to the ground. The news broke his heart. After the Babylonian captivity, a remnant of the Jewish people had returned to their homeland, but a city with broken walls revealed a defeated people.

In his book, *Holy Discontent*, Hybels explains that whenever something breaks the heart of a follower of Christ, it is God's way of firing them up to join the playing field and fix something that is broken in the world.

Hybels referenced his favorite cartoon character, Popeye. Other than his massive forearms, Popeye has an average physique and mild manners, but should something or someone threaten or actually harm his beloved Olive Oyl, watch out! Then he would finally snap, saying, "That's all I can stands! I can't stands no more!" and "duly pulverize" the villain to save his girl. Hybels reflected that Nehemiah had a similar reaction to his frustration. If he could rebuild the walls of Jerusalem, it would would send a message to the enemies of Israel, and more importantly, would be a turning point to show Israel that God would protect His people.

Hybels related several stories of times when God tapped someone on the shoulder to change the world for the better. His friend Bono—of U2 fame—was on a surfing trip in Ethiopia when he saw the unbelievable poverty there. It prompted him to establish various philanthropic programs to fight global poverty. David saw Goliath mocking the Israelites, prompting him to run into the fray like a madman and slay the giant. When Paul learned that the apostles wanted to confine Christ's message, he camel-tripped to different cities throughout the Middle East to spread the Good Word. Martin Luther King, Jr. reached the point where he could no longer accept the extreme racial discrimination in America and led a revolution. It was his passion for this cause that led to his assassination. Candy Lightner was a Californian mother whose daughter was killed by a drunk driver, and she harnessed her sorrow to create Mothers Against Drunk Driving (MADD), a group that lobbies for stricter laws against drunk driving. All of these people were unwavering in harnessing their broken hearts into a "firestorm of frustration to get off their couches and into the boxing ring to fight for something that should have been fixed a long time ago."

Hybels asked the congregants of Willow Creek that morning to identify our holy discontent and have a Popeye moment—we need to find out what it is that He wants us to do. Hybels coached us to approach this the same way Nehemiah did: first, fully reflect on our pain; second, pray with a clear mind; and third, obey God, who is the source of our spiritual spinach strength.

This was all very inspirational, but it's what Hybels did at the conclusion of his sermon that really set him apart from other pastors I'd heard. He actively challenged the Willow Creek community to stir up their hearts by identifying three different issues that they wanted to fix and then outlining the next steps they needed to take to initiate real change.

This call to action was what really stuck out about Hybels's sermon. His message was intelligent, polished, and relevant, drawing on both modern and Biblical stories. But what was most telling was how precisely Hybels identified the holy discontent that preceded the actions of Nehemiah, David, MLK, and others. It made me wonder what Hybels's holy discontent had been when he set out to modernize several aspects of American Christianity.

After service, leaders in each seating section hosted a fun social get-together with cookies and coffee, getting to know one another and forming friendships on the spot. The congregation was buzzing after the sermon, and I overheard another first-time visitor tell a friend how amazed she was at Hybels's message. It didn't just touch on the surface level, no—instead it drove deep down and "stirred the warrior's heart."

114

. . .

A few weeks after my visit, I blogged about my day at Willow Creek on Medium.com, titling it "Bill Hybels is a Man You Should Know." I quickly received a tweet from the associate pastor, Steve Carter, who thanked me for joining and couldn't wait to hear more about my findings. Months later, I met a friend who also had attended Willow Creek and shared the article. Then, Willow Creek's lead musicians caught wind of the article, which went viral within the church. A flurry of positive comments flooded in, many indicating a shared sense of pride about their faith-led community and founding pastor. Even after *52 Churches in 52 Weeks* had long since passed, I was willing to drive the six hour round-trip to return to be a part of this community again.

But fast-forward three years to September 2018 (at the time this book goes to distribution), I can't help but drop my head at the growing number of sexual misconduct allegations against Hybels.

In March 2018, *The Chicago Tribune* published an article that detailed allegations of sexual misconduct by Hybels that spanned decades. *The Tribune* wrote that the elders of Willow Creek had conducted an internal review of Hybels' behavior which led to no findings of misconduct. Two weeks later, Hybels announced he would accelerate his retirement by six months by resigning immediately to avoid distraction, not before getting a standing ovation on his way out. After all, this was no ordinary man. This was Bill Hybels. No way could such a visionary pastor ever put himself in such a shameful situation.

But new misconduct allegations followed, with the board performing a second internal investigation and finding there was more to the allegations than they originally thought. Nothing was done until August 2018 when a former executive assistant descriptively detailed his unwanted advances by Hybels in *The New York Times*. Unlike the previous accusations, this article was the final straw.

Steve Carter, who was assumed to be the heir apparent to the Willow Creek pulpit, felt that the information had been withheld from him and posted his resignation on his blog (since then, Carter found his holy discontent and created a campaign to help sex abuse victims). The following day, on the eve of the Global Leadership Summit where thousands of church leaders would be visiting, the entire elder board also announced they'd resign by the end of the year, apologizing to the church that they had failed to hold Hybels accountable, especially when the allegations first came to light.

Now in the court of public opinion, Hybels no longer looks like Luke Skywalker or a white-hat hero who modernized "an Empire of boring churches." No——he gained too much power, became too big to fail, and if all allegations prove to be true, everything he attained was being gambled for desires of skin. Now he has fallen from his pedestal, resembling more of a broken, crippled Anakin Skywalker who just had his arms cut off while drowning in a river of lava. His alleged affairs have been outed, each accusation being denied while those who defended him are having their own lives flipped upside down. Now, everything and everyone at Willow Creek has been left behind in the Dark Side he created. Now a man who has written 50 best-selling books and countless sermons throughout his 40 years of living the Christian life, is left with nothing else to say.

So now what?

Like Jerusalem in Nehemiah's day, Willow Creek's walls have been destroyed to bring humiliation at its doorstep. We don't know how far Hybels's alleged affairs and the blind eyes of the elder board will impact the church. If Willow Creek's once-thought invincible leadership couldn't get it right, then how else do churches weather the storm when sexual misconduct is blowing inside their midst?

If Father, Son, and Holy Ghost are the three persons of the Trinity——then Sex, Money, and Power have become the Triangle of Temptation. During the Me Too movement, the Hybels story is teaching us how unchecked sexual desire damages relationships, marriages, and even megachurches. At the deepest core of the issue, this is about power and how individuals wield it while using institutions (like the church) to protect its most visible employee.

Whenever Christianity has gotten in bed with power, it has always been destined to fail. Christianity has never been a sad religion, rather one of hope and restoration that shares power with the powerless, including those who have been mistreated. After all, Christians believe in an upside-down Kingdom where the poor shall inherit the kingdom of heaven while the rich will find it easier to fit a camel through the eye of a needle rather than enter in themselves.

If the church is to learn anything from Hybels and the Me Too movement, it needs to latch that concept NOW. Live it, breathe it, and do it. No one is too big to escape judgment, even iconic spiritual leaders who learn the hard way of coming back down to earth.

BIGFOOT SIGHTING AT SYNAGOGUE

MOUNT SINAI CONGREGATION • WAUSAU, WISCONSIN

Bigfoot does exist. He hangs out with Spock at Jewish celebrations.

On March 8, 2015, at approximately 7:16 P.M., I was eating complimentary M&M's while attending a Purim festival at Mount Sinai Congregation. It was here that I was confronted by an apelike creature that was hunched over, covered in thick black hair, and had arms that swung like wrecking balls. The feral Sasquatch turned his eyes on me, scaring the Yiddish out of me. My heart started racing faster than Sonic the Hedgehog getting coffee at a Starbucks drive-thru. He was no more than 20 yards away from me when he could be heard breathing in-and-out with guttural-like moans. He was visible for only a few seconds before he turned and just...vanished. Either Spock teleported him to another forest, or he stomped off to the greeting hall to grab the last of the hamentasch pastries. Either way, I'm certain it was Bigfoot. Apparently, he's also Jewish, as evidenced by the kippah he wore.

This traumatic experience took place at a synagogue during Purim, one of the most joyous holidays on the Hebrew calendar. It commemorates Esther saving the Jews, as detailed in the Megillah, which is the Biblical Book of Esther.

According to the story, King Ahasuerus of Persia—more famously known by the Greek translation of his name, King Xerxes I—wished to display his kingdom's wealth to all through a lavish celebration that would have made Las Vegas look like a library convention. Having gotten thoroughly drunk, Xerxes commanded his wife, Queen Vashti, to dance in front of the populace to display her beauty. She refused. Rather than wait 25 centuries to hash out their marital issues on Dr. Phil, the king banished his wife from the kingdom and then ordered all the beautiful young virgins of the kingdom to be presented to him so he could choose a new queen.

At this time, a Jewish man named Mordecai lived in Persia with his cousin Esther, whom he raised as his own daughter. According to the Scripture, Esther was very attractive and "lovely in form and features" (Esther 2:7), which is basically the Bible's way of saying she was smokin' hot. If this story couldn't get any more sexist by today's standards, Mordecai persuaded Esther to compete in the queen-making beauty pageant for the oogling eyes of King Xerxes and his nobles. Esther's beauty pleased the king's testosterone, and they were married in front of the entire nation. Today, this custom is called *The Bachelor.*

Now, Mordecai had an archnemesis named Haman, who was depicted in this synagogue as a child-drawn illustration set along a wall with all the other story's characters. He was pictured with a pencil-thin mustache, yellow serpent eyes, and a three-cornered hat made of what looked like a giant football. Haman hated Mordecai because he didn't bow down to him—the Old Testament equivalent of giving him the finger. Haman somehow learned that Mordecai was a Jew, and he plotted to destroy Persia's Jewish population.

Getting wind of this evil plot, Mordecai persuaded Queen Esther to speak to the king on behalf of the Jewish people. Despite knowing that the last queen had lost her throne by confronting the king, Esther risked her livelihood to appeal to the king. She revealed that she was Jewish (Say whaaaat?!) and pleaded that her people be spared from Haman's genocidal plot.

Since Esther had at this point won the love (or lust?) of her new king husband, King Xerxes was appalled by this revelation that his wife's life was in danger and had Haman immediately hung. The Jewish people were saved, and everyone lived happily Purim after.

. . .

Mount Sinai Congregation in Wausau, Wisconsin
March 7, 2015 – 7:00 P.M. Purim Costume Party

My knowledge of the Jewish faith is limited, which is another way of saying I watched a performance of Adam Sandler's "The Hanukkah Song" as my initial research.

Although this wasn't technically a church service—it was instead a festival at a synagogue—visit number 22 was by a friend's request.

The three-hour Purim festival was publicly promoted as having "live music, belly dancers, and lots of fun!" Purim is considered the Jewish Mardi Gras, and it's customary to dress up in costumes to hide one's identity during the festival. After all, God "disguised" His presence in the Book of Esther, since the name of God is never mentioned in the entire book.

The master of ceremonies this evening was The Big Lebowski. Despite having misplaced his infamous Persian rug from the movie, he really held the room together between the live band, the belly dancers, and the yeti. Between the band playing song covers like "Burning Down the House" and "Gold on the Ceiling," The Dude officiated a trivia contest and provided insight into various Purim traditions.

For instance, any time the name "Haman" was mentioned aloud, everyone was instructed to stamp their feet, pound the tables, and use the provided noisemaker graggers to obliterate his name. Everyone was also encouraged to celebrate with a festive meal of hamentasch, a triangular pastry designed to resemble Haman's hat; kreplach, a ravioli-like filled pasta; and beer dip (I'm still trying to figure out the religious significance of that one). I was also encouraged to drink until I could no longer tell the difference between saying "Cursed be Haman" and "Blessed be Mordecai." This sounded like a great way to schedule a future AA meeting, until the gentleman at the concessions stand poured me a $2 plastic cup of Miller Lite that had more foam than beer. Cursed be Haman, indeed.

The highlight of the night was the belly dancers, who wore fitted sequin-covered tops, harem pants, and three-armed candelabras on their heads. They danced to Hebrew folk songs, shimmying their ribcages in time, balancing lit candles on their heads and in their hands, and prancing about on their tippy-toes.

The night concluded with loud music and the belly dancers grabbing the attendees to join them in awkward arm flailing and shaking motions. One dancer even grabbed my arm to pull me to my feet. "Come on, it's fun," she urged, making me feel like a party pooper. But I politely refused the dance, not being one to draw attention to my man-beauty.

Unlike Queen Vashti, fortunately I was not banished.

Much like Bigfoot playing the world's longest-running game of hide-and-seek, the Book of Esther resides in a deep forest of hidden meaning. Why is the name of God hidden throughout this particular story? Why did Esther hide her Jewish identity from her husband king? Why was Haman not hung earlier for his poor fashion sense regarding triangular hats? These are the questions that have worn holes in my carpet after much pacing and pondering.

The Book of Esther is like a spiritual hike to explore God's hidden presence. Its underlying theme is that God works in ways that often appear to be pure chance or coincidence and, frankly, will not be believed. To believe requires embracing the mysterious, where anything is possible. You can never prove it, and you can never disprove it.

Although Bigfoot remains a mystery, every now and then, you can witness indisputable proof of God's hand at work in the world. Now if God's hand could just pour me a proper cup of beer, I'd be set.

CHURCH 23:
SCIENCE TO PROVE THE EXISTENCE OF GOD
CREATION EDUCATION CENTER AT HIGHLAND COMMUNITY CHURCH • WAUSAU, WISCONSIN

I was 15 years old when I was taught Darwin's theory of evolution for the first time. Kermit the Frog's cover of "Put the Lime in the Coconut" was stuck in my head as I operated on a dead amphibian's opened chest. While I poked around the frog's organs like unwanted peas on a dinner plate, my high school biology teacher interrupted the dissection to launch into a lecture on how our human species has evolved over millions of years from our little cold-blooded friends.

Had he gone loco? No way was I gonna cross-reference my family tree with the Teenage Mutant Ninja Turtles. The coconut song in my head got progressively kookier the more he talked. My mind felt like it was spinning and had been twisted into a Mesozoic rainforest overrun by dancing sock puppets. As the imagined stuffed animals in my mind began hissing, hooting, and hollering, my biology teacher reigned supreme as the classroom's tribal chief, casting Darwinist spells to possess my classmates' minds. I hypothesized that he had gone cuckoo to believe that humankind's first words were derived from "ribbit."

My defensive reaction had been triggered by my strict Christian upbringing, coupled with VHS tapes of *The Muppet Show*. I had been taught to take the Bible literally, including the part about the world being created in six days and God taking a much-deserved day off on the seventh. As a result, Dave's Theory of Evil Evolutionary Scientists deduced that science teachers were plotting to add the Bible to the endangered species list—especially those science teachers who gave me a grade below a B. I hypothesized that the only solvents that could save my biology teacher's contaminated soul was baptism water mixed with Tide Ultra Plus Bleach.

I retained this line of thought throughout my late 20's. However, I often found myself befriending people who were skeptical about the idea of a Great Puppeteer in the Sky pulling all the strings. My attempts to convince these nonbelievers of the power of faith often led to discussions about the origin of the universe. I quickly learned that combating scientific arguments with my literal Biblical interpretation of Eden's talking snakes and Noah's vegan lions sounded about as logical as Kermit and Miss Piggy conceiving Neil deGrasse Tyson. If I wanted to put the lime in the coconut and make my argument feel better, I needed a doctor to relieve my creationist take.

I thought my wish was granted when Dr. Ken Ham debated Bill Nye over the age-old question: how did we come to be here? I was certain that the back-and-forth arguments would be like a professional wrestling match—minus "God's Number One" foam fingers on the spectators' right hands and sweaty men climbing on top of each other in spandex underwear.

I felt strange about Bill Nye's role in this debate, though. He had been one of my childhood heroes. Every day, I'd jump off the bus after school and challenge the speed of light in a mad dash to get home before that catchy *Bill Nye the Science Guy* tune started. Now, 20 years later, Nye was arguing against my very belief system by publicly declaring creationism to be false. *How dare he grapple with the opening narrative of the Bible*, I thought. His stance felt like a piece of my childhood being ripped away, similar to when André the Giant ripped the crucifix from around Hulk Hogan's neck to set up their WrestleMania III clash.

Fortunately on "God's side," Christians had Ken Ham, a creationist champion who would enter the scientific ring to body slam Nye through a periodic table. I was certain that when Ham pinned Nye, evolutionists would have no choice but to eat their vitamins and say their prayers, "cause whatcha gonna do, brother, when Ken Ham-amania runs wild on yooooouuuuu!"

I watched the debate livestream on YouTube. It didn't go very well for the Christian camp.

I had hoped that Ham would explain creationism in a new scientific light, thus helping me explain my faith's position that the earth is only 6,000 years old. Instead of compelling evidence though, Ham mostly brought quotes plucked from Genesis. In essence, he dragged Nye out to call him the Eve of our day, taking a bite from the fruit of the Tree of the Knowledge of Good and Evil. And in two instances, he replied to Nye with a condescending, snarky, and dare I say it, un-Christian-like smugness. "Uh, Bill, I do want to let you know, there is a book out there," Ham said at one point, clearly referring to the Bible while inciting self-professed loving Christians to laugh at the silly children's TV-show host who had devoted his life's work to science and bowties. Nye glared at him; Ham snickered to the crowd. I didn't see how this debate was leading people to heaven.

By the time the debate ended, I got the impression that Ham was expecting Jesus Christ Himself to descend from the heavens in a referee shirt and make a cameo appearance just to raise Ham's arm as winner by celestial decision.

After the Ham/Nye debate, I struggled with the idea of Adam and Eve sitting in a tree (of knowledge), K-I-S-S-I-N-G. Don't get me wrong: I still believe that Jesus died for my sins and that God ornamented the universe brighter than the Rockefeller Center Christmas tree. Yet, I could not deny the scientific evidence just a few clicks away from my Millennial fingertips. As a result, I've become skeptical of any literal interpretations of Genesis. You mean to tell me that God wiggled his nose and said "Presto," and in a few days, Eve was seeing a talking snake behind Adam's naked rump? Do I have to believe that part, too?

In the past, I had checked my intellect at the door whenever I walked into church. I failed to entertain rational scientific thought. I feared that if I dared to veer from what the church taught, God Himself might question my faith. My salvation passport might be revoked, and I'd be stuck in the afterlife airport.

Now, as I reexamined my spirituality with *52 Churches in 52 Weeks*, I also sought to strengthen my understanding of science. My curiosity led me to explore everything from abiogenesis, to gravitational constants, to Sheldon Cooper. The more I read and learned, the more my intellect couldn't deny its worth. So I was left asking: as a Christian, where is the good scientific data to support intelligent design?

. . .

Creation Education Center at Highland Community Church in Wausau, Wisconsin
March 15, 2015 – 6:00 P.M. Creation vs. Evolution (The Case from Science) Presentation

It's not every day that you go to a church service that includes a PowerPoint presentation featuring images of the Big Bang, Richard Dawkins, and a T-Rex. Yet this was a part of the scene when Highland Community Church hosted Jay Seegert of the Creation Education Center.

Raised Christian, Seegert pursued a physics degree, and his professors frequently challenged his creationist views. This sparked a passion and led him to study creation science for nearly 30 years.

Mixing Sunday School class with a science lecture, Seegert prefaced his presentation by saying it was not his intention to twist anyone's arm, but rather to suggest that the Bible isn't mere mythology. He started with a nod to a recent article that used quantum theory—which compliments Einstein's theory of general relativity—to challenge the theory that the universe was created in a Big Bang. This new model accounts for dark matter and dark energy, neither of which the Big Bang theory could explain, and concludes that the universe had no beginning.

Seegert used this as a warning against accepting the Big Bang theory, which suggests that the universe started as a super-dense singularity containing all the mass of the universe packed into a space smaller than a proton. Then, suddenly, BANG!!!!!!!!! Without warning, that singularity just magically burst, expanding outward to create space and time faster than my editor can delete all my extra exclamation points!!!!!!!!!!! Astronomy shows us that the universe is still expanding, like the exclamation points in this paragraph!!!!!!!!!!!!!!!!!!!!!!!!!!!!!!!!!!!!!!!

Seegert asserted that, in many ways, the Big Bang theory isn't based in science at all, as the first law of thermodynamics is that energy cannot be created or destroyed. The energy to set off the Big Bang must have already existed within the tiny singularity that became the universe. So where was it? In what form did it exist? And what caused that energy to set off the Big Bang? To quote astronomer David Darling, how can scientists magically "pull a hundred billion galaxies out of their quantum hats?"

Seegert transitioned into discussing the probability of life arising merely by chance, mentioning Stanley Miller's experiment that has become the textbook model for the origins of life. Miller recreated the conditions of primitive Earth using methane, ammonia, and hydrogen, and then exposed this environment to an electrical discharge similar to lighting. As a result, many different amino acids—which are the building blocks of proteins—formed.

This experiment led to the theory that all living organisms originated from a chemical soup. Seegert argued that Miller had the wrong materials. While Miller may have found a compelling theory for how the most basic organic compounds formed, the probability that these chemical compounds would accidentally arrange themselves into even the simplest life form is infinitesimally small. In fact, it's practically a miracle.

Astronomer Sir Fred Hoyle, who derisively coined the term "Big Bang," found his atheism greatly shaken after calculating the chance of obtaining even a single functioning protein from such a primordial soup: it's similar to 2,105 blindfolded people solving a Rubik's Cube simultaneously. According to Hoyle, the likelihood of success is an astronomical number with a lot of zeroes, to one. Hoyle admitted that one theory to explain this seeming impossibility was a word forbidden in science: God.

Seegert wrapped up his presentation by turning to the origin of our species. When most people think of evolution, they tend to think of a creature like my frog patient that slowly evolved over millions of years to become mammals and then the humans of today. But if Earth started out in a molten state and slowly cooled to become solid rock, that would mean that water came from rocks, water formed cells, cells formed organisms, which eventually evolved into a variety of animals, which evolved into you and me. So in theory, we are the descendants of rocks.

Seegert also went into mathematician William Dembski's concept of design inference to argue that one could mathematically differentiate between the work of God and the work of natural processes. He also mentioned some of the outrageous claims of atheist scientists, such as Francis Crick, who co-discovered the structure of DNA. Upon seeing the intricate design, Crick thought it was the result of alien migration through the universe.

Seegert ended by recapping that there is good science to support trusting the Bible from cover to cover. If you ask someone to just believe in God, you're asking them to believe you. "We do need reasons to support what we believe in," Seegert concluded, hoping his presentation could help others who may have a similar struggle with their faith against scientific views.

. . .

When Albert Einstein was asked about his pantheist views, he said:

> *Your question is the most difficult in the world. It is not a question I can answer simply with yes or no...The problem involved is too vast for our limited minds. May I not reply with a parable? The human mind, no matter how highly trained, cannot grasp the universe. We are in the position of a little child, entering a huge library whose walls are covered to the ceiling with books in many different tongues. The child knows that someone must have written those books. It does not know who or how. It does not understand the languages in which they are written. The child notes a definite plan in the arrangement of the books, a mysterious order, which it does not comprehend, but only dimly suspects. That, it seems to me, is the attitude of the human mind, even the greatest and most cultured, toward God. We see a universe marvelously arranged, obeying certain laws, but we understand the laws only dimly. Our limited minds cannot grasp the mysterious force that sways the constellations.*

You don't need to agree with Einstein—or with my laptop theology—

125

on this, but my increasing interest in science has challenged my previous literal interpretation of the Bible, especially regarding things like the stories of Adam and Eve and Noah's Ark. Why can't we understand that the beginning of Genesis is an allegorical explanation for a world whose greatest invention was the wheel and still believe in God? Why are we as Christians not more accepting of the sound science that many have done over the years to explain our world in further detail? Some will say, "Anything is possible through God." I don't disagree, but we must also remember that God's Word was inspired by God, not written by God. He wasn't some Almighty Witch Doctor who possessed the bodies and minds of Jewish scribes like they were Muppets. They were still human beings writing what they believed God wanted them to write.

As Christians, we've fallen into the trap of believing that the Bible should explain everything in a straightforward way, still clinging to Israel's origin stories to make sense of modern scientific questions about the origins of the universe. In reality, the Bible is so much more than that. The Bible is a collection of texts by different authors from different backgrounds, transcribing oral stories from different time periods and in different styles—including historical accounts, letters, songs, and warnings—all to help us understand God's nature in relation to human nature's consistent pattern of disobedience and need for repentance. That still applies today.

At the end of the day, rather than pick out Bible passages to suit my beliefs, I would prefer to look at the grand design of life when it comes to the question of the origin of the universe. There's too much consistency, too much law and order to suggest random chance. That said, I believe science can strengthen the faith of many believers with more understanding and less bias.

Still, while I can throw lots of scientific theories around, I know one thing for a fact: the next time I'm posing for photo in a church directory, my family portrait will not include a frog.

CHURCH 24:
PRESS START TO CONTINUE
DOWNTOWN WAUSAU CHURCHES • WAUSAU, WISCONSIN

The first time I ever stole something was when I was eight years old. Indiana Jones showed me how to do it.

Reenacting the opening scene from *Raiders of the Lost Ark*, I quietly tippy-toed into my brother's room and looked eye-to-eye with his piggy bank perched atop his dresser. My forehead dripped with beads of sweat, and my hands shook nervously as I seized the ceramic swine and uncorked the rubber plug on its underside. I shook all the change out of his four-years-of-life-savings and made an illegal withdrawal of several quarters. Then, with treasure in hand, I replaced the remaining money, covered my tracks, and tipped my imaginary fedora before leaving.

But something seemed terribly wrong about the whole thing. My conscience was a booby trap, triggering a giant boulder of guilt to barrel down on me for my thievery.

The embezzled quarters were used for my family's Sunday morning ritual. Before church, we'd stop at The Donut Shop, where I could choose any two donuts. Once I was done eating and acquired my sugar rush, it was here that I'd head over to the lone arcade game there, *Ms. Pac-Man*.

I deposited my stolen quarters in the slot, pounded the white 'Start' button, and wrapped my little right hand around the bright red ball of a joystick. Suddenly, I was immersed in an 8-bit wonderland of flashing dots, bouncing fruit, and the almighty power pellets. Unfortunately, after several minutes, my yellow female chomper was cornered by the four colored ghosts and exploded in yellow fireworks. The music momentarily stopped and then played a depressing tune to signify she had been laid to R.I.P. (Rest In Pixels).

In the back of my adolescent mind, I knew Ms. Pac-Man's death was because of my sin. She would have never exploded if I hadn't stolen. When I was out of quarters, I ran over to my dad and asked him for just one more quarter, but it was time to go to church. I looked back over at the screen, which taunted me with two words: "Game Over."

As I privately mourned the loss of Ms. Pac-Man (and my role in it), our family piled into our Chevy station wagon and *Oregon Trail*ed it to church. After the service, Dad took us on a joyride through the countryside. Between thinking, *How am I gonna break the news to Mr. Pac-Man?*, I'd get bored and look out my window at all the different churches that we drove past: Catholic, Baptist, Methodist, and Presbyterian—the denominations could have been called Blinky, Pinky, Inky, and Clyde for all I cared. I'd wonder why we didn't go to church anywhere else, but was taught that they didn't preach the Bible like our "One True Church," so they were automatically "bad."

As an adult, before I started visiting different churches, I was turned off by the segregation of American Christianity divided into different regimes. After falling out of favor with my former church, I assumed that all other churches were the same with rigid rules and policies, thus chomping away at an individual's personal spiritual walk. I didn't understand why this was. If we're all brothers and sisters in Christ, why are we divided by denomination?

Then something unexpected happened. As it turned out, my hometown actually felt the same way.

. . .

St. Paul United Church of Christ, St. Stephen Lutheran Church, The Episcopal Church of St. John the Baptist, Church of the Resurrection, First United Methodist Church, First Presbyterian Church, and First Universalist Unitarian Church in Wausau, Wisconsin
March 30, 2015 – 6:30 P.M. Stations of the Cross

A coworker informed me that seven downtown churches from different Christian denominations would be collaborating to host a Stations of the Cross procession in advance of Good Friday and Easter. Catholic, Lutheran, Methodist, Presbyterian, Episcopal, Universalist Unitarian, and Church of Christ churches would all be represented. Having already attended services at three of the participating churches, I was intrigued to see what would happen.

The Stations of the Cross is primarily a Catholic practice that consists of

14 stations that are traditionally depicted along the walls of the church. As we were told at the start of the procession, the Stations not only represent Jesus' walk to His crucifixion, but it also depicts those who followed Him to His final destination. Although there are officially 14 stations, our event was limited to seven—one at each church—to make it more accessible to everyone and to keep the walk under a full mile.

The procession started at St. Paul's United Church of Christ in front of a humongous window with an overhanging giant cross. The friendly rector from St. John Episcopal was leading the event, and explained that we would be making our way through the streets of Wausau, following a large, light, wooden cross during our church-to-church pilgrimage. For me, the Millennial translation was that my Google Maps app looked like a *Pac-Man* level, where each church was dotted as a power pellet.

Each church had complete creative freedom for the station it was assigned. Most turned it into a bite-sized church service, with a hymn and a short sermon. First United Methodist had three of its members dressed in tunics like those worn by citizens during Jesus's time, all looking up to a cross while another member sang a solo. First Presbyterian Church had the clergy and congregation recite a litany that went back and forth like a liturgical version of Pong.

But it was St. John Episcopal, which I had previously visited during week 13 that really spoke to me. As everyone piled into the church from a light rain outside, we all lined up around the walls of the church. Everyone was given a large metal nail, which served as a sobering reminder of what had pierced Christ's hands and feet. And that was it. There were no words, just everyone in the church standing silently with a nail in our palm. It definitely put the price He paid into perspective.

My route home took me past that same Donut Shop. It had closed more than a decade ago and had been replaced by, coincidentally, a video-game store. I found myself thinking back over the variety of donuts I had to choose from every Sunday morning and how I preferred some types of donuts to others. I now realized that the same can be said when it comes to church and denominational preferences.

God gives us variety.

Before starting *52 Churches in 52 Weeks*, I was very much against the idea of denominations. To me, it was a modern-day Tower of Babel that only served to divide us. After 24 weeks, I was beginning to change my view and see the positive aspects of religious diversity.

Even though we're united brothers and sisters in Christ, we don't need to be identical twins. If we were, we'd all be conformists. Churches offer different preaching styles, different music, and different programs to reach different groups of people. What's important is that despite the diversity in form, the overall substance must remain the same and focused on Christ.

After the 14th Station of the Cross, we found that Jesus had gone the way of Ms. Pac-Man, laid to rest in a tomb with no lives left. The death screen of His life was flashing 'Game Over.' What's important though is that when Jesus asked His Father for just one more quarter to keep on playing, his request was granted.

He got to play one more time.

CHURCH 25:
UPON THIS ROCK I WILL BUILD MY MEGACHURCH
ROCKFORD FIRST • ROCKFORD, ILLINOIS

The Egyptians had theirs, then the Greeks, and then the Romans. Today, superheroes have swooped in to become the new American heroes of mythology. Originally created by pen, ink, and imagination, comic-book tales have increasingly come to life on the silver screen in the last few years, pitting Good against Evil.

But unlike the mythological heroes of ancient civilizations, today's six-pack-blessed gods with their seven-figure paychecks and CGI superpowers live in a society that is somewhat influenced by Christian belief. To second Captain America's response to Black Widow's warning about getting in the middle of a fight between two Norse gods, "There's only one God, ma'am, and I'm pretty sure He doesn't dress like that."

Avengers: Age of Ultron was released around this time, and I knew it had a Hulkulean task ahead of itself if it was going to measure up to the original. Unfortunately, my inner fanboy wanted to throw Thor's Mjölnir over how ridiculous some of the movie's explanations were. For example, why was Samuel L. Jackson hiding in Hawkeye's barn? How was it that Black Widow was the only one who could calm the Hulk? And (spoiler alert) why couldn't Quicksilver dodge that bullet?

But my biggest nitpick was with how the villain was set up:

"Hey, Banner, let's make Ultron."

"Okay, Stark."

"Uh, it's not working."

"Shoot, let's go to a party instead."

As soon as the Superhero Science Bros left for cocktails, the artificial intelligence known as Ultron uploaded all he could chew from the apple of The Web of Knowledge of Good and Evil. He emerged firing lethal shots of repulsor beams and sarcasm, firmly establishing himself as the villain by being a party pooper.

While the Avengers played the blame game, Ultron ascended the throne of a desolated church in a fictitious European country. It's here that Tony Stark's man-made creation developed a God complex to foreshadow the battle to come: "They put [the church] in the middle of the city, so that everyone could be equally close to God. I like that: the symmetry, the geometry of belief."

Ultron recruited his apostle twins, Pietro and Wanda Maximoff, and then put his ideological plans in motion. His mission to achieve world peace led him to conclude that mankind must become extinct. Ultron wasn't diabolically evil; rather more fascinated by the beauty of a clean slate. He wanted to take a page from Darwin and evolve——both himself and the world—into something better, but doing so required some inspiration from Genesis. When Wanda learned of his plans to cleanse the human populace in order to start over, she asked him why this was his solution. Ultron's retort is simple: "Ask Noah."

Before nicknaming Captain America "God's Righteous Man," Ultron's most affecting sound bite came when he tossed a canister full of vibranium to his personal Peter, Pietro Maximoff. Ultron then quoted Matthew 16:18: "Upon this rock, I will build my church."

I had come to the movie theater for a superhero movie. I left having seen a twisted tale full of religious symbolism that had been narrated by a soulless theologian robot.

. . .

Rockford First in Rockford, Illinois
April 5, 2015 – 1:00 P.M. Easter Worship Service

A few weeks before *Age of Ultron*'s release, I attended a massive worship service at Rockford First (which has since been renamed to City First Church) to see how one of the nation's fastest-growing megachurches did Easter. Despite my original negative perceptions of such over-the-top venues, I had grown quite fond of them by this point. Megachurches feel like the movies, bridging Christianity with our modern sensibilities. They're like a spiritual box office that seeks to gross the highest number of souls, listing Christ as the top attraction on the marquee.

One of my "experiments within the experiment" was to see how a church welcomed first-time visitors. For large churches like this one, a system is already in place. When I first drove into the parking lot, nearly two dozen volunteers were stationed outside, outfitted in bright-yellow safety vests and waving their hands to direct traffic and welcome everyone to church. Inside, a lady greeted me at their welcome desk, and in exchange for my email and mailing address, she gifted me a black-and-yellow swag bag that included a coffee mug with the church's logo, a DVD, a 28-day full-color devotional, a welcome card, a coupon for a free coffee at the church cafeteria, and various colored brochures about the church's various ministries. She even gave me a mini tour, taking me past their bookstore and some of their life groups before leading me into the worship auditorium to find a seat. I'd seen this before, but still found it as a great personal touch to help feel less like a stranger.

What's fascinating about megachurches is how much micromanagement goes into every little detail. From the coffee shop's branding to the pastor's denim jacket, everything seemed designed to deliver the grandest blockbuster production for the spiritual seeker. That said, I was beginning to notice that megachurches often tried a bit too hard in their attempts to cater to audiences entranced by pop culture.

Here, passing around a collection plate is soooooo 2003. If you wanted to tithe, you could do so with your PayPal account. Who needs hymnals when all the song lyrics are projected up onto the overhead IMAX screen? Organ music may have been all the rage during the Protestant Reformation, but here, the musicians—silhouetted by a laser light show that featured more zips and zaps than a *Guardians of the Galaxy* opening fight scene— pumped the congregation up with a MacBook Pro-powered techno dance beat combined with a cello in a piece that could go on Star-Lord's next mixtape.

After the music, a New Year's Eve-style countdown led into the service itself. The church's Mr. and Mrs. Head Pastor were introduced as "Rockford First's Couple," while their Twitter and Instagram handles (apparently, email and Facebook were too passé) were projected on the overhead screens. The superpastors promoted the church's new DVD that was included in my gift bag, which they had recently filmed on Route 66 and were giving away for free upon request. The screens transitioned to showing a trailer for the high-octane-for-a-Christian film, in which the senior pastor was re-imagined as Vin Diesel driving fast and furiously in a Dodge Challenger RT while still obediently maintaining the speed limit. In a voiceover, he talked about going on a journey and using a road trip as a metaphor for building a relationship with God. "When you start a journey, you need a destination", he said before asking everyone to invite Jesus to ride shotgun. The camera then zoomed out to show the pastor (presumably) driving donuts in a blocked-off area of the Nevada desert.

The trailer ended, and the lights transitioned to show the stage set up with trendy sermon furniture for the Easter message. In the middle of the stage was a table just small enough to prop a Bible on it and a chair so ergonomically impossible to sit in, I was sure the church was required to take out an Allstate policy before anyone could use it. Next to this was a 50-inch HDTV that had been rolled out on caster wheels, used as a giant reading visual for the pastor and congregation to reference Scripture.

The sermon itself focused on the resurrection and Jesus proving to a doubting Thomas that He is God, as only He could resurrect Himself from the dead. It was a bit weird to get through, as I had become so distracted by all the countdowns, flashing lights, and noise. It felt like going to a website, only to get barraged by pop-ups.

After service, the church and its Easter message reminded me of *Age of Ultron*. Stark and Banner eventually took a second stab at creating an A.I. savior, breathing life into it with Thor's godlike lighting. The result was Vision, half-man, half-something else, who was puzzled by the world he came into. When the Avengers questioned his purpose, Vision responded, "I am," a Biblical reference in itself. Having been deemed worthy by an all-powerful hammer, Vision joined the Avengers for the final battle of Good versus Evil. In the film's grand finale, the Avengers fended off Ultron's robot army, which would send a flying city crashing toward Earth. And at the center of it all was a church.

While I may poke fun at Rockford First's production design, doesn't God design our lives? While traditional churches are stuck in the mud with conservative mindsets, places like Rockford First seek to breathe new life into our faith by engaging with new cultural norms. Sometimes it can feel like a bit much, but I appreciate that this church isn't afraid to go out on a limb to reach new believers.

In Vision's final scene, the last Ultron robot tracks him down. Running out of power, the only ammunition Ultron is left with is his words: "Stark asked for a Savior and settled for a slave."

Vision retorts that Ultron missed the point of humankind, saying, "There is grace in their failings."

Just like Vision, there's a certain beauty in the fact that Jesus settled to slave for our sins by living among us and our own failings, despite having all of God's power. Through such association, He was actually our Savior all along.

As Vision says, "A thing isn't beautiful because it lasts."

"YOU DON'T KNOW IT, BUT THE WORLD LOST A GIANT"
WASHINGTON NATIONAL CATHEDRAL • WASHINGTON, D.C.

I was never good with plants.

After buying a house, Tiff's mom tried to get me excited about starting a garden. I knew enough about gardening to know that I should never garden. I barely get enough water and Vitamin D as it is. Why leave me in charge of a living, breathing plant that requires me to keep it alive? At least start me off with a Chia Pet.

I feared that if this garden ever came to pass, the Arbor Day Foundation would come by my house and gasp at my neglected flowerbeds. They would film a TV commercial there with a Sarah McLachlan soundtrack, zooming in on a lone, anorexic-stemmed daffodil who'd look innocently into the camera with its center eye. With the gentlest of breezes, its dried petals would slowly wither away as a 1–800 number would flash across the screen, urging people to help save the remaining petunias in my backyard.

It would have helped if I'd known Bonnie sooner.

The first time I said hi to Bonnie, I was saying bye to Patrick. I'm never good with goodbyes, especially when it comes to my best friend. They were going to uproot from Madison and move to greener pastures in Washington, D.C. Bonnie was passionate about gardening, so much so that she wanted to landscape a new life by going back to college in her 30's and major in plant science at the University of Maryland.

While my visit with Patrick soon degraded into a religious debate—as it

135

usually did—Bonnie gathered supplies for the going-away picnic they were hosting. Rather than directly weighing in on our theological debate, Bonnie made a few comments that planted new thoughts in Patrick's mind regarding his indifference to religion. Bonnie had a remarkable gift, something that I couldn't do. It was the first time I'd seen someone (ANYONE!) weed his mind on the subject. And she was so gentle about it. I could immediately see why Patrick was so drawn to her. It wasn't just the plants in her garden that were growing; Bonnie was growing on me, too.

A few years later, *52 Churches in 52 Weeks* enabled me to cross paths with Patrick and Bonnie again, this time in D.C. Their relationship didn't ultimately work out, but they remained close friends. I had just completed a visit to the Washington National Cathedral, and the three of us had lunch at an organic restaurant and then visited the White House on the peak day of cherry blossom season. Before venturing any further, she gave up her role as the third wheel and bid us adieu.

"See you later," I said.

Again, I'm bad with goodbyes. Given that Patrick was planning on moving to Portland and Bonnie lived over a thousand miles from me, I knew it was likely the last time I'd ever see her in person. It bothered me that I didn't give her an appropriate farewell, but I didn't know what else to say. As we walked along, I mentioned this to Patrick: "I think that's the first time I've ever said goodbye to someone that I know I'll never see again."

A few weeks later, Patrick updated his Facebook profile picture to be of the two of them in a loving hug. I was curious: had they had gotten back together?

I texted him and asked. His reply came back: "Bonnie was killed by a truck."

. . .

Not many people, on a global scale, know who Bonnie is, but the outpouring of stories and pictures from around the world is astonishing. i sit here and think about her and there's a range of emotions and thoughts that happen...and setting aside my own personal thoughts and feelings about her and boil it down to something...man has the world lost out on a great amount of knowledge and ideas contained in her head. from how to treat people (which her actions more than fully embodied) to her research (which was so far above my head it took her graduate sponsor at her memorial on campus to make me fully realize how important and unique it was) to the way she approached life. i can tell you there are days where she cried because she was so stressed and so frustrated but she never gave the fuck up. no matter the obstacle or how unlikely a favorable outcome there was in front of her she fought. never anything less than with her full head heart and body. no one and nothing would keep her from capturing the thing she set out to do, ever. she was crazy in the best possible way and i can't tell you how many times i shook my head at her. she'd give a knowing laugh, and continue on.

you don't know it, but the world lost a giant. — Patrick

. . .

Washington National Cathedral in Washington, D.C.
April 11, 2015 – 12:00 P.M. Holy Eucharist (Bethlehem Chapel)

Three hours before I met up with Bonnie and Patrick, I was craning my neck to look up at the second largest cathedral in the United States for the halfway point of *52 Churches in 52 Weeks*.

The Washington National Cathedral serves as a spiritual Christian home for America, while also paying tribute to its history and values. Seeing everything of note in the cathedral is literally a scavenger hunt, as it is filled with memorial bays commemorating leaders and events of national significance. There's a bronze statue of Abe Lincoln with a floor inset of pennies, all 50 state flags hanging above the nave's ceiling, and stained-glass windows commemorating everything from Creation to the moon landing. It's the only place of worship where, if you look to your right, you can see the tomb of former president Woodrow Wilson right there inside the church with you. I even tried to locate the Darth Vader gargoyle perched on the northwest tower by borrowing a random kid's binoculars.

At noon, I attended a low-key Episcopalian service inside the Bethlehem Chapel, located downstairs in the crypt of the cathedral. Services have been held inside the Bethlehem Chapel nearly every single day since it opened in 1912—barring national tragedies. When the service started, I was outnumbered two-to-one by the presiding pastors. Eventually, my lone-congregant status changed as more parishioners came in late, as the walk to even find the chapel was nearly two football fields in length.

There wasn't much to the service. The sermon was a quick six minutes, and it didn't immediately resonate with me. Yet, as I reflected on everything that happened afterward with Bonnie, I realized that the pastor had spoken so elegantly on the human condition: "Love is real. It really is stronger than death. Love can help us to go on...and trusting that our work and relationships with others is worth the effort."

When I received Patrick's text, I could tell that the life had been sucked out of him. I stared at my cell, desperately struggling to think of the exact right thing to say to help him deal with the pain. I searched for words, wanting to give him a manly verbal hug through the phone and break him out of his stunned trance. Instead...I had nothing.

Bonnie genuinely wanted to help people, and I was pissed that I had to watch a 30-second biking ad in order to watch a 23-second news blip about how her life ended. I didn't have the words to break the trance that such a tragedy brings. I didn't know what to say to my best friend who was grieving. Or her friends. Or family. I was just a guy who spent all of three days with her. That Saturday was one of them.

So instead of focusing on the pain, I'm going to focus on what Bonnie did to help others. She did that through gardening. She lived it. She breathed it. She loved it. If there's any metaphor to explain humanity, it's the garden.

At its root, a garden is about life and beauty. It's a place where you can put your hands in the dirt. It requires that you pour everything you have into it to make something of it. It's a reflection of your hard work. With your hands, you craft life and growth, while also protecting it from Mother Nature and Father Time.

As I looked at comments on her Facebook wall from friends and family, I realized that what Bonnie had been planting in her garden had begun to sprout. She planted seeds in the hearts of all those she touched. She watered those seeds with her kindness, gave them sunlight with her smile, and weeded what negativity she could in this silly garden we call life.

Like a flower that loses its colors, our outer physical attributes wither away when we cross over. We leave behind our bodies, culture, ego, material possessions. Once these are gone, another sort of beauty shines through. What's left is the stem of our essence.

The essence of Bonnie's life was rooted in growth. For those she touched, her essence is still growing. To quote the sermon I heard that day, love is stronger than death, and Bonnie's work has proved that.

SYMBOLISM OF THE CROSS
THE BASILICA OF THE NATIONAL SHRINE OF THE IMMACULATE CONCEPTION • WASHINGTON, D.C.

I was never good at buying gifts for women.

During my relationship with Tiff, I got her things she couldn't use. I bought her *Guitar Hero* for my Wii (she didn't have a Wii). Since she liked all things J.K. Rowling, I bought her the *Harry Potter* Blu-ray collection for my Blu-ray player (she didn't have a Blu-ray player). I also got her socks. I wasn't buying gifts for her; I was buying the gifts for Me. Me. Me. Except for the socks. Her feet were always abnormally cold.

To truly communicate my feelings that would also put all my past gift-giving to shame, I wanted to get her a romantic emblem to signify my love. Something rich, beautiful, and with actual thought behind it. At first, I was going to purchase a cross necklace to signify our keeping Christ the center of our relationship. The problem was that I was still hung up on Me and selfishly distanced myself from the cross idea. Instead, after a considerable amount of research, I found just the thing: the journey necklace.

Forested with diamonds and paved in 14K white gold, the journey necklace was shaped like a winding "S" shape. The smallest stones were at the bottom to represent the beginning of our journey together, with each ascending stone growing slighter larger than the last, symbolizing how our love and connection was becoming increasingly intertwined through the twists and turns of life. As our relationship was nurtured over time, our souls began to swirl together to create more and more magical memories. Tiff loved it. Not a day went by when she didn't wear it.

One summer day, she called me with so many tears streaming down her face, she could have melted the Wicked Witch of the West. She had lost the necklace at the beach while swimming with friends. When I drove out to meet her, she was searching the mud on her hands and knees. When it got dark, the search was called off. Losing it seemed like a disaster to her. I couldn't stand to see her punish herself over something like that. I purchased a new one for her a week later.

For me, it wasn't about the necklace. It was about the journey. Over time, our connection was layered with love, passion, hope, joy, ups and downs, the good and the bad, and yes, even bad gift-giving.

Then one day, Tiff gathered the courage to tell me that our journey had reached a dead end. She wanted to create her own path. I had to find my own.

When she came to say goodbye in person, I took a quick glance at her neck and noticed something different. For the first time since I had given it to her, she wasn't wearing the necklace.

I never truly understood the vastness of the human soul until our relationship ended. I was able to accept that it didn't work out, yet I was still certain that we were important souls to one another and had helped each other, even if it was for a finite period of time. I wanted the best for her, even if that didn't include me. To me, that was love. What we had experienced together had not been a waste of time.

I started sending emails to God's celestial inbox, praying that He was keeping her safe. Four months after the breakup, I received an email from her. The subject line was a simple "Hello." I think she was reaching out for comfort, to get closure, and to seek validation that what we'd had was mutual.

She wanted me to know about all the great things she was doing. She had run a charity event to raise funds to fight cancer, she was succeeding in her academic major, and her biggest achievement was about to come: she was going to Washington, D.C. for a leadership symposium.

I was immensely proud of her. She was making her dreams come true, and the greatness I saw in her was blooming faster than D.C.'s cherry blossoms in April. She was making her mark on the world and making it a better place. My joy was short-lived though. Her successes proved that she had made the right decision to split. She was becoming more without me.

I was wary that my interference would hinder her current journey of self-discovery, yet my emotions got the better of me, and I wrote back:

Tiff, I need to let go for myself and for you to let go to be true to yourself and whatever it is you're searching for. I hope that I could give you the closure that you needed, but I need to gracefully bow out of your life, possibly forever. I am still rooting and praying for you, but...I need to disappear. Good luck with your new life and I hope you find what you're looking for. I'm very proud of all the good things you do.

I couldn't be a part of her life when she was reaching her greatest heights.

. . .

Basilica of the National Shrine of the Immaculate Conception in Washington, D.C.
April 13, 2015 – 12:10 P.M. Mass (Crypt Chapel)

I never really had any desire to visit D.C. In the past, driving an hour to the nearest Olive Garden was my idea of a road trip. Yet, when my best friend Patrick moved there, it changed my tune regarding the nation's capital.

While riding the metro train, I spotted a massive dome decorated with a colorful pattern of blues, yellows, and reds, right next to a magnificent tower that shadowed the neighborhood. A crucifix topped both structures.

"What kind of church is that?" I asked Patrick.

He replied that it was the National Shrine of the Immaculate Conception, one of the tallest buildings in the nation's capital and the largest Catholic church in the United States. I knew I had to see it up close, and it certainly didn't disappoint.

A nun had to pick up my jaw from the ceramic tile floor. The sheer size of this basilica was astonishing, with its towering marble chancel and the numerous statues, paintings, and mosaics featuring traditional Catholic iconography. There were over 70 chapels throughout the church and the downstairs crypt, most honoring the Virgin Mary in various international representations.

As a lifelong Protestant, my understanding of the Catholic tradition mirrors my ignorance in gift-giving. At the few Catholic masses I've attended, I felt more out of place than Honey Boo Boo during Jeopardy! Kids Week. I missed the cues for when it was time to make the sign of the cross, I sat alone when members went up to receive the Eucharist, and I failed to understand several important church doctrines that were the result of papal supremacy.

But now, rather than focus on what I didn't understand, I decided to focus on what I did—the same symbol I had rejected years ago when it came to buying a necklace for Tiff: the cross.

The sermon this day was about the very first Christians who witnessed the dramatic double event that was the death and resurrection of Christ. Nothing resonated with me until the priest explained, "Whenever we discover something new, we tend to look at it by comparison to something old and familiar. We try to make connections with thoughts. And immediately, people began to look back and connect the new with what was immediately preceded."

The same could be said for any kind of breakup. It's a serious matter, a tremendous loss, and a deep wound that takes time to heal. The human soul, eternal and vast, often cannot comprehend such a severe reaction when so much that has been invested in another person is suddenly taken away.

The basilica's sermon didn't teach me this immediately, but it helped me start making connections regarding the symbolism of the cross. The cross symbolizes everything that Jesus stood for and everything we should stand for. The entire Biblical narrative takes us on a journey that leads us to the revelation of God's love on the cross at that moment.

This is how we know what love is. Jesus died on the cross for us so we could live for each other. The cross defines the very nature of God. The depth and quality of a person's love for another is measured by the degree to which they will sacrifice for them. By dying, Christ went to the furthest degree for us.

In pain, our shells break so that our hearts can be exposed to the sun. When our hearts are broken, they are broken open so that we may feel more love, more pain, more life. It deepens who we are. We have the ability to feel deeply, to grieve to the core of our beings, and to know love in all its totality.

If you can understand the cross, you can understand love.

A WHOLE NEW WORLD

THE RELIGIOUS SOCIETY OF FRIENDS • MADISON, WISCONSIN

One frustrating thing about prayer is that God isn't some kind of magic genie wearing parachute pants and speaking with a Robin Williams voiceover.

As a wee li'l tike, I imagined God granting prayers like they were Aladdin's wishes. Instead of praying for important things like world peace, feeding the hungry, or ending male pattern baldness, I selfishly prayed for myself. Part of this mentality was due to my parochial school upbringing. One Bible passage that was superglued to my cerebellum was, "Ask and it will be given to you; seek and you will find; knock and the door will be opened to you." I only comprehended the "Ask and it will be given to you" part and zoned out for the rest.

This continued into my teenage years. I expected my prayer requests to be handed to me like Jesus guest-hosting for Oprah: "You get a car! You get a house! You get a college degree! You get a sidekick monkey with a fez hat!" I waited, certain that soon I'd be giddier than Tom Cruise jumping on Oprah's couch and that my legs would bicycle kick with glee. As for One Thousand and One Nights, I asked God to open the magical Open Sesame door and grant me countless material blessings. Each granted prayer would be gift-wrapped with decorative bows and handwritten name tags that would read: "To: Dave. From: Jesus."

But that never happened.

When the Princess Jasmine of my life ended our magic carpet ride with the words, "I need to see other guys," leaving me in A Whole New World of singleness, my prayers began to change. My guiding principle became to pray for her. Not me. Her. Every night when my head hit the pillow, I prayed and prayed and prayed. Before drifting off into la la land, my last request was that God command some guardian angels to ensure that Tiff was safe, happy, and most importantly, macing any and all guys who dared talk to her.

Then one December night, our paths crossed again for the first time in over a year.

The temperature was dipping below zero when I stepped out of my car in a mall parking lot. As I made my way to the front entrance to start my Christmas shopping, my heart slipped in my chest like a bad guy on an animated banana peel.

It was her.

She stepped through the automatic exit doors, lifted her hood over her head, and burrowed her eyes in text messages while walking straight toward me. Anticipating that she'd stop in her tracks at my smiling face, I strolled toward her. This was a moment that I hadn't anticipated. Still, I wanted to encourage her, learn what she'd been up to, and tell her how proud I was of her accomplishments. I wanted to let her know that I was doing okay, and I hoped she was, too.

"Hi, Tiff," I mumbled when our paths crossed. My voice had apparently abandoned me, giving my greeting as much force as a fart from Abu.

Instead of looking up from her phone, she walked right past me, her cold shoulder nearly brushing mine. There was no "hi" in return. No recognition. Not even a quick-draw of mace from her purse.

Did she even hear me? Did she even see me?

I briefly stopped and looked back at her with the same bewilderment as Bruce Willis at the end of The Sixth Sense. I took one step toward her, but then instead of seeking and I shall find, I stopped at the imaginary 'Do Not Disturb' sign on her back. That's when it hit me: we were headed in different directions, both that day and in life.

When I got home that night, I just lay in the darkness, thinking. My Disney romance had become an M. Night Shyamalan film. I was invisible to the girl that I had previously planned to spend my life with. I was hoping some sort of Jesus-ish feeling would swoop over me when I needed it most. Was God even listening to my prayers? Did God even care?

That night, I desperately wanted my prayers to be answered. That night, I stopped praying for her. That night...I stopped praying for anything.

. . .

Madison Meeting of the Religious Society of Friends (Quakers) in Madison, Wisconsin
April 26, 2015 – 8:00 A.M. Meeting

The game plan for visit number 28 was a worship meeting with the Madtown Quakers. Long story short, I tried to pray in silence for a full hour while my butt cramped up.

There's not a whole lot to write about a Quaker meeting. No one talks when they walk in. You find a comfortable seat and start meditating. That's it. There are no worship songs. No elaborate sermons. No Scriptures read. I was glad I hadn't attempted to eat a big breakfast; I would have hated to have my digestive system play a solo concert for those silently praying around me.

By the time everyone had arrived, there were approximately 30 people peacefully turning toward their inner light in an effort to discover God in their thoughts. I was the only one at this 8:00 A.M. meeting under the age of 40.

From my online research, I had learned that in some Quaker meetings, members might be inspired by the Holy Spirit to stand and speak briefly about a topic they were praying about. Afterward, the person sits down, and an awkward silence ensues. That didn't happen here, and I certainly wasn't going to stand up and break the silence.

During the stillness, I realized that I was actually pretty rusty when it came to praying. Even surrounded by so many introspective thinkers, I had trouble calming my mind. All I could think of was Steve Carell in *Anchorman* pointing at random objects and announcing that he loves them. I heard a robin chirping outside, and I prayed for the bird. I heard the wooden floor creak, and I prayed for the floor. I heard the lady in front of me get up to use the restroom, and I prayed that she wasn't self-conscious about the fact that everyone could hear her bowel movements from the next room.

I tried to pray. I really did, striving to create the kind of mental stillness in which I could tune into my own spiritual frequency. Instead, my roving thoughts were scattered everywhere. When I looked up, I got stares from "prayer-ers" looking in my direction. I looked down again and started tracing mental patterns in the carpet.

After an hour of steady silence, a designated person broke the silence with a handshake to the person next to him. Then the others in the room followed suit. Those around me introduced themselves and were very friendly. Several asked why I was visiting, and I gave a brief account of my faith expedition. They seemed genuinely interested, even giving me some suggestions of where to visit next.

After visiting some of the biggest megachurches and largest mainline churches in the country, I had become accustomed to loud, pumping worship music and wordsmith preachers. Here was a completely new world where prayer alone was the focus.

Looking back, my mindset was all wrong when I walked in. I often feel like I'm obligated to pray for someone less fortunate, forcing my mind to frantically search for things and people to pray for while hoping God will magically make my prayer come true.

Before I left, I was talking with one gentleman and learned that, like me, he had grown up in a Lutheran church. "Why did you join this type of church?" I asked, still unsure why Quakerism would appeal to him.

"Church was where I worshiped God. But here—here is where I commune with God."

Amen, I thought.

WATER UNDER THE BRIDGE
VALLEYBROOK CHURCH • EAU CLAIRE, WISCONSIN

So there's this story in the Bible. Elijah and Elisha are strolling down the road, talking about prophet stuff, when a flaming chariot appeared and separated the two. It carried Elijah away, never to be seen again.

I'm convinced this is also what happened to the majority of the women I've dated since using online Christian dating sites.

As a Christian single who desired a faith-based relationship, I figured that dating sites like eHarmony and Christian Mingle made sense. I'm not naturally an extroverted person who is bold, loud, and proud. I'm an introvert. Self-checkout lanes at Walmart were invented for people like me.

Using online Christian dating sites, I hoped to attract a Proverbs 31 woman: someone who is authentic and honest with others and with herself. Someone who is confident in who God made her to be, but also willing to be vulnerable about the brokenness we all have in our lives. I wanted to connect with someone about life, faith, challenges, and passions. I also wanted a girl other than my mom who would laugh at my bad jokes and call me "handsome".

I figured it wouldn't be too daunting to form a deep connection with a woman of faith. But in my experiences, online Christian dating has been anything but Christ-like.

This is how it goes. After swapping a few smiley-face emojis in emails and texts, you make plans to meet your self-described Christian woman in person. Imagining the other person with impossible expectations, you meet at a place like Olive Garden and then load up on complimentary salad and breadsticks. The entire time, you're hoping you don't have the logo from the Cabbage Patch Kids wedged in your teeth when you smile.

Vince Vaughn described dating perfectly in *Wedding Crashers*: "You're sitting there, you're wondering, do I have food on my face, am I eating, am I talking too much, are they talking enough, am I interested, but I'm not really interested. Should I play like I'm interested, but I'm not that interested, but I think she might be interested, but do I want to be interested, but now she's not that interested. So now all of a sudden, I'm starting to get interested."

After some other date activity, the clock strikes midnight, and if you are interested, you're forced into an awkward goodbye where you're unsure if it would be displeasing to the Lord to go in for a first kiss or if you should go with a play-it-safe hug. You go home, cordially send your date a quick text to thank her for the evening, and wait for a reply. And you wait. And wait. And you wait until you conclude that the object of your interest was swept up in a whirlwind of fire, taken up to heaven, and now enjoying a triple-chocolate mousse with Elijah.

And there you are. Alone. Left in the dust like Elisha, except you have ice cream in the freezer.

Nothing says "Jesus loves you" quite like staring at the grayed-out box of your Christian love interest after he or she has blocked you on the online dating site the next day. "But this just means you're even closer to finding the right person for you," the eHarmony message says, which is really a subtle way of a girl communicating, "I'm praying that you remove my number from your phone and never text me again." You click the X to remove that footnote from your life and then get a reminder that it's time to renew your membership at a rate of $59.95 per month so you can do it all over again.

As bad as those generalities are, I was worse. You know that scene in *Seinfeld* when Elaine tells Jerry that he's too picky when it comes to dating? That was me. There was the pre-school teacher whom I found strange because she talked about frogs too much. I canceled a second date with an accountant because she was a diehard Minnesota Vikings fan. And I will never forget my Noodles & Company date with the freckled stage-five clinger.

It was love at first noodle... for her. She fell head over heels as soon as I received my mac n' cheese. I learned everything about her way too fast, beginning with her entire family medical history. Ten minutes into the date, she told me there was a good probability that "our offspring" would have MS, said she was done with her last boyfriend of ten years because he ruined her Christmas when he was admitted to the psych ward, and topped it off by channeling her inner Heath Ledger Joker, describing in excruciating detail how she got this scar down her chest while playing with one of her cats. She claimed the amount of blood she lost nearly killed her.

I sat there thinking, *The only way a scar could be located in that region is if you had been topless with your cats.* Running out of red flags, I wanted to plug forks in my ears and ring the fire alarm to get out of that date. She texted me nonstop for the next week. I didn't know how to tell her that she was psycho in the most loving-Christian way possible. I took the easy way out and didn't reply at all.

If that weren't bad enough, my most humbling online dating moment came when a girl with only one picture in her profile popped up. In it, her face was turned to look up as she flung snow in the air. All I could make out was her chin, but I figured I'd take a leap of faith, considering she was Christian, lived in the same town, and had an attractive jaw line. What was the worst that could happen? I messaged her. She replied, "Um, Dave. This is (such-and-such). Remember me? Tiff's old roommate?"

I was done, ready to throw in the towel and live under a rock. After 20 first dates in a year, I was inadvertently making a move on my former girlfriend's former roommate. I had two weeks left on my Christian Mingle membership before I would wash my hands of it.

Then I got an email from a girl in Eau Claire. Her name was Kacie.

She was cute and had a thicket of curly blonde hair with a smile so bright, it could melt Antarctica, wipe out the polar bears, and spark new legislation on global warming. When I met her for a bowling date, I had no expectations. I just wanted to drink a Captain and Coke, flaunt the latest fashion in bowling shoes, and not look like a social outcast. We talked about the outdoors, I teased her for the pet fish she unoriginally named Fishy, and we got into a heated debate about cows and their ability to swim. She texted me a YouTube video to prove they can. Apparently, she was right.

Later in the evening, Kacie excused herself to freshen up in the restroom. I took this as a sign that she was interested. When it was time to say goodnight, I felt like I had nothing to lose. I was like Mel Gibson in *Braveheart*, rebelling against my introversion. I rallied my troops, painted my manliness in blue war paint, and raised my sword to do something I'd never tried on a first date: going in for a first kiss.

By divine intervention, she was able to deflect my incoming lips by using her cheek as a smooch shield. Still, judging by her smile, I knew she liked that I had gone for it. Suddenly, instead of being a courting gentleman, I was an assertive Christian bad boy with a bit of an edge.

The following week, I took her to a romantic comedy starring a shirtless Gerard Butler. I went for it again, and this time, she reciprocated my affection.

On our third date, I brought up church. From what I had encountered from past dates, I thought spirituality would be a natural topic after meeting a woman on a faith-based dating website. Surprisingly, it was often the best way to get friend-zoned, especially when religious denominations didn't match. But Kacie's response was different. She said something no other Christian girl had said: "We don't need to discuss that."

Our relationship was Facebook-official a few days later. We had convinced ourselves that we were in a "Christian relationship," but only in the loosest sense. We called ourselves Christian, yet we rarely talked about our faith. I don't even remember where she went to church.

Instead, we explored Eau Claire. It's an amazing Midwestern town with plenty of twisting rivers, deep gorges, and hills. The downtown area is along the merging of the Eau Claire and Chippewa Rivers, making it the perfect area for walking and biking. Everywhere we went, there was some kind of bridge we had to cross.

As I began to fall in love with Kacie, I also began to fall in love with Eau Claire. Every bridge, whether it was for train, car, or recreation, had a monumental impact on the city. After all the rejection I'd experienced through online dating, I took it as a metaphor that I'd finally crossed over to something worthwhile. My past was finally water under the bridge.

Or so I thought.

. . .

Valleybrook Church in Eau Claire, Wisconsin
May 3, 2015 – 6:00 P.M. Worship Service
I had no idea what I was walking into. I wanted to pay Eau Claire a visit, and my first Google result for downtown churches with a Sunday night service was Valleybrook Church. It was situated in a converted former movie theater. Posters featuring a dove with the tagline, "Beautiful Beginnings," adorned the outside. I snapped some pictures and immediately caught the attention of a lady inside who marched out to meet me.

"Hi there, are you with the media?" she asked.

Given that I've only ever been questioned once for taking pictures—and for looking like a potential stranger danger in the Sunday School area of the church in Texas—I knew she was being protective. I disclosed my project of making a visit to a different church every week and my habit of taking pictures to document my travels. She asked if I was aware of the news coverage of their church. I wasn't, but it was apparent that something bad had happened.

When I flipped down a theater seat inside, settled in, and pulled up the church's name on my phone, I saw that Google was littered with articles about the resignation of Valleybrook's previous senior pastor. An investigative report by the local media alleged that the pastor had been practicing spiritual abuse, encouraging church members to sever ties with their families in order to "knit" together with unrelated people in the congregation. Words like "cult" and "brainwashed" were used. One couple came forward to talk about their adult son, who was the same age as me and who had been an associate pastor. Apparently, the senior pastor had legally adopted him, along with his wife and four children. The grieving parents stated that they hadn't even known something like that was possible. The last time they spoke to him, he berated them for their beliefs. He had since moved to Texas to be with his adopted father/pastor/coworker.

The interim pastor was soft-spoken, but kept the sermon light-hearted. He preached about Jesus dining with Simon the Pharisee, when a sinful woman anointed Him. The pastor used *The Lion King* as a metaphor to explain light versus darkness, complete with an intentionally horrible rendition of "Circle of Life." He explained that Mufasa was painted lighter as the hero, while the villainous Scar was painted with scary dark colors. In Jesus' times, the Pharisee would have been painted as the white-hat hero for being a member of the cultural elite, while the sinful woman would have been stained in dark gray colors, being pushed to the outside margins of society. But Jesus' response to the "sinful" woman's anointing by forgiving her sins was startling to the society of that culture.

The pastor explained: "The Pharisee had a good reputation, which certainly merits value, but it doesn't ensure a relationship with God. Likewise, neither does a stained background like [that of] the sinful woman somehow disqualify [her] from fellowship with God."

To the church's credit, the worship team and interim pastor were piecing the church back together after corruption had drifted in. Attendance appeared to be fine, but I'm sure several congregants had left due to the controversy, feeling disillusioned with the very leaders they had entrusted with their spiritual inspiration every Sunday. Still, all I could see was an eHarmony-style message: "Your pastor has moved on, so his profile is no longer visible. But this just means you're even closer to finding the right pastor for you."

When I think about the rejection I experienced through "Christian dating" and the spiritual abuse from Valleybrook's past leadership, it's easy to get caught up in the currents of sin. Just because we put a "Christian" label on something, that doesn't necessarily mean it is Christ-like, just like the white-washed reputations of the Pharisees during Jesus' time.

When I left church that night, I had to sprint to my car, as it was pouring cats, dogs, horses, cows, fishies, and every other animal from Old MacDonald's Farm. In the span of an hour, a beautiful day had given way to a severe thunderstorm warning, with the sky lit up and emergency sirens blaring in the distance.

I had planned to take a picture of the bridge at Phoenix Park that I had so often crossed with Kacie, so despite the storm, I drove over and parked, peering out at the bridge and the rain pounding down into the rushing rapids below.

In addition to everything at Valleybrook, I had a lot on my mind: what could have been with Kacie, my foiled attempts at courtship afterward, and where my faith had gone after all the ensuing rejections. Suddenly, it struck me: if you don't pay attention, anyone—even church leadership—can be caught off-guard and swept away from God by the rivers of sin to drift away in an endless sea. Even Elijah and Elisha were stuck in front of the Jordan River before Elijah's faith summoned a divine Uber. What's reassuring is that no matter who you are or how far you think you've drifted, you're never beyond Christ's love.

CHURCH 30:
UNDER CONSTRUCTION
THORNCROWN CHAPEL • EUREKA SPRINGS, ARKANSAS

There's this tall tale in Genesis. Many manly men wanted to make a name for themselves by building a tower so tall it would reach the heavens, allowing everyone to spy on God's lawn ornaments. The men went to their local Home Depot, grabbed supplies from the DIY section, and began construction on the Tower of Babel. God looked down and recognized that this was a dumb idea, so He hit the SAP button on His celestial remote control to scramble the world's language. Because Rosetta Stone hadn't been invented yet, everyone was confused and went their separate ways, abandoning the project.

When I was five, I also attempted to build the Tower of Babel. Sadly, my mom thwarted my efforts when I ran out of LEGOs and she refused to buy more. Plus, the living-room ceiling was in the way. And I was short. Regardless, after I was done crying into my Frosted Flakes, I never had the urge to undertake such a massive project again.

Although my dreams of a Tower of LEGO were never realized, I did buy a starter house 20 years later as part of my efforts to live the American Dream. That was all fine and dandy, but I wasn't prepared for the amount of maintenance that is required with home ownership. I've slammed my car into the garage door, found plant life in the gutters, and nearly killed myself trying to do electrical work. Sadly, my previous relationships hit the same wire.

As the living embodiment of the anti-Bob Vila, I've broken more than I know how to fix. I neglect issues and hope problems go away on their own. When something gets worse, I patch up cracks with false affirmations like duct tape, hoping that "Everything will be okay" is a long-term solution.

Just like with a house, when relationship problems become so bad they're impossible to ignore, that's when the whole thing is about to fall apart faster than a demolition crew operating a fine china store. I was hopeful that wouldn't happen when I started dating Kacie.

One night during the early stages of our relationship, we went to a local bar in search of a grasshopper drink. As soon as we walked in, my night fell apart.

Standing in front of me was Tiff, the woman I had once planned to someday call my wife, standing with the Voldemort-esque snake she had foreclosed our future for. They both looked at me with "Oh shit" expressions. It was brief. Awkward. Shorter than this sentence. But the three of us knew what was going on. When I handed Kacie her grasshopper in exchange for her adoring puppy eyes, all I could think was, *How could Tiff still be with this guy? How could she have moved on so easily? What does she see in him that I don't have?*

Envy gripped me. Instead of remembering the good time, my mind flashed back to the gut-wrenching pain, the fierce betrayal, and the cold shoulders. I channeled my emotions to spite them. I got cocky. Arrogant. I started making out with Kacie, a giant "F you" to Tiff and He Who Shall Not Be Named on the other end of the bar. I wanted them both to see how I had remodeled myself after they had built the foundations of their relationship atop my bulldozed heart.

When it was time to call it a night, I walked out with Kacie by my side, but anger in my heart. Tiff and Voldemort were seated next to the door. In my peripheral vision, I saw Tiff turn her shoulder briefly—possibly to give me one last look. Could I let bygones be bygones and at least say hi?

No. I couldn't talk to her. I had loved her, and we had hurt each other deeply. I couldn't forgive her. I looked straight ahead and kept on walking.

. . .

Thorncrown Chapel in Eureka Springs, Arkansas
May 24, 2015 – 10:00 A.M. Worship Service

Walking through the winding terrain of Eureka Springs, I was greeted by the outstretched arms of the 66-foot-tall Christ of the Ozarks, the tallest Jesus mega-statue in the United States. Critics contend that it looks like a giant milk carton with a head and arms. Either way, "Our Milk Carton with Arms" saw me and summoned rain clouds as soon as I arrived at Thorncrown Chapel for visit number 30.

If you Google search for the most beautiful churches in the world,

Thorncrown Chapel ranks at the top of nearly every list. The chapel is nestled in the pines and soars skyward with abstract zig-zag architecture. Although it looks like an open-air structure, it's actually enclosed by glass, with a large skylight providing natural light. Since it opened in 1980, the chapel has won numerous awards for its use of glass, allowing nature to be an integral part of the spiritual experience. The result is an incredibly relaxing, quiet, and unique setting for a church service.

With the rain tapping on the roof above, the organist opened the service by giving a brief history of the tourist chapel. She mentioned that the architect didn't realize the interior cross-shaped lanterns would create several cross-shaped ghosts outside the chapel, a feature that is as mysterious as it is eerie.

An interim pastor, who opened the service by slipping on a wet spot and nearly breaking his neck, gave the sermon. Fortunately, he was okay and quickly moved on to preaching about the Pentecost. He prefaced his message by saying that he would replace the word "kingdom" for the more active word "reign." He quoted several gospel passages with the word substitution to proclaim the "reign" of God and talked about how we need to build ourselves from the inside to strengthen our faith and be ready for heaven.

I wasn't as interested in the sermon as I was in the glass chapel itself with construction that captivated me more than any preaching could. After the service, I paged through a pamphlet that gave a brief history of the chapel. Thorncrown was the brainchild of Jim Reed, a teacher who had purchased the land to build a retirement home. After noticing admirers taking in the view of the Ozarks Mountains from his land, he was inspired to do something crazy. He set in motion a plan to build a glass chapel in the woodlands to give visiting Christians an inspiring setting where they could commune with God.

Midway through construction, Reed's funds were exhausted and he couldn't obtain more. Many within the community ridiculed him. When it was finally time to throw in the towel, he took one last walk through his half-finished chapel, looking down at the ground and feeling betrayed by his own ambition. He broke down, got down on his knees, and prayed to God more earnestly than he ever had in his life. A few days later, Reed's prayer was answered when a generous woman provided a loan to cover the remainder of the project's costs. Since then, Thorncrown has hosted visiting churchgoers from all over the world who want to see the little glass chapel that was built to honor God.

When it comes to building anything—whether it's a house, a Tower of LEGOs, a glass church, or, to quote Ron Burgundy, a glass case of emotion—you need to start by constructing a strong foundation. This has multiple parts that must fit together perfectly. A pipe has to be an exact length. The hinges on a door have to be in the right place. All the parts need to come together to make the final product.

When it comes to relationships and my takeaways from Thorncrown Chapel, I realized that Christ is the one who designed the blueprint for a dream house in heaven. When He got his Hands in our mess, He started building a place in the Kingdom of God for us by raising pillars made of kindness, supporting us with forgiveness, and cementing it with His love.

But Rome wasn't built in a day, and that took a long time to construct within myself. I thought I was building something good with Kacie, but I wasn't. After the breakup with Tiff, I was constructing walls around my heart with envy, mortaring them with jealousy, and bricking them with hate.

How could I show my vulnerabilities in a new relationship when my heart was fortified better than Alcatraz?

CHURCH 31:
SEX BEFORE MARRIAGE
LIFECHURCH.TV • EDMOND, OKLAHOMA

My chest sucked in from excitement as the lower region of my pants started to feel tighter. Kacie flipped her brunette curls over her shoulder; her blue eyes told me what she wanted—what we both wanted. I clicked the TV remote, casting the living room into darkness as her body became a silhouette in the dark. She walked over to me, her thin hips begging to be grabbed as she draped her hands across my legs. She slowly crawled into my lap wearing nothing but a mismatched bra and panties.

"I want this so bad," she whispered into my ear before sucking it. Her hands wandered under my shirt to feel my chest, then she leaned back to graze my pants with her fingertips to sample what was clearly escalating. She was a minx, pouncing with her lips, her hands exploring my face as she kissed me. I seized her in my arms and pulled her in close. My lips retaliated by gliding down her neck. She gasped in pleasure as I stroked her skin with my tongue. The aroma of her perfume triggered my instincts to take control of the situation.

After several long minutes of wandering hands and deep kisses, I couldn't take it anymore. I grabbed her thighs and pulled her upright, lifting her in my arms as I stood. She wrapped her legs tightly around my waist and her arms around my neck. I transported her through the hallway, past the cross on the wall just outside my bedroom. In that moment, I wasn't thinking about the cross or Christ. All I could focus on were the feelings and hormones raging through our bodies.

I dropped her onto my bed and took a full view of her body. Planting a trail of kisses up her stomach, I slipped my tongue into her mouth when I reached her face and slightly nibbled on her lip before rolling her over on top of me. I could feel her body getting hotter and hotter as she became more and more excited. She arched her back to push her chest out. Our breath danced in rhythm; our hearts beat in sync.

"I want to have sex with you," she purred into my ear, sending shivers down my spine. She gazed into my eyes; her own filled with lust. She was fully prepared to give herself to me, and she tightened her core, pushing it into mine.

Sweat was dripping off her body and onto my chest. I could feel how wet she was, how much she wanted me to consummate our relationship by thrusting into her. I could have done it. I wanted to do it. But there was a voice inside my head that I couldn't ignore.

I reached out, placed my hands around her waist, and blocked her advances by pulling her off me and setting her to my side. I had tried to ignore my conscience, but I just couldn't. Finally, I laid it on her: "I've been saving myself for my wife."

She stopped.

"That's awesome," Kacie replied, looking at me like a unicorn who'd been raised in a monastery by Steve Carrell from *The 40-Year-Old Virgin*. She caressed my cheek, trying to not kill the mood entirely. "What made you decide to do that?"

I was in love with her. At least, I was reasonably sure I was in love with her. But I wasn't ready to tell her why I chose to wait. It was too deep. Too personal. I couldn't tear down that wall around my heart yet.

As a Millennial guy, revealing that you haven't done the Cupid Shuffle under the sheets feels like the new coming out of the closet. Sometimes I feel like I'm in the wrong generation. Today's culture preaches "try before you buy."

Over the last few years, some of the most common viral blog posts about Millennials and the church have been by young women providing testimonies about abstinence pledges, purity rings, and becoming "perfect Christian girl mascots." They made it to the marriage finish line with their virginity intact and an expectation that the fairy God the Father would roll up in a pumpkin carriage and waive His magic wand, making K-Y Jelly magically appear in the bedsheets like manna. They had assumed that once God had given them the green light after marriage, it would lead to loads of hot, steamy, satisfying sex, forever and ever, amen! But when their marriages had been consummated and a chorus of angels didn't sing hallelujah after they finally rounded third base, they ended up deeply regretting their decision to wait.

As a Christian guy saving myself for marriage, it was a different set of thoughts that raced through my head when I considered the issue of sex. I hoped that waiting would express my undying loyalty and love to my future wife and that it would be intimately attractive to my One and Only. But instead, today's culture has scrambled my intentions and turned them sunny side up.

Millennials are more open about casual giggity-giggity (Christians included), so by waiting it feels like I'm saying that I'm "better" than everyone else. I had to consider what would happen if my future wife hadn't saved herself for me. Would that be putting her in a shameful situation? If I continued to wait, was I merely trying to "one-up" her in the life-long loyalty department?

In prior relationships, we had gotten frisky, yet the choice to postpone hanky-panky had been mutual, despite raging boners. But now, with Kacie, things were different. We both wanted it; it was just this whole religious thing that was in the way.

After that night, I seriously grappled with my decision to wait. I discussed it with Patrick, who told me to cut religion's apron strings and tap dat ass. YOLO! I examined my last two relationships, where desire always loomed, yet we ultimately held back. Those relationships still ended in heartbreak, and I didn't want that to happen to Kacie. I hoped that she would be my wife someday. Would sinning and having premarital sex actually strengthen and improve our relationship, leading to a better Christian marriage down the road? My hormones told me yes. My faith told me no. Which was the lesser of two evils?

. . .

LifeChurch.tv in Edmond, Oklahoma
May 24, 2015 – 6:30 P.M. Worship Service

After trekking through the Ozarks at Thorncrown Chapel for visit 30, I still had enough time to pull a doubleheader and drive to OOOOk-lahoma that same day for a night service, where church number 31 came sweepin' down the plain, and the free coffee sure smelled sweet after the wind came behind the rain. That sounded better in my head.

A 163-foot-tall giant cross towered over the prairie, making a powerful statement as I drove up to the headquarters of Life.Church, which was known as LifeChurch.tv at the time of my visit. Craig Groeschel is the church's larger-than-life pastor, presiding over one of the most influential churches in the United States thanks to its creation of the world's most-downloaded Bible app. Called YouVersion, it's on more than 192 million mobile devices and available in nearly 800 languages, enabling users to bring God's Word with them anywhere and read it any time. Thanks to cornering the market on digital real estate, Life.Church was able to expand its *real* real estate, and it now has 24 (and counting) franchise campuses spread across seven states. Featuring free refreshments, high-tech satellite video, and amplified concert-style music, Life.Church has become one of the largest megachurches in the United States.

Pastor Craig was on a vacation during my Memorial Day weekend visit, so associate pastor Sam Roberts was called in to relieve him via a pre-recorded video message to close out a four-week series called, simply, "Pray." Prefacing Paul's letter to the Philippians, Pastor Sam talked about the challenges we all face in life. We hope we're doing the right thing, but when it comes to choices, how do we know what's really best?

Paul had an "agape love" for the Philippians' church, an unconditional love that ranks as the highest level of love possible—and not the same way someone would "love" Krispy Kreme donuts. He further explained that God expresses agape love in different ways and can utilize people to speak love and truth. This happened to Pastor Sam, when Pastor Craig confronted him about his intense work ethic and refusal to take a vacation. He told Pastor Sam that while his devotion was admirable, he would eventually burn out. God made use of Pastor Craig to show him love and make him hear what he needed.

Using the story of when he and his wife were wrestling with the decision to adopt a child as an example, Pastor Sam suggested we all seek Christian counsel, pray, and read the Bible to find an anchor verse to help us when making important choices. When wrestling with the choice, he found his anchor verse in Numbers. The Israelites were complaining about eating manna every day after having been delivered from Egypt, and Moses was pretty annoyed with them about it. As Moses communed with God on his spiritual radio, God answered Moses in Numbers 11:23: "Is the Lord's arm too short? Now you will see whether or not what I say will come true for you."

For Pastor Sam, he realized he had been asking the wrong question all along. He thought he knew what was best and had really been asking, "What's easiest? What makes me feel good?" This realization began to transform him from the inside out. Instead of asking, "How do I know what's best?" he found the key to knowing what's best is knowing God.

"What do you think makes us a good couple?" Kacie asked as I dipped a tater tot in nacho cheese sauce.

The question didn't surprise me. After multiple hints over our last few dates, I knew this was coming. Every statement about the future that didn't include me was a red flag. The issue of my abstinence certainly contributed to our problems, but it went deeper than that.

I didn't want to have this conversation at Taco John's, so we went to her apartment to talk privately. I learned more about her in the hour-long conversation that followed than I had in the entirety of our six-month relationship.

We decided to take a brief break. It was set to expire in a week, but the break never ended. That afternoon before I drove away, we hugged as tears dripped from her eyes like a leaky faucet. "Keep going to church," was the last thing I told her. Then I stopped going myself.

I was glad the relationship happened for the lessons it taught me. Instead of feeling ashamed about waiting, I had come to realize that I had stockpiled a significant amount of love for my future marriage. Whether a Christian has sex before marriage or not, shame should never be a part of that decision. Virginity isn't something you either have or don't have, keep or lose. It's a way of life, filled with twists and turns, mistakes and growth, just like anything. It takes a certain kind of person to value a person of God. For me, the great thing about waiting is that it allows me to take time to understand my future wife. To get to know her, to value her, to appreciate her, and to love her. There's more to a relationship than sex, and I want to appreciate the value she has from the inside.

The reason I'm waiting is that I'm deeply in love with my future wife. Knowing God, that's how I know what's best for me.

DEAR LAURA

PRECIOUS MOMENTS CHAPEL • CARTHAGE, MISSOURI

D ear Laura,
You don't know who I am. We've never met and never will. But I've heard about you my entire life. After all, we came from the same womb.

Mom told me the story of how, when she was younger, she was infatuated with her high school sweetheart. I picture him having upward-swept hair like Elvis, given the way he topped the charts of her heart. One night, they got all shook up and found a place for some hunka hunka burnin' love. Her skirt breezed up like she was Marilyn Monroe standing over a New York City-subway grate, resulting in some shake, rattle, 'n' rollin' between the bedsheets. That's when the jukebox stopped. Mom was stung and soon had a baby on the way. That baby was you.

She turned to her parents, who were well-respected members of their church. They were known as good, generous people who exemplified Christian values. But when Mom begged them for help after learning of your unplanned arrival, the pressures of judgmental church doctrine in those days were too much for them to withstand. Having premarital sex was the death knell for any hopes that Mom might have a good, Christian marriage. Your biological father was blue suede shooed away for being nothing but a hound dog, and when he had left the building, Mom checked into the Heartbreak Hotel in Disgraceland.

Our grandparents had to cover-up your impending existence. You were like Watergate; if the news broke that Mom bore you out of wedlock, it was feared the family would go the way of Nixon and be impeached from the church. An executive decision was made to keep the baby bump confidential to protect the family from scandal. Mom was condemned to stay hidden at home, never to risk that someone might see that you had infiltrated her belly.

In the black of night, Mom's parents drove to Milwaukee to meet with their own Deep Throat. Instead of crossing hearts and dotting foreheads in the name of the Father, Son, and Holy Spirit, you were signed away with crossed t's and dotted i's. The deal was done. Mom never even got to meet your adoptive parents. She protested the arrangement and begged to keep you. She wanted to love you.

You came into this world kicking and screaming. Mom named you Laura and baptized your forehead with her tears. She only had a few precious moments to hold you after her womb was empty and before her arms were empty, you having been given to your new parents. When she left the hospital, kicking and screaming at herself, a piece of her heart was empty. It's been empty ever since.

She never saw you again.

Several years later, Mom married my dad, and I was born into the world as a "firstborn." Dad was on the road a lot for work, so I became a miniature therapist with a PhD in Mom's feelings. She would talk about the few moments she had with you as I scribbled away on my Etch A Sketch. She would reminiscence about how beautiful you were and how healthy you were, perfect in every way. Some days, she was happy. Most days, she was depressed.

The only thing she knew about your adoptive parents was that they were Christian. Nevertheless, her soul was tortured with guilt for not being the mother you deserved. I remember her frequently saying how much she missed you. All she could do was pray and hope that God and His guardian angels were watching over you.

Even knowing what happened to you, it took me a long time to see what church doctrine gets wrong in its attempt to preach what's right. I've always believed in God, but over time, I felt my faith deteriorating due to the persecution some churches perpetuate. Look at you, for example. The church chose to look at the sin, not your life. How could a church do that? How could it practically encourage separating a mother and her child? Jesus certainly wouldn't have promoted such a strategy. Rather than discard church entirely, I went all-in to explore other faiths, sermons, and churches. There had to be something missing. But what?

On Memorial Day, I was passing through Missouri when I saw a billboard featuring a familiar teardrop-eyed doll and an invitation to visit the Precious Moments Chapel. Mom owned a figurine similar to the one on the billboard, which she placed next to my baby pictures. I had a vague memory of having heard of this chapel, but never really thought about it.

Given that I was on a road trip to visit a variety of churches, it made sense to take a slight detour and make an unplanned visit.

. . .

Precious Moments Chapel in Carthage, Missouri
May 25, 2015 – 12:00 P.M. Tour

At first, I kept asking myself why I was at a doll church. After all, I had a made-up rule that I needed to attend an actual service for a visit to count. But the more time I spent at the chapel, the more I paid attention to what it was saying. I felt inspired—not by words—but by how the chapel proclaimed Christ's love for His children through art. By the time I left, two hours had ticked away. I left thinking about you.

At noon, a tour guide came into the chapel to narrate the story of the Precious Moments Chapel and the artist that created it, Samuel Butcher. Butcher married his high school sweetheart, had six children, and adopted a seventh. He was a struggling artist for years until he created a line of greeting cards using teardrop-eyed figures. In 1978, he launched a Precious Moments collectible figurine line with the same design. They became an overnight success. Perhaps your adoptive parents even bought you some. You would have been seven years old when they first came out.

Although he accumulated instant wealth, Butcher was worried that the Christian message behind his work would be lost. Deriving inspiration from the Sistine Chapel, he decided to build his own chapel so he could praise God with his own unique artistic talents. He purchased a piece of land with gentle rolling hills, trees, and a tranquil stream. Several buildings were built, and he spent years working tirelessly to paint the chapel's interior with murals.

When you walk in, the left side of the chapel is covered with murals depicting stories from the Old Testament: baby Moses being rescued by Pharaoh's daughter, an infertile Hannah bringing Samuel to the temple, and Queen Esther celebrating the redemption of her people. On the right side are murals depicting parables derived from New Testament stories, including one of the baby Jesus, Mary, and his stepfather, Joseph.

As I looked at these images, I couldn't help but think about those memories of you. For years, I had tried to understand and rationalize why my grandparents let go of you. I never got to know them. Grandpa died before I was born and grandma passed away when I was ten years old. While family and friends still beam when they think of them, I've long struggled with resentment for the emotional damage they inflicted on my mother. How could they have lived peacefully after exporting you in order to maintain their own "perfect" religious reputations?

If there's one thing Mom could take solace in, it's that you were placed in a Christian family that could love and support you. I hope that's true. Despite Mom's desire to raise you herself, she simply couldn't support you as a teenage kid herself.

With Butcher being an adoptive parent himself, I think he understood the blessing of adoption, which was especially evident in his murals in the chapel. In the stories he portrayed, those who were adopted served a greater divine purpose. He could have picked any story for Moses, such as God giving him the Ten Commandments or him parting the Red Sea. But instead, he picked the one that centered on his adoption.

In the center of the sanctuary was a mural called "Hallelujah Square." Although cute, it's intimidating based on its gargantuan size alone. The tour guide said that it took Butcher 20 years to paint, but he knew he wanted to paint a scene featuring people who had gone to heaven. In the very center of the portrait was Jesus. Butcher didn't intentionally do that in front of such a massive blank canvas; he only realized it after taking several steps back. Christ is painted in a very different style from all the other child-like characters in the mural, and He's depicted extending His arms to welcome all His children home.

Laura, I hope you know that your biological mom loves you. Although we're half-siblings, I've heard about you so much over the years that you became my sister-in-heart. You will likely never read this, and I doubt we'll ever meet. But someday in the far-off future, I hope to meet you in Hallelujah Square. Through love, Jesus adopted us both.

CHURCH 33:
IS HEAVEN FOR REAL?
CROSSROADS WESLEYAN CHURCH • IMPERIAL, NEBRASKA

My former church had a sign out front that needed a collection plate for how many eye rolls it got: "Looking for a sign from God? Here's one."

It was displayed out front for months. No one in the church cared to change it. After a while, the message began taunting me. Endless questions spun through my head like the Tasmanian Devil twirling through a merry-go-round factory:

When will God show me a sign?

Why isn't Jesus Christ revealing His divine image in the tortilla of my Taco Bell crunch wrap?

Would I see "The Sign" if I opened up my eyes and started singing Ace of Base on karaoke night?

So I went to church, selfishly thinking God owed me a sign since I kept showing up. During the sermon, I'd daydream about going to heaven after watching the *Blue Collar Comedy Tour* the night before. In such moments, my personal revelation involved God looking down on me wearing a Jeff Foxworthy mustache, surrounded by angelic harp-playing 5th graders with better geography skills than me. I'd look up at my Maker and mutter something stupid like, "Is this heaven?" Right on cue, Bill Engvall would fly down on angel's wings only to snap, "No, it's Iowa. Here's your sign."

But God was a good God, and I was His dutiful follower. I knew that, upon my arrival, Simon Peter would check my name off the judgment list and lift the velvet rope to admit me into heaven's pearly gates. Jesus would greet me at the front, take my hand, and give me the tour. We'd board an ark to splash through Noah's Water Park, whirl around in Elijah's Fire Chariot Ride, and pump iron in Samson's Weight Room. Upon learning that I had been single my entire life, My Savior would correct my lifelong singleness and yoke me up with an angelic woman that literally fell from heaven. We'd finalize our vows with a kiss to gross out the 5th graders, then float down the aisle to our honeymoon suite, followed by the voice of a halo-wearing Larry the Cable Guy shouting, "Git-R-Done!"

At that, I'd snap back to Earth. Still, trusting in Him began to animate my faith. I started to wonder: is heaven for real, or is it just a bunch of Looney Tunes?

If God exists, why did He drop off a cliff like Wile E. Coyote after the Bible was completed? Suddenly, a TNT fuse had been lit in my spirituality, ready to go KABOOM! at any moment regarding the reliability of the Bible. So I'm supposed to believe the vengeful God of the Old Testament who destroyed Sodom and Gomorrah turned into the loving God of the New Testament and gave us His one and only Son, then wrapped things up with Porky Pig bursting through the last page of the Book of Revelation with "Th-Th-Th-Th-Th-That's all folks!" before disappearing from the stage?

As *deth-spicable* as it sounds, why did it feel like I needed to be Bugs Bunny for God to throw me a carrot? How come He hasn't shown Himself since Biblical times? And even if He has, I'm sure someone in today's social media age would have recorded it on a smartphone. When it comes to going viral on Facebook or YouTube, how is it that the Great and Powerful God is still behind the curtain? My disordered Millennial heart wanted a modern spin from God to bolster my faith. Lord, give me a sign!

Then I did see a sign—a sale sign at Walmart for a book with a yellow cover featuring a smiling little boy. It was called *Heaven is for Real*.

Heaven is for Real is told through the eyes of Todd Burpo, the senior pastor at Crossroads Wesleyan Church in Imperial, Nebraska. Burpo recounts the near-death experience of his son, Colton, during an emergency appendectomy when he was four years old. During the surgery, Colton temporarily slipped from life up to heaven, and Todd escaped the waiting room and went to a separate room, where he angrily prayed at God, questioning why He would take his young son after Burpo had given Him a lifetime of servitude. Miraculously, the family's prayers were answered, and Colton made a full recovery.

Colton soon started talking about his experiences in heaven, describing them as only an innocent child could. From spending time with Jesus and His "red markers," to meeting deceased loved ones that he couldn't have known about, to witnessing his dad's meltdown with God, Colton's account gives readers a small glimpse of what's to come in the afterlife.

I was unconvinced by the book's claims until we see Burpo showing Colton picture after picture after picture of artistic interpretations of Jesus, and Colton not recognizing any of them—except for a painting by a child prodigy named Akiane Kramarik, who painted it when she was eight years old after having visions of heaven. To both Colton and Akiane, what remained with them the most was the beauty in His eyes.

This story struck a chord with me, and I wasn't the only one. With so many people wondering what happens after we die, the book became an overnight success, ascending to the top of *The New York Times* Best Seller List. The movie rights were sold a year later. With Greg Kinnear starring as Burpo, the film was released during Easter 2014 and became a box office hit, grossing over one hundred million dollars worldwide.

It became my favorite book, renewed my faith, and pumped up my spirit...for a while, anyway. As I continued my *52 Churches in 52 Weeks* voyage, I couldn't help but think, *Since I'm visiting different churches to find people who are strengthening others' faith, why don't I visit the church that ignited the mainstream curiosity about heaven?*

So I went to find out if the church was for real.

. . .

Crossroads Wesleyan Church in Imperial, Nebraska
June 14, 2015 – 10:30 A.M. Worship Service

Revelation 7:9 speaks of heaven like this: "I looked, and there before me was a great multitude that no one could count, from every nation, tribe, people and language." This could also describe Nebraska, except take "from every nation, tribe, people, and language" and replace it with "corn, corn, and more corn."

Desperate to see anything other than another cornstalk (at least give me some soybeans), I was relieved to see the sign welcoming me to Imperial, Nebraska, population 2,071. Rolling into downtown on a Sunday morning felt like I was pulling into a ghost town. All the small businesses were closed, a line of American flags whimpered above vacant parking spaces, and the storefronts featured hand-painted signage cheering on the Huskers.

Given that the Burpo story had gained national exposure, I had expected the entire town to be lined up outside Crossroads Wesleyan Church. Instead, Crossroads was hidden away in a corner of town. Both the road and parking lot were worn down to gravel. It looked nothing like the movie version, though that shouldn't have come as much of a surprise, given Hollywood's penchant for pizzazz. The nearby Catholic and Lutheran churches probably outnumbered Crossroads in the number of cars in their parking lots.

Walking into Crossroads felt a little surreal, in part because it's where the film's apex takes place. In fact, I was more confused than the writers who penned the last episode of Lost. I wandered around the deserted worship area aimlessly, a little freaked out that no one was joining me, despite the worship service starting in just 20 minutes.

I stopped to examine a small portrait of Akiane's Prince of Peace painting in the foyer. It was displayed directly above a Bible that had been opened to Isaiah. Further into the commons area was a *Heaven is for Real* movie poster that had been autographed by the Burpos.

While examining these symbols of the church's fame, a kind woman approached me and introduced herself. She informed me that Imperial is just a few minutes into the Mountain Time Zone, and as a result, I had arrived extremely early. Our conversation eventually touched on Heaven is for Real, and I asked if Todd Burpo was preaching that day.

"Would you like to meet Pastor Burpo?" she asked. Given my natural shyness and current star-struck mood, I was going to decline, but she continued, "Well, what do you know? Here he is now!"

In walked Todd Burpo, moving with a noticeable limp from a broken leg he suffered during a softball game gone wrong. We shook hands and matched each other quite well in the awkward introversion department. Neither of us quite made direct eye contact, and he rocked back-and-forth before excusing himself to prep for Bible study.

The kind lady resumed my tour and asked me to sign their friendship register, where only a handful of entries had been penned over the last several months. Apparently, Crossroads didn't get many visitors.

Since I had arrived so early, I was invited to attend Bible study with Pastor Burpo and seven other church members. The study was a part of an Andy Stanley sermon series, though the focus eventually turned to the church's long-term goal of bringing in farmers for services during peak harvest times.

Eventually, it was time for the worship service to begin. Colton Burpo, having just turned 16 and earning his driver's license, sat in the front row surrounded by friends. His left forearm was in a cast, and he looked a little depressed about it, even though he was the small-town celebrity and was sitting next to a few girls who weren't shy about flashing the occasional smile his way. When the service began, Colton and his classmates took the stage to perform some contemporary worship music. Each student specialized in their own instrument, and Colton grabbed a mic and sang backup.

After the music ended, Pastor Burpo begin his sermon with a simple question: "How many of you have prayed a prayer that didn't get answered the way you prayed it would be?" He pointed out that sometimes we think we know what's best, but we don't always get it. This can leave us so frustrated that we might even give up on prayer. While God answered his prayer and saved Colton, God didn't answer his prayers to help Burpo repair his strained relationship with his father before he passed away. He still struggles with that to this day. So why doesn't God give us a sign when we ask for it? Does He even care?

Burpo countered that with a question of his own: why did Jesus leave the comforts of heaven and come down to Earth to be born in an animal's trough? He suffered poverty, persecution, misunderstanding, abandonment, and more. He experienced our pain. We can't say He didn't care after reading what He endured for us. When we go through pain and say to God, "This hurts," He can say, "I know! I've been there. I've done that, too. I know."

Heaven isn't real here on Earth. Not all prayers will be answered. Burpo said that when we're placed in difficult circumstances, we have two options: we can run to God or run away from God. We can blame God for the problem, or we can go to God for help.

After the service, Pastor Burpo made sure to come over to me and wish me luck on my journey.

I walked out of Crossroads, never having gotten a "sign" or accidentally opening the bathroom door to a portal to the throne of God. Instead, I learned that I needed to develop patience. The worst part about waiting for a sign is the waiting part. We all want instant gratification these days, and even asking God for a sign is a sign of selfishness. Plus, even if we do get one, like Gideon did, we'd probably doubt it and ask Him for another one, just to make sure it wasn't an accident.

Before I drove away, I looked up into the sky, where the sun was hiding behind the clouds. It cast a shadow, yet no one could control that cloud and move it in order to see the light behind it. So I simply waited for the cloud to drift by, waiting for the light to shine. Waiting patiently. Still waiting.

CHURCH 34:
GOD'S B**** TO ACCIDENTAL SAINT
THE HOUSE FOR ALL SINNERS AND SAINTS • DENVER, COLORADO

E very January 1, my New Year's Resolution is to not make a New
Year's Resolution.

This is mostly due to my gym rat days. I'd be busy gutturally
roaring while lifting heavy objects in front of mirrors, and the New Year's
Resolutionists would suddenly come out of the woodwork to crowd the
gym at the very beginning of January. They were the people who polished
off the last of the Christmas cookies, drank too much champagne before
the ball drop, and made ballsy claims about getting in shape after the Rose
Bowl. They'd show up a few times and do 20 minutes on the elliptical, but
never made it past two weeks.

This also happens in the church, especially around Easter and
Christmas. Pews fill with people dressed in their Sunday best who exercise
their minds with a 20-minute sermon and then vanish until the next holiday.
Being a self-righteous Christian with his nose in the air, I swore that this
would never be me.

Until it was. I would religiously go to the church every week for a while,
only to fumble my church-going ways during NFL season and binge-watch
football instead. It's like I had achieved spiritual six-pack abs, but then
stopped going to the gym and replaced my workout regime with a Shake
Weight. My hunger for the bread of life was replaced by a hunger for junk
food, and my waistline slowly expanded along with my sugarcoated excuses
for why I wasn't opening those church doors. Eventually, the theology

button of my pants was ready to burst. Something needed to change. It was time to show up again and get back in spiritual shape.

If anyone knew how to show up in the right place at the right time, it was Mary Magdalene. She was a hot mess, a homeless schizophrenic with personal demons that prostituted her mind as much as she let men prostitute her body. She had no business being next to Christ. Why was someone like her allowed to even associate with the Bible's greatest hero? After all, women were basically property back in those days, and as a fallen woman, her status was lower than a slug competing in a limbo contest. And yet, in all the gospels, there she is! Matthew, Mark, Luke, and John all mention her. Her passion for Christ—a grand devotion that howled for His love—left her sobbing in the dirt. She was the last one to leave the cross and the first to arrive at His grave on the third day.

Why her?

. . .

The House for All Sinners and Saints at St. Thomas Episcopal Church in Denver, Colorado
June 14, 2015 – 5:00 P.M. Worship Service (Blessing of the Bicycles)

Holy crap, was my first thought. *What am I doing here?*

I had arrived at an emerging church which its own pastor deemed "a freak show." Its membership included transgender teens, LGBT couples, and bankers in khaki shorts. Apparently, it wasn't uncommon to witness an elected official receive the Eucharist from an ex-convict.

I reached the trendy Denver neighborhood that housed the church after 15 hours of driving, googly-eyed and with my body spazzing out due to sleep deprivation. I was tired, red-faced, and out of place, and my demeanor resembled that of a cranky Tickle Me Elmo. I was in no mood to talk to anyone, but I'd shown up anyway.

Nadia Bolz-Weber, the ecclesiastical ringmaster of The House for All Sinners and Saints, had been the one to pique my interest in the church. Standing over six feet tall, with stone-cold blue eyes, and sporting spiked Cruella de Vil highlights, Bolz-Weber has been raising hell to save people from it. She had a jawline made for the UFC women's bantamweight division, and you'd be forgiven for assuming she spends her free time in the octagon, training to cave in Ronda Rousey's face. However, instead of hitting opponents in the ring, Bolz-Weber preaches a gospel that hits even harder.

Bolz-Weber has become an original voice in postmodern Christian America, gaining an apostle-like social media following after pulling no punches in her spiritual memoir, *Pastrix: The Cranky, Beautiful Faith of a Sinner and Saint*. In it, she is both bold and vulnerable, writing about her past as a stand-up comedian when alcohol and drugs had a full mount on her life, fully expectant to be tapping out and saying uncle by the age of 30. But instead of focusing on those wounds, she writes about what brought her back before the ten-count. When a close friend committed suicide, she was asked to give the eulogy. Seeing her friends' brokenness and feeling the desire to reach out to them and help in whatever way she could, Bolz-Weber discovered her calling. She threw in the towel on her past life and used it to clean up, get sober, and reverse the suffocating chokehold of her hypocritical Christian upbringing. Eventually, she revolutionized her theology, found a path and a purpose, and got in the corner of people who wanted the same. She was given a second chance at life—one that was better than she could have ever believed—all by starting a church to give glory to God. But before any of that happened, in her words, "I'd have to become God's bitch."

For far too long, I maintained a prejudiced, Pharisee-like faith that warranted persecution of those who allowed—let alone publicized—female leadership. My ultra-conservative WELS upbringing molded me into believing it was necessary to frown upon churches that ordained female preachers. Even at congregational meetings when church members had to vote on some matter of business, women were expected to remain silent so the men could say "Aye" or "Nay." It always felt like there was a wish to add an 11th Commandment, as though Moses was walking down Mount Sinai when God quickly reappeared in a wisp of smoke in front of him and said, "I almost forgot! Thou shalt not have a woman lead a church. Wish Miriam the best in her future endeavors."

My former church and others like it prefer to hang their hats on selected passages from 1 Timothy 2:11-14, which trace original sin not back to Adam, but to the silly woman who was duped by a talking snake. In such traditions, it's all Eve's fault that the world fell into a sinful downward spiral.

As a result, while I knew about Ruth's and Esther's heroics in Scripture, I was clueless about Deborah, who led Israel as a judge; Tabitha, who was called to be a disciple after helping the dream team of Peter and Paul; and Phoebe, whom Paul acknowledged as a deacon in Romans. There seemed to be a contradiction that I was still learning about.

Now, for the first time, I was open to the idea of a female leading a church, and I hoped this service would help me confront and change my lifelong prejudices.

The House For All Sinners and Saints is an emerging ELCA Lutheran church, which at the time, was renting space from a traditional Episcopal church. When I stepped into the church, the first thing that caught my eye was a note card taped to a gold-framed portrait of the King that read, "Elvis welcomes you to The House for All Sinners and Saints." Just inside the door, three balloons rubbed against each other next to a lesbian couple that stood in a tight embrace. A transgender usher handed me a bulletin and asked if I wanted to sign-up to volunteer in the service. I politely declined.

Before the service started, Bolz-Weber entered wearing a clerical collar and a shirt that wasn't long-sleeved enough to cover the Mary Magdalene tattoo on her forearm. After making small talk with a nearby couple, she looked in my direction, and I turned away to avoid her gaze. Due to her increasing celebrity status and CrossFit-chiseled shoulders, I was self-conscious and overcome with the paranoid feeling that she wanted to beat me in an arm-wrestling contest.

I isolated myself in a seat in the back, focusing on people-watching as a wide mix of worshipers walked in. There were families with children, gay couples, and older folks who reminded me of my mom and dad. They seemed to have nothing in common, yet here they were: approximately 150 people jam-packed together, making small talk. Suddenly, a hymn broke out, and the community joined together to sing a cappella.

The seating arrangement was unique, as it was "in the round," with every folding chair facing the altar at the center of the converted gym. At any other church—traditional or modern—pastors are usually given the special perk of sitting off to the side onstage or in a front-row seat. But here, there was no special reserved seating for either Bolz-Weber or the associate pastor. Instead, they sat among the congregation. As a result, volunteers played a large role in the service: one read the Prayer of the Day, another led a liturgy that was reminiscent of the traditional chants like "Kyrie," and others distributed Communion. All Bolz-Weber did was make the opening announcements, give the Eucharist prayer, and playfully scoop up babies that she was handed.

And that's what made the House so different. It was a community that was clearly passionate about combining deeply rooted traditions with quirky slants to fit its unique demographic mix.

After the service, everyone went outside, where the excitement mounted higher than the Rocky Mountains. Standing near the portrait of Elvis, Bolz-Weber and the associate pastor held the Blessing of the Bicycles, praying for bikers' safety on the roads after the church lost one of its own in an accident. One-by-one, nearly 50 bikers rode a few blocks around the neighborhood before settling down at the outdoor patio for free slices of pizza and red Solo cups of Fat Tire. Exhausted, I headed back to my car so I could find a hotel and crash.

As I drove away, I considered what Bolz-Weber was doing with her church and felt ashamed. It was filled with a cast of characters who would be deemed social outcasts in a traditional church setting and spit out by the church machine. Yet they still chose to surround themselves with Christ in uniquely passionate and deeply devoted ways. And yet, persecutory religious upbringing encouraged me to disapprove of all of this, based solely on what lay between the senior preacher's legs.

On my drive back to Wisconsin, I listened to an interview with Bolz-Weber by Krista Tippett from *On Being*. At one point, Bolz-Weber explained the meaning behind her forearm tattoo and how Mary Magdalene—whom she described as "the patron saint of showing up"—fit into the gospel for her: "She is announcing the resurrection. She was the one, this woman who was delivered from so much, who was broken and could do nothing but follow Jesus. She didn't hightail it out when things got hot. She showed up. And she was the one who was chosen to be the first witness of the resurrection. She was the one who was told to go and tell."

As much as Mary Magdalene loved Christ, she never would have found Him if He hadn't come to find her first. Christ chose her to witness His victory over death—not the Apostles, not the high priests, not even a ruling king. He didn't put on some big, elaborate public display. In John 20:16, Jesus gracefully and humbly walked up to her and just said, "Mary."

He didn't say, "I'm back," thus putting the emphasis on Himself. He put her name first. In effect, He could be saying, "You." He revealed Himself to the one person who kept showing up. Gender, status, money, past mistakes—these meant nothing. They didn't matter. Her slate was clean.

"I have seen the Lord!" she then exclaimed to the disciples, becoming the first "preacher" of Christ's return.

MAN OVERBOARD!

ST. ANNE CATHOLIC CHURCH • WAUSAU, WISCONSIN

During my first relationship, my poor gift-giving skills led to the emotional reenactment of the Titanic sinking.

Remember when, in the movie, a wide-eyed Leonardo DiCaprio sketched Kate Winslet wearing nothing but a blue diamond Heart of the Ocean necklace? I do! I was still new to puberty when I saw that scene on VHS. Since I couldn't write poetry and my artistic ability was limited to smiley faces, my impressionable mind deducted that jewelry was the ticket into a lady's heart. Being an immature 14 years old, I was just excited about the new meaning to the term "boob tube."

Fast-forward a decade later, Celine Dion's voice was echoing in my head when I bought my first girlfriend an open-heart pendant necklace. I told her that no matter what happened to us, it was to symbolize how "My Heart Will Go On" (barf). I placed the pendant around her neck, and she passionately replied by navigating her lips onto my mine. At that moment, I was the king of the world.

Later that night, her fingertips softly caressed my neck, and she started whispering sweet nothings into my ear. Staring at the necklace, she tested the oceanic depths of my romantic nature by asking, "How much did something like this cost you?"

Like a moron, I replied, "$7.98 at Target. It was 50 percent off!" I followed that up with a quick kiss. "Love you, honey."

My intuitive understanding of the female psyche informed me that she was upset, and it soon felt like an iceberg had slammed into our cuddle. I'm surprised she didn't attempt to signal an SOS through Morse code via her eye-twitching. Alas, the necklace broke a month later, and a few weeks after that, her Atlantic-blue eyes flooded with tears when she realized we were on a ship that would never reach its matrimonial destination. The relationship capsized, and it was man overboard for me.

That was the first time I ever actually got down on my hands and knees in a Gethsemane prayer stance. I begged God to help me weather the storms of heartbreak. Lost in a sea of emotions, I was struggling to keep my head above water.

Unfortunately, "relationshipwrecks" have crushed me more than once. When my heart is forced to walk the plank like that, I become a human bobber without a line, floating helplessly in the waves and desperate to come up for air. The only spiritual buoy I ever had within those tumultuous currents was God, and I held onto Him for dear life.

After what seemed like the time needed to proofread *Moby Dick*, my body would wash ashore an island of singleness again. I often half-hoped Jesus would see me from His lifeguard post and run toward me in slow motion like David Hasselhoff with the *Baywatch* theme song playing in the background. He wouldn't even need to swim; He'd just run atop the water and drag my lifeless body to the beach, where Pamela Anderson would be ready to apply CPR and resuscitate me.

Then I'd look up. Boobs.

. . .

St. Anne Fest at St. Anne Catholic Church in Wausau, Wisconsin
June 21, 2015 – 10:30 A.M. Polka Mass

For my first-ever polka mass, I found myself in a giant white tent about the size of Jonah's fish. This was unique, as I got to hear about the King of the Jews while sitting next to banners for the King of Beers.

Polka masses are a big thing during Wisconsin summers, especially in the Roman Catholic Church. Every weekend, there's at least one Catholic congregation pitching tents, frying bratwursts, and tapping kegs while members polka the night away. On Sunday morning, the festivities halt for mass, and the musicians alter their accordion music to be more appropriate for a spiritual setting.

The liturgy and the ritual of Catholic mass was still something of a mystery to me. This was my fifth Catholic experience, and I still wasn't picking up the cues on what to say and when to sit, kneel, or stand. It's like playing Simon Peter Says, except here I could purchase a Bud Light Raz-Ber-Rita and blame my ignorance on the 8% alcohol by volume.

What was odd about this day though was that I wasn't the only one who was clueless. The polka band leading mass didn't know what to do, either. The band members looked at their leader with stares of concern as they tried to get on the same page. Each musical misfire formed another bead of sweat dripping down their foreheads. I couldn't help but envision Wisconsin's premier polka band on an episode of VH1's Behind the Music, discussing their breakup after the 20th mistimed "Hallelujah" or "Amen." After a while, the congregation thought, "Screw it!" and decided to cover for the lead singer by leading instead.

The priest prefaced his sermon with a reading from Mark 4, telling of how Jesus was getting some much-needed beauty sleep in a boat while crossing the Sea of Galilee. When a furious storm came along, the waves nearly capsized the boat. His disciples woke Him and said, "Teacher, we know your Sleep Number is right where you want it, but don't you care if we drown?"

Jesus woke up, rebuked the wind, and said to the waves, "Quiet! Be still!"

The wind died down and it became completely calm, thus also reducing the disciples' Geico boat insurance rates when word of this miracle spread.

Jesus turned to his disciples and said, "Why are you so afraid? Do you still have no faith?" Then Jesus went back to counting sheep.

The disciples were terrified though, and they asked each other, "Who is this? Even the wind and the waves obey Him!"

The priest then turned to his sermon, which was based on a recent encyclical letter—a kind of official document stating the Catholic Church's position and doctrine on an issue—from Pope Francis, titled *Laudato si'*, which translates to "Praise be to you." He spoke of the pope's vision of everyone praising the God who gave us gifts like the wind, sun, and rain.

As I listened to this message, I thought of all the times when I saw God's hand in my life when the elements were beating down. I'd be stuck in the middle of the high tides that hit everyone, asking "Can I really trust God's plan for my life?" It's difficult for me to trust that He's the screenplay writer, the director, and the producer in our lives. What exactly does *my* life's script entail?

But when I look back at the adversity I faced, I know that I came out better for having faced the rain and the wind and having used the Bible as a compass to navigate me move forward when there was only dark clouds ahead. He has a way of helping us through every storm. Just commit to keep moving forward and paddling one stroke at a time. God does some of His best work when we're lost at sea.

In pain, there is also healing, an ever-deepening deep blue sea to search for our own Heart of the Ocean. In many ways, whoever is fortunate enough to dive into this ocean will both grieve deeply and rejoice in the core of their being, knowing the ecstasies and agonies of love in all its totality.

There are moments when I feel like it would be better off to lock my heart away in a dead man's chest, throw away the key, and let it sink to the bottom of Davy Jones' locker, never to be seen again. In today's culture, grief is a very misunderstood—and sometimes even taboo—emotion. We are told to get over it and move on as quickly as possible, especially as men. But when it comes to love, the soul loves with reckless abandon with feelings that are unpredictable and impossible to control.

There's a line from *Pirates of the Caribbean: At World's End* that has always stuck with me. As Will Turner is talking to Captain Jack Sparrow about his relationship with Elizabeth Swann falling apart, he confesses, "I'm losing her, Jack. Every step I make for my father is a step away from Elizabeth."

Jack, likely smelling of rum and wearing a touch more eyeliner than is absolutely necessary, looks at him and says something I'll never forget: "Mate, if you choose to lock your heart away, you'll lose it for certain."

The same chest that would protect me from disappointment would also block out the wonderful treasures of life.

CHURCH 36:
IT'S ALL GREEK ORTHODOX TO ME
ANNUNCIATION GREEK ORTHODOX CHURCH • WAUWATOSA,
WISCONSIN

Millennials get a bad rap about their religious life.

The news often covers my generation's religious life by leading off with a headline like "Millennials are vacating the church faster than a <insert snarky comment here>," and then they simply <insert a declining Pew Research Center survey statistic here>. To add visual flair, they often include a stock photo of a teenager in saggy pants riding a skateboard (who should obviously be going to church). And just like that, you have another trendy clickbait article profiling everything wrong with our generation for conservative Christians to freak out over.

I soon realized that I was one of those statistics who escaped the church, a spiritual *Fugitive*, like a dapper young Harrison Ford on the run from redundant liturgy and droning hymns. My pastors always seemed to know I was a congregant on the loose, too. Probably because my mom told them. I'm sure they pinned up 'Wanted' posters with my church directory mug shot, equipped themselves with holstered catechisms, and earnestly began the manhunt to bring me back to the "One True Church."

Remember the scene where Tommy Lee Jones traps Harrison Ford near the edge of a storm drain? That's sorta what happened to me—except it was in the cereal aisle at the local Target. When I bumped into my associate pastor, he gave an Oscar-worthy mini-sermon on why I was Cocoa Puffs for not coming to church. Instead of being told to stick my hands up and turn around, I felt like I had to fold my hands and kneel on the ground to pray right then and there next to Cap'n Crunch. But rather than return to a pew without parole, I looked down at the dam's raging waters as my only escape. My knees trembling, I closed my eyes, pulled up my saggy pants, and fell. Fell away from the church.

I can't speak for every Millennial who makes a break from the church, but what I can say is that we don't know the full movie script God has written for us. We don't know the ramifications of what we're praying for. And we sure as H-E-double-hockey-sticks don't know the countless other factors that God is considering. Yes, we're smart, but we're also clueless. We scope things out before diving in, but sometimes we say, "Screw it," and dive in anyway. We're walking contradictions, juxtapositions in the flesh. We always know what we want. Except when we don't. Then we write paragraphs like this where we don't even know where we're going with this. Unless you do make sense of this. Then great! If not, well, that's the point. I'm not even sure I know my point. Anyway, this is getting wordy. Moving on.

We're taught that the only reason to do something is if we're somehow validated for doing it. Then, the social and professional pressures of young adulthood squeeze the passion right out of us. We are constantly pushing away uncomfortable experiences and instead seeking only what brings us pleasure and instant gratification. We do this with relationships, jobs, everything. We seek hourly affirmation through Facebook likes, Instagram hearts, and Twitter followers. To quasi-quote our social-media forefathers, "Give me notifications, or give me boredom." At the core, we've become a selfish generation that has focused on self-identity, self-gratification, and selfies. We're searching for the next high without realizing that it will never last. As a result, we tend to lose touch with what really matters, and our spirituality begins to slip.

For many of us, the enemy is just good, old-fashioned complacency. We settle into our routines. We distract ourselves. The couch is too comfortable. The Fruit Loops are too fruity. Nothing new happens, and when Sunday morning arrives, we silence the alarm clock in favor of the gravitational pull of our bed.

We've become cynical regarding everything 'big.' We grew up during a time when bigger was better. Go big or go home. Super-size me. And we've seen the failure of 'big.' We now have no trust in big institutions like the media, the police, Congress, banks, big business, megachurches, and even marriage. We see police brutality, government shutdowns, bank bailouts, crippling divorce rates, and Catholic child-abuse scandals. Now social media has opened the floodgates of doom and gloom. When something 'big' isn't authentic, we see right through it.

So how can we believe in an institution as big as the church?

. . .

Annunciation Greek Orthodox Church in Wauwatosa, Wisconsin
July 12, 2015 – 9:30 A.M. Divine Liturgy

The theme for visit number 36 was to go retro and observe the ancient traditions of the Greek Orthodox Church. Admittedly, I was skeptical going in. From what I researched, the religion believes itself to be free from all error and distortion, tracing its linage directly from the very first church founded by the Apostles. This type of perfectionist thinking is what turns me off from organized religion. Nevertheless, I tried to keep an open mind.

The church building itself was the first thing that stood out. It looks more like a retired UFO than a place of worship. Annunciation was one of the last works of Frank Lloyd Wright, considered by many to be the greatest American architect of all time. When he consulted his wife, who was brought up in the Greek Orthodox faith, her advice was to focus on the cross and the dome. On the outside, a golden cross stands atop the flattened dome, which is typical in Byzantine architecture. Inside, the floor plan is based on an equilateral Greek cross. Through simplification and abstraction of the forms, the church pays homage to tradition with a modern twist.

I walked in half-expecting to be greeted by all the Greek stereotypes one could think of. Would there be smashing plates? A free gyro? Maybe even a lifetime supply of feta cheese? Of course, none of this happened. Instead, I got culture shock from the pre-service Orthros, which consists of a priest singing litanies and psalms in traditional Koine Greek, the original language of the New Testament. I didn't understand a word, but was fascinated to hear a worship service in a foreign language.

The Greek Orthodox Church prides itself on its Divine Liturgy, a service that dates back to the 4th century. It's comprised of blessing, praising, and glorifying God the Father, Son, and Holy Spirit. Any time the Holy Trinity was echoed by the priest, celebrants used their fingers to make the sign of the cross. This one service called for making the sign of the cross more than all the Western Christian services I had attended combined. My estimate exceeded 100 times during the service.

Annunciation was in the process of bouncing back after an alleged embezzlement at the time of my visit. A former priest was accused of improperly spending thousands of dollars from a church trust fund, and then the priest who exposed the embezzling allegations was reportedly given the pink slip, too. This was exactly the sort of thing that caused people like me to distrust the church at large.

This was the new priest's first service, and he stated that he wanted to reassure the parish and draw them all closer to Christ. He used Romans 5:3–5 as his base text for his message: "We rejoice in our sufferings, knowing that suffering produces endurance, and endurance produces character, and character produces hope, and hope does not disappoint us, because God's love has been poured into our hearts through the Holy Spirit which has been given to us."

It felt like visiting a friend's house, but then your friend's parents get into a big fight at the dinner table. The congregation seemed sick of the scandals that had plagued the church for the past two years and was just trying to keep it together and move forward.

But things changed during the Eucharist, an elaborate sacrament that reenacts the Last Supper. This is where Eastern Orthodox Church services separate themselves from any other church service I've seen. The priest came out flanked by several children of different ages, dressed in decorative robes to serve as acolytes. Everyone in the church came forward and, one-by-one, placed a four-foot-long Communion cloth under their chin and opened their mouth. The priest then dipped a teaspoon in the chalice and spoon-fed the recipient like Gerber baby food. The recipient then wiped their lips with the cloth, made the sign of the cross, and handed the Communion cloth to the next person in line. This took a full 20 minutes. At the end of the service before exiting, the congregation did it all over again, this time with a cube of bread to represent Christ's body.

Did I come away with a deep, divine understanding of the Greek Orthodox traditions? No. I was an outsider peeking over the upper balcony rail to see how this parish followed traditions that were foreign to me. I can't always leave a church service with a new spiritual revelation or a feeling of renewal and blessing.

Sometimes, there still is confusion on this spiritual trek.

But the thing I appreciated about this church was their appetite for God. Sin spoils our appetite, as we saw with the priest who dipped into the church's cookie jar one too many times. But the way they conducted Communion served as a reminder of how sacred we become through the sacrament. The same Christ that died on the cross now lives in all of us.

A MATCH MADE IN HEAVEN

CHRISTIAN WRESTLING FEDERATION AT GENERATIONS CHURCH •
FATE, TEXAS

Many don't know this, but God is a huge professional wrestling fan. Back in the Old Testament, God was seated in His celestial box suite and booked a match made in heaven, pitting Jacob against Esau.

At the time, Jacob was being a jerk because he couldn't grow a beard and his older brother Esau could. One day, he tricked their dad into giving him the firstborn's inheritance by impersonating Esau with so much body hair, it would have made George "The Animal" Steele look like the official spokesman for Gillette. Afterwards, Jacob fled the city, got married, and made lots of babies. Meanwhile, Esau spent years in therapy due to self-esteem issues, since manscaping wasn't a thing yet in Genesis.

Several years passed, and Jacob found himself on the run from his father-in-law. He had nowhere else to go, so he decided to return home and pay the piper. Awaiting him was an embittered Esau with 400 men, all ready to lay the smackdown at the family reunion. Karma had finally caught up with Jacob.

The night before the grudge match, Jacob sent everything he had accumulated over the years to Esau, hoping to make peace with his brother. Alone, Jacob was sneak-attacked by a stranger, and they went toe-to-toe in a battle for the ages. They wrestled all night, pulling out body slams, Ric Flair-style knife-edge chops, and even some suplexes on the Spanish announce table. After a while, it became evident that Jacob would not go down for the count. Before the timekeeper could ring the bell at daybreak, the stranger love-tapped the socket of Jacob's hip when the ref wasn't looking, crippling him as a result.

Despite the injury, Jacob would not give up. Wanting to maintain his identity before daybreak, the stranger uttered his favorite John Cena catchphrase, "You can't see me," and tried to escape. But Jacob held on to his attacker, saying, "I will not let you go unless you bless me."

Finally, the mystery opponent had had enough and blessed him. It was then that the stranger revealed Himself to be the omnipotent creator of the universe.

Jacob pissed his loincloth.

. . .

Christian Wrestling Federation at Generations Church in Fate, Texas July 18, 2015 – 7:00 P.M. CWF Champions Cup Tag Team Tournament (Night 2)

I never thought searching for God would lead me to a bunch of sweaty men climbing on top of each other in skintight spandex, yet in the name of Christ, that's exactly what happened at my next church visit.

Growing up as a little Hulkamaniac, I said my prayers, took my vitamins, and dreamed of one day having Hulk Hogan-like 24-inch pythons. I took "Macho Man" Randy Savage's advice, snapped into a Slim Jim, and watched wrestling every Saturday morning to see feats of strength combined with fake punches and kicks. Now, I drove more than a thousand miles to rediscover my childhood pastime combined with my current spiritual undertaking. My destination was Generations Church in rural Texas for the wacky world of the "cross-denominational" Christian Wrestling Federation (CWF).

One of the greatest things I've learned to appreciate during my *52 Churches in 52 Weeks* journey is the different entry points people can take inside a church. The CWF is an outreach ministry that aims to spread the Scripture using professional wrestling as a progressive and innovative way to get new butts in seats.

I was curious about how over-the-top the CWF would be. I had grandiose, Andre the Giant-sized visions of it turning into *The Passion of the Christ* as directed by Vince McMahon, with good-guy wrestlers dressed in animal skins and being besieged by Biblical villains like Cain and Pharaoh, bringing pet snakes into the ring like Jake "The Snake" Roberts. I pictured them handcuffing the hero to a steel cage, arms outstretched to symbolize the crucifixion. A toga-wearing Judas would blow him a final kiss, and the bad guys would stomp the hero's face into a pool of his own blood, symbolizing how Christ's blood was shed for us. Just when all seemed lost, a spotlight from the heavens would shine down upon the man who would become God's Champion and unleash a Samson-esque rage by furiously tearing apart the handcuffs and wildly wielding a donkey's jawbone to scatter his opponents.

Fortunately, none of this happened. Instead, the CWF consists of indy wrestlers from across the country who preach the Gospel through their actions in the ring. Sportsmanship is the name of the game here.

The evening of my visit was the second and final outing of the CWF Tag Team Champions Cup Tournament. The victorious pair would take home a towering trophy accented with a crucifix.

The biggest reaction of the night went to Lodi and Scotty Mathews, better known as Team Fearless. They are a pair of bald-headed, spray-tanned witnesses who vowed to wrestle anyone, anywhere, anytime to make some noise for Jesus. When their music started, kids flocked to the duo as they struck their signature poses.

Lodi was the main event's biggest draw, having earned fame during the late 90's by coming to ringside with a variety of signs to mock his opponents. Nowadays, his signs are meant to inspire, with messages like "Lodi 3:16 says read John 3:16," "Make your dreams a reality," and "Get strong, Philippians 4:13."

Scotty Mathews, on the other hand, was new to me. I had no idea who he was. All I knew was that after he shouted at his opponents from the entrance door, he displayed an impressive range in projectile spit, nearly hitting me in the crowd with a goober of saliva.

In the tournament finale, Team Fearless faced off against the makeshift team of Caprice Coleman and "Sweet Dreamz" Marcus Howard. Several of the wrestlers left the locker room to watch the last match, including former WWE superstar Michael Tarver. Tarver is a 300-pound, bald-headed behemoth of a man known for body-slamming opponents with such concussive force, it would register on seismographs. He came over to my seat not wearing a shirt, just wearing shorts, shoes, and a small wash cloth on his shoulders to wipe the sweat from his chest. He tapped my shoulder to take the open seat right next to me, making me fear that his post-match protein snack would be me.

The atmosphere for the final match was electric, largely thanks to Caprice Coleman. He was a preacher outside of the ring, but had made a name for himself during the tournament with his high-risk moves. He could dish out offense from anywhere in the ring and pulled off an incredible you-had-to-see-it-to-believe-it triple rolling suplex on Lodi. He then finished it off by wrapping his free arm around Mathews and hauling both opponents vertically over his head, which earned a wild reaction from the crowd—including Tarver, who still hadn't eaten me for a snack at that point. In the end, Coleman was knocked off the ring apron and crashed to the ground like Jack and Jill down a hill. Not a moment too soon, Scotty Mathews executed a kick to Sweet Dreamz's jaw, which sent him bouncing off the rope and into the air. Lodi then hit him with a clothesline from the top turnbuckle to make Sweet Dreamz see stars. It was purely academic after that, as Mathews lay on top of him to get the pin count for the 1-2-3 victory.

A chant of "Thank-You Je-sus!" broke out in the auditorium as Team Fearless celebrated with their newly won Champions Cup. While the ring crew checked on Coleman, Sweet Dreamz joined in the chant for a show of sportsmanship.

After a quick photo op, a sweat-drenched Lodi gave a sermon about the power Christ can have in all of our lives. It was the first time in my life I've ever felt inspired by a shirtless guy in his underpants. In the background, Scotty Mathews hoisted the Champions Cup and pointed up to the spotlight above them to thank his Savior.

That night, Team Fearless were champions. One month later, things took a turn for the worse when Scotty Mathews was blindsided by a car.

He suffered a wrenched hip.

. . .

"God gives me the strength to conquer this because without you," tweeted Scotty, "it wouldn't matter if I won the fight anyway."

Scotty's pelvis was busted and needed immediate surgery. The only thing holding his body together was metal plates and screws. In spirit, his faith held together much more. His inability to walk had wiped out his source of income, forcing him to find other means to support his four children.

This is where many would struggle, calling God out into the ring. In such circumstances, many of us might call Him fake or a gimmick and shift the blame onto Him.

But Scotty didn't do that. Instead, he maintained both his faith and his integrity while laughing at his biggest blow. "Iron sharpens iron," he posted at one point, tagging Lodi as his tag-team partner in life. He used his trials and tribulations to inspire others, posting photos on social media and writing about how God was working inside his spirit. Lodi and several other indy wrestlers showed their support by praying before shows for his recovery. Despite a life-changing event that required significant time to heal a broken body, Scotty never allowed the pain to harden his soul.

You will never see who you truly are or gain any strength, character, humility, and perspective unless you suffer and experience weakness. Real growth always involves struggle and pain. In such circumstances, you can either embrace the victim mentality or become a victor and fight through the pain. By choosing to fight, you will be humbled in ways you couldn't begin to express, and yet sometimes that pain is truly a blessing in disguise.

As Scotty Mathews posted about his journey on social media—from the hospital visits, to the physical therapy sessions, to the painful workouts as he tried to get his health back to its previous condition—it wasn't hard to see a direct correlation between Scotty's struggles and Jacob's. For one thing, they both learned that wrestling with a wrenched hip isn't easy.

Jacob spent his entire life wrestling with himself, with other people, and with God. What he needed was God's blessing, and he wouldn't stop wrestling until he obtained it. Many of us would tap out. But not Jacob, and not Scotty.

Eventually, Scotty did reunite with Lodi and revive Team Fearless over a year later—the name now meaning even more than it did that night that I saw them.

Before God left Jacob, He left him with a word of encouragement: "Your name will no longer be Jacob, but Israel, because you have struggled with God and with men and have overcome."

CHURCH 38:
HARRY POTTER AND THE POTTER'S HOUSE
THE POTTER'S HOUSE • DALLAS, TEXAS

I remember the night Cedric Diggory died.

I was late in boarding the Hogwarts Express, waiting until well after the Harry Potter hype train had left the station. The first three Potter films were irritatingly kid-friendly, but Tiff convinced me long before our breakup that *Harry Potter and the Goblet of Fire* was different, claiming that it shook the Wizarding World to its magical core. She raved about Cedric, a character who symbolized kindness and honesty. His death ushered in a world that would become progressively darker, with bigger stakes, strained loyalties, and mounting deception. I didn't know it at the time, but the same things would soon come to pass in our relationship.

Before Voldemort appeared and offed the beloved Hufflepuff teen, the four Triwizard Tournament champions prepared to enter a maze as the third and final task. Dumbledore's stern warning to Harry and Cedric was symbolic: "In the maze, you'll find no dragons or creatures of the deep. Instead, you'll face something even more challenging. You see, people change in the maze. Oh, find the cup if you can. But be very wary. You could just lose yourselves along the way."

Like life, the maze itself was the obstacle. Harry and Cedric entered lost, alone, and overruled by a binding and scary silence. What didn't happen was the most terrifying part, as mystery lurked behind fog and shadows, forcing their imaginations to fill in the blanks of what was around the next corner. The walled hedges were seemingly alive and moved at random times unpredictably. They would waste no time in unleashing their roots and snatching up any wizards who stood in one place for too long.

Near the end, both Harry and Cedric spotted the Triwizard Cup. As they raced toward it, branches reached out and lassoed Cedric's ankles, slamming him into the ground. He ate dirt, and the roots gripped him, reeling him. Cedric's fingers clawed the ground as he tried to save himself. Harry could have left him behind, abandoning his integrity in pursuit of material victory. But instead, Harry turned around to witness Cedric struggling. Harry extended his wand and uttered a spell, saving his friend.

"For a moment there, I thought you were gonna let it get me," Cedric said.

"For a moment, so did I," Harry replied.

A year after Tiff broke up with me, she sent me an email, saying that if I ever had a change of heart and wanted to be friends, I should reach out to her.

I never did.

For the longest time, I didn't want to look inside her Chamber of Secrets. I still avoided peering at her social media doings with my Mad-Eye so that I wouldn't see anything that could hurt me. After all, He-Who-Shall-Not-Be-Named was still slithering in the picture. My mind was like a Time-Turner, constantly replaying the past to figure out what went wrong.

But at the same time, I realized that her heart must have felt like a prisoner of Azkaban. She needed to find her inner Sirius Black and escape from the thought of wedding bells chained to her ankles. I had been holding her back, a boyfriend in Dementor's clothes that was sucking the soul out of her future. She still wanted me in her life despite the breakup, and I would have done anything to cast a Patronus charm to protect her heart.

But breakups don't work that way.

When she made a break for it, I knew I had to put on a Cloak of Invisibility and disappear so she could live the life she wanted without my interference. I was convinced it was the right thing to do. But was it the right thing to do for so long? Somewhere along the way, it stopped feeling right.

. . .

The Potter's House in Dallas, Texas
July 19, 2015 – 9:00 A.M. Worship Service
Due to my innate ability to get lost, I started my 38th church visit by getting chased by the cops at the largest African-American megachurch in the U.S.

This was all based on a misunderstanding. In Texas, the police serve as traffic control for megachurches, especially ones the size of The Potter's House in Dallas. Attendance often exceeds 20,000 for its Sunday morning service. I happened to take a wrong turn when they waved me through, and the next thing I knew, three police officers were running after me, shouting "Stop! You can't go in there!" as I lay the pedal to the metal at a blistering five miles per hour in the church parking lot.

After the Dallas police made me U-turn and find another parking lot, people from all over the country were walking into the Potter's House to hear T.D. Jakes preach the Word of God that morning. The bishop developed a huge following over the years for his deep-voiced motivational sermons, inspiring even NFL Hall of Fame players like Michael Irvin to attend, who was spotted in the front row to catch some of Jakes' preaching.

The sermon started out focusing on a passage that was all too familiar: Tiff's favorite, Matthew 17:20: "I tell you the truth, if you have faith as small as a mustard seed, you can say to this mountain, 'Move from here to there' and it will move. Nothing will be impossible for you." It's as though he was preaching forgiveness for the one person I had trouble forgiving.

But then, before Jakes went any further, he twisted it, using Luke 17:6 to compare the same mustard seed to the stubborn roots of a sycamine tree: "And the Lord said, 'If you have faith as small as a mustard seed, you might say unto this sycamine tree, be plucked by the root, and be planted into the sea, and it should obey you.'"

As Jakes detailed, Jesus said that you can tear down a sycamine tree if you have the faith of a mustard seed. He used a sycamine tree for a reason. It can grow to be 20 feet high, but it grows far deeper underground. You could cut off branch after branch, but it would still keep growing because the roots are so deep. Because sycamines can grow quickly in any climate, the wood was often used for caskets. As Jakes put it, "If you don't kill the sycamine tree, the sycamine tree will kill you."

Like the sycamine, the thoughts and feelings we plant within ourselves grow deep within our hearts. They can cause us to become hateful, bitter, and spiteful. With time, they can bewitch us and change us into someone we aren't. Unresolved bitterness will kill opportunities that arise in our lives, and if we let it go for too long unchecked, it will bury us. If we don't pull it up by the root, we will end up being entombed by it. In order to be free, we must cast out our hatred and bitterness. Of course, that's easier said than done.

After my visit to The Potter's House, I realized that I had to put on my Sorting Hat and categorize my thoughts. Despite my best intentions, the more time passed, the more I noticed that bitterness had grown within my heart. When you try to numb your heart, bitterness will put down roots and begin to wrap itself around your heart, choking out all happiness. The mind will tell you that it's a wall to protect you, but that's a lie. The consequence is the opposite. Hate and bitterness will destroy those who don't deserve it. Their roots dig deep into the past, choking out the present, and wiping out the future.

Only forgiveness could destroy the Horcrux that had latched onto my heart. Forgiveness meant that it would no longer matter if I hit back. I finally understood that if I kept fighting the past, I would stay trapped in the maze. I had to uproot the bitterness. I would forgive and grow from the experience, letting it teach me.

After writing this, I sat at my computer, finally ready to write back to Tiff. *Forgive and grow*, I told myself. But I just sat there. I stared at the keyboard and couldn't touch a key. God help me.

CHURCH 39:
ARE WE THERE YET?
ST. LOUIS CATHEDRAL • NEW ORLEANS, LOUISIANA

One observation one could make after studying the Bible is that everyone who played a role is dead now.

Take, for instance, the children of Israel. They were born into slavery, begging their Heavenly Father to be liberated from Egypt's chains. God answered their prayers by sending a series of miraculous plagues, which would be dramatized centuries later in a 2014 film adaption that would receive mixed-to-negative reviews on Rotten Tomatoes. The worst of these plagues was the decision to cast Christian Bale as Moses.

But still, the children of Israel were free! They all piled into God's Prius, buckled their seatbelts, and Christian Bale's Moses (who was riding shotgun) told them in his best raspy BatDad voice, "Kids, we're going to the Promised Land!" This was exciting news, because back in those days, the Promised Land was like the Old Testament's version of Disneyland. Ticket prices were cheap, Donald Duck was considered a quail delicacy, and rumor had it that they sold sunscreen. So off they went, merrily singing "99 Bottles of Beer on the Wall of Jericho."

But the children of Israel never made it to the Promised Land.

They complained from Day One. They griped about the water, grumbled about the food, and quarreled about the leadership. They cried that it was too hot, too cold, too far. When things started to get hard, they begged to turn around and go back to Egypt, where things had been predictable. The Israelites' behavior was so utterly insane, it nearly caused

Christian Bale's Moses to go full *American Psycho*. In short, they acted like spoiled brats.

To quiet their complaints, God's hand extended from heaven and gave them manna to snack on. But no, they still threw temper tantrums from the backseat, whining, crying, and disobeying throughout the entire trip. "God, are we there yet? Are we there yet? Are we there yet?!"

Finally, even God, with His infinite patience, had had enough. Fed up with the nonstop bickering on the worst road trip in the history of mankind, He pulled off to the side of the desert and told them they wouldn't go any further.

Long story short, the children of Israel wandered in the desert for 40 years. Nearly every man, woman, and child who walked out of Egypt ended up dying without setting foot in the Promised Land. Failing to put their trust in God behind the steering wheel, the children of Israel died in the desert, choking on the dust of their own mental enslavement.

. . .

St. Louis Cathedral in New Orleans, Louisiana
July 20, 2015 – 12:05 P.M. Mass

Church visit number 39 took me to the heart of the Big Easy. As soon as I exited my car, a homeless man approached me and begged for five dollars. I gave it to him and asked where the Cathedral was. His name was Damon, and he repaid me by becoming my impromptu tour guide to the church. On the way, he told me about some of the local Catholic churches that provided food and shelter as we passed a freak show of sights and smells in the French Quarter. There were endless XXX strip clubs on Bourbon Street, where bars and restaurants served all manner of delectable fare and overpriced alcoholic beverages. In the streets, cleaning crews washed vomit down the sewers while homeless locals took a whiz on the opposite corner. I never knew Southern decadence could smell so strong.

Damon took his leave when we arrived at St. Louis Cathedral, which looked incredibly photogenic in front of Jackson Square. Despite Hurricane Katrina's best efforts a few years earlier, the cathedral is still standing tall as the oldest Catholic church in the United States, having been built by French colonists in 1718. According to urban legend, it even inspired the design for Disney's Cinderella Castle. Whether the story is true or not, the cathedral is an impressive structure. Three spires top its radiant white façade and shadow the world's prime destination for having a good time.

It serves as an interesting contrast in the French Quarter. By day, tourists line up to see the cathedral's interior. When the sun goes down though, nightlife festivities break out from Bourbon Street's balconies as tourists let their hair—and their tops—down. Against this seedy backdrop, the St. Louis Cathedral is certainly an interesting place to hear a sermon about sin.

The sermon this afternoon compared the children of Israel's slavery to our current culture. The priest asked the congregation to mediate on the fundamental aspect of human nature, using the Exodus experience as a liturgical compass. As he put it, "When we hear the word 'freedom,' we often think of it as synonymous with liberty. But liberty and freedom are not synonymous." He explained that freedom is a state of being in which we are capable of making decisions without external control. Liberty, on the other hand, is our God-given gift of freedom, which has been granted by externally by God.

I wasn't sure I understood the difference, but he continued, pointing out that we all have free will. We can make decisions, whether good or bad, right or wrong, prudent or foolish. But the way in which we exercise that freedom is very important for today's younger generation. We have the notion today that as free human beings, "I do what I want, when I want, and how I want." As a result, freedom gets confused with selfishness and narcissism.

I walked out scratching my head, enjoying the cathedral more than the confusing sermon. I'd like to think the children of Israel taught us a valuable lesson, which reflects our ongoing struggle with ourselves. Without trust in God, we can wander aimlessly in the desolation of our minds, chasing after mirages for upwards of 40 years, while still never finding our own Promised Land. We witness God's hand in our lives, yet all too easily forget about Him when things go south. Instead of looking toward the unknown of the future, we cling to the past or what's missing. We are either surviving or thriving—whining for God to make things better, or taking to the desert and making sandcastles with what God does give us.

CHURCH 40:

NINE RELIGIONS IN ONE

THE BAHÁ'Í HOUSE OF WORSHIP FOR NORTH AMERICA •
WILMETTE, ILLINOIS

D uring the course of my *52 Churches in 52 Weeks* project, the most
frequent question I was asked was, "How do you pick which
churches you visit?"

The truth is, I winged it. Some caught my eye as I drove by, but most of
the time, I had zero idea of where I'd be on Sunday morning until I started
researching Saturday night. If something about a church piqued my interest,
I'd answer the call and go.

Originally, my plan was to slowly break out of my spiritual shell by
dabbling outside of Christianity and exploring houses of worship from all
different faiths: Buddhism, Hinduism, Sikhism, Taoism, and even Jediism.

Yes. Jediism, a religion derived from *Star Wars* lore. This was a top
request from several friends after I learned that it was Britain's fourth most-
prominent religion during a recent UK census. The Jedi Creed eventually
made the jump to hyperspace and into different parts of the United States,
where *Star Wars*-themed weddings became all the rage, complete with
Storm Trooper groomsmen, Ewok flower girls, and R2-D2 ring bearers.

The Jedi live by the Jedi Code, which encourages one to free themselves
of emotion. In fact, the very first line of the Jedi Code states, "There is no
emotion, there is peace." If emotions get in the way, it can lead to the Dark
Side.

I have to admit that the idea of visiting a Jedi church gripped me like
Darth Vader choking the windpipe of an incompetent Imperial officer. I

looked into channeling my inner Obi-Wan Kenobi and considered mingling with members of the Maryland Jedi Order, which was one of the most prominent Jedi religions found online. But during my research, I found that the "church" was listed on GoMeetMe as "Stan's House," with "services" scheduled on Thursday nights for "mixed martial arts practice."

My initial reaction was similar to Luke Skywalker's when he found out the girl he had the hots for was his sister. I was taken aback, concluding that this was likely located in a parent's basement far, far away. I envisioned hanging out with Stan's friends while trying to harness the energies of all living things and tapping into The Force's unknown powers to pass each other the Chex Mix through levitation. Oh, and we'd talk with Yoda's speech syntax.

Bad idea, I decided this was.

. . .

The Bahá'í House of Worship for North America in Wilmette, Illinois
July 26, 2015 – 12:30 P.M. Afternoon Devotion

Even though the Jediism idea exploded faster than the Death Star on the Fourth of July, my Episode XL marked the start of my wishy-washy efforts to sample other faiths. I had a New Hope that I would be able to shift my mindset away from Christian churches, but that was easier said than done. During an earlier visit to a Jewish synagogue, I had felt a sense of desolation without the presence of the cross in the building to center my faith. In my mind, going to a place of worship without Christ at the center felt stranger than cosplaying Captain Kirk at a *Star Wars* convention.

My captain's log for this day recorded me ten miles north of Chicago's Wrigley Field at The Bahá'í House of Worship for North America, one of nine continental temples that currently exist in the world.

The Bahá'í faith is a melting pot of the world's most recognized religions, all sliced, diced, and blended together to achieve the oneness of God. Christianity is one of its ingredients, but I didn't know how much, so I decided to find out for myself.

I arrived at the Bahá'í House early to beat Chicago's morning traffic. It is surrounded by landscaped gardens and fountains, which serve as a sacred space where visitors can pray and mediate with Jedi-like peace. This didn't happen for me, though. I must have gotten too close to a nest, as a momma Angry Bird took issue with my proximity to her homestead. She started attacking me with beaked X-wing fighter intensity, forcing me into a Bruce Lee-esque defensive stance. After two swooping attacks at my head, I decided to throw in the towel and hightailed it out of the garden.

When I reached safety, my eyes were drawn upward by the soaring white temple topped with an intricate lacey dome, which several black birds were using as their nesting headquarters. Nine pillars outlined the structure. Nine seemed to be the number of the day, as Bahá'ís believe the digit symbolizes unity and perfection. Many features of the building designed in groups of nine: nine pillars, nine fountains, nine dome sections, nine entrances, and a nine-pointed star as the religious symbol.

When I walked in, an usher stood next to a sign that prohibited the use of cameras and electronic devices inside the House, marking the rare instance when I couldn't take snapshots inside.

The sanctuary was enormous, but despite its size, it was surprisingly calm and peaceful. Harmony was the theme here, and the vibe succeeded in stilling the heart.

The service was the shortest of any I attended, clocking in at 20 minutes. There was no clergy and no sermon. Instead, five members of the Bahá'í House sat up front and took turns reading holy passages at the lectern. After every fifth reading, the musically gifted of the group graced the room with an a cappella solo. There were only ten readings in total: eight from Bahá'í sacred writings, one from the Bhagavad Gita of the Hindu canon, and one from the Christian Gospel of Matthew. Given the prominence of the number nine, I was surprised they went with ten readings.

After the service, I visited the House's welcome center for a presentation on the Bahá'í faith. There were about 15 people in attendance, all newcomers who were curious about this religion. According to our instructor, Bahá'ís believe that throughout history, God has revealed Himself to humanity through a series of messengers that have appeared every 500 to 1,000 years. Each messenger established a religion that was suited to the needs of the time. The list of God's messengers was basically a Who's Who of recognizable names from religions throughout history, including the likes of Abraham, Moses, Krishna, Buddha, Zoroaster, Muhammad, and Jesus. In the 19th century, a man named the Báb became the eighth messenger by serving a role similar to John the Baptist in the Bahá'í faith, prophesying that the "manifestation of God" would soon be revealed. The Báb was executed by the Persian government for his teachings, but not before one of his followers, Bahá'u'lláh, was recognized as the ninth and final divine messenger sent to be an intermediary between humanity and God. According to Bahá'í tradition, Ottoman authorities imprisoned him for agitating the local population, but tensions eventually eased, and he was allowed to finish his sentence in exile, spending the rest of his life writing from within the comforts of a mansion in modern-day Israel.

I enjoyed the calmness and tranquility of the Bahá'í faith and its practices, but this visit made me realize that I didn't want to continue exploring different religions. Despite setting myself up to be a human guinea pig, I couldn't come to terms with the idea of complicating my beliefs. It would distract me from the original purpose of my wayfaring journey: to reset my faith in God by exploring who Jesus was. With that in mind, I saw no point in further pursuing Eastern religions.

My understanding of non-Christ-based faiths was as clear as Chewbacca's five greatest lines. You don't know what you don't know you know when you don't want to know. Ya know? Religion can be a dangerous topic to discuss, and I came to the conclusion that if I didn't understand— or didn't want to truly understand—I wouldn't be able to give such worship centers a fair chance.

When I got home after this visit, I felt liberated to a certain extent. I could do what I wanted to. The more Christian churches I visited, the more Christ would be at the center of everything I was searching for.

CHURCH DATE

S hadrach, Meshach, and Abednego had nothing on me.

Something seismic was happening within me. My faith was on fire. After 40 weeks of blazing new trails in my spiritual quest, each new church experience only added more fuel to the flames. The impurities of my past were melting away, and my faith was being forged and reshaped by the refinery of the Holy Spirit. I felt new. Stronger than the Man of Steel. I had a burning passion for Christ, and it lit up my life. I was no longer afraid of the coulda, woulda, shouldas of my past that were choking my present and my future. Instead, I was radiant with fireproof confidence, certain that I was destined to live out God's purpose as I crushed the coals beneath me. Transformed, yet not consumed, I had emerged from my own fiery furnace anew, walking tall and baptized by fire.

When you burn the midnight oil going all-in for Christ, it's amazing what kindles inside of you. When you have determination and you know that what you're doing is right, you begin to find meaning and newfound power in your life. There's a slow waiting period at the beginning when you feel like you're moving forward inch-by-inch, like a fuse attached to a firework, slowly traveling upward toward the shell. Then, without warning, BOOM! You explode in your faith.

Just as this was starting to happen for me, a new blessing walked into my life. You can encounter tens of thousands of people in your life, yet it's rare to be seeking someone that also is seeking you at the same time. But if you can have a little patience and a whole lot of faith, God will divinely orchestrate things to happen in His perfecting timing and bring two people together through faith.

This particular week, I had a church date, and boy, did she have the hots for me.

Her name was Rachel, and wow, she was stunning. Earlier in the week, she had found my profile on eHarmony and immediately reached out to me. She was fascinated with *52 Churches in 52 Weeks*, asking where I'd visited, what I'd learned, and how it was impacting my faith. Unlike other girls who would usually wait a day to respond back, she would reply to my messages immediately. We soon spoke on the phone and she invited me to her church in Onalaska. Recalling how this whole thing started when I refused to go on a church date, I wasn't going to let that happen again.

On the drive to her church, I hoped to smolder any unrealistic first-date expectations—for either of us—by focusing my mindset by listening to a sermon from Tim Keller of Redeemer Presbyterian Church in New York City. I had recently came across Keller for his compelling insights about the moral challenges facing many Christian singles, myself included. We aim to abide by Christian values in dating, yet are frustrated and disillusioned by society's acceptance of hook-ups and one-night stands.

Keller's sermon was titled "The Struggle for Love," and it made use of one of the first soap operas in Genesis. Jacob was *The Young and The Restless* member of his family, running away from home penniless and empty inside. As he navigated through life as a wayfaring stranger, things finally began to look up when he met *The Bold and The Beautiful* Rachel. Suddenly, his heart was overtaken by lust. "If I can just have Rachel, everything will be okay," Jacob told himself. To earn her hand in marriage, Jacob worked for her dad/his uncle, Laban, for seven years. However, Laban pulled the old switcheroo the day of the wedding and tricked Jacob into marrying his unwanted first daughter, Leah, instead. Jacob was furious, and luckily for Laban, Thanksgiving family get-togethers weren't a thing in the Old Testament. Eventually, they reached an agreement whereby Jacob would work for Laban for another seven years, and at the end of that time, Jacob could finally marry Rachel, thus initiating the world's first love triangle.

Now Leah was the girl nobody wanted, the ugly duckling to Rachel's swan. God saw that Leah was unloved and opened her womb, while Rachel remained barren. Leah gave birth to three sons and hoped that each son would help her gain her husband's love. But Jacob always preferred Rachel. "*Look at All My Children* I've given him," she cried. "What must I do for my husband love me?" She was distraught and lonely, ready to check-in to a *General Hospital* for how badly her heart was emotionally wounded.

But as Keller explained, Leah experienced a breakthrough in her faith when her fourth child was conceived. She looked into the deepest parts of her heart, removed the adoration she felt for her unloving husband, and instead went all-in for the Lord. After all, she only had *One Life to Live*, and she finally realized that all the men in her life had, well, sucked.

When God became her *Guiding Light*, that's when the light bulb clicked on, and Leah took her life back. As Genesis 29:35 says of her fourth birth: "She conceived again, and when she gave birth to a son, she said, 'This time, I will praise the Lord.'"

. . .

First Free Church in Onalaska, Wisconsin
August 2, 2015 – 10:30 A.M. Worship Service

"This time I will praise the Lord," was on auto-repeat in my noggin when I entered First Free Church to meet Rachel for our first date. After swapping texts and calling each other earlier in the week, I could tell that her attraction to me had reached Ascension heights. She even told me that I gave her goosebumps. And why not? I have a fast smile, a dorky personality, and a penchant for cheesy humor that cracks my mom up. Oh, and did you catch that Oxford comma? I'm a man who's got grammatical game! What more could a girl want?

When I first saw Rachel in person, I thought I was dreaming with my eyes open. Not since Jesus told the disciples to cast their nets into the Sea of Galilee had the world seen such a catch. She was absolutely spellbinding; I had never met anyone like her. Her green eyes held me in a trance, and her a summer tan made her look like the sun itself had kissed her. She had a heart for Christ and a voice like a siren that spoke of the gospel. Her father and ex-husband had failed her. But now she was walking out of her own fiery furnace of life's experience as an unshakable woman of God who could survive anything. As I looked at her, I had to remind myself, "This time, I will praise the Lord."

I strolled up and flashed her a smooth James Bond smile, and we exchanged pleasantries. We were both a little nervous; her, for meeting a guy who actually knew what an Oxford comma was, and me, for meeting a beautiful Christian woman who was so passionate about her faith.

We entered the worship area just as the opening number was about to begin. Rachel was excited to see the return of First Free's senior pastor, Shane Holden, who had been away on a months-long sabbatical. He was starting a new expository series that morning, beginning with the very first passage of Hebrews. As Pastor Shane forewarned us, the Book of Hebrews is an incredibly difficult book to understand and is often the least-preached book in the New Testament due to its warning passages and the mystery as to who even wrote it. As a result, he wanted to tackle it head-on.

Part One was intended to lay the framework for the sermon series that was projected to last the next six-to-eight months, providing insight into the kind of persecution faced by new Christians who had migrated to Rome. They paid a high price for following Christ in a polytheistic culture. In general, Judaism had gained the immunity idol in this religious game of Survivor, since its leaders had managed to get into the good graces of the Roman government. The Christians, on the other hand, had no such protection, and as a result, many considered going back to their old ways. They were in a dark season of their lives, asking God, "Where are you? Do you care? Why are you allowing us to suffer? Why are you being silent?"

Apparently, Pastor Shane was known to have a motormouth, pumping out Scripture at Indianapolis 500 speeds. He was animated and passionate in his delivery, even at one point getting down on his hands and knees to make a point.

He explained how the message to the inaugural Christians in Hebrews is still relevant to the church today. We all occasionally find ourselves in situations where we ask, "God, why are you allowing _____ to happen?"

What I appreciated about Pastor Shane was that he kept his sermon light-hearted and fun, even sneaking in the occasional snarky comment to get a rise from the congregation. But even with the bad jokes, and there were several, he was still reverent in the way he taught the Scripture, carefully pulling out the truth, even if it was hard to hear or fell on deaf ears. He had no problem preaching about the heavy-hitting challenges of today and was open about his own sins, faults, and difficulties.

After 40 weeks of purposeful church-hopping, I realized that something felt different about First Free. I found myself mentally checking off a list of things I was searching for in a church, some of which I didn't even know I was looking for. Empowering preacher? Check. High-spirited contemporary worship music? Check. Bad jokes? Definite check. Sermon references to the story in 2 Chronicles about King Jehoram's bowels falling out (don't ask)? Check, check, and check!

After church, Rachel and I went out for coffee. It was too early to tell if we had chemistry, but I went in with a different mindset than I'd had on other dates. In any type of healthy friendship or relationship, you want to give and support the other person. In this case, I wanted to enhance her faith, no matter the outcome. I had been on too many first dates to know that most don't work out. That used to be depressing, but I've come to realize that every person that comes into our lives, whether good or bad, for one day or a lifetime, is there to teach you something about yourself. They help prepare you for the person you must become. Typically, when the right person shows up in your life, and you're right for them, they'll want to stick around, no matter how many bad jokes you tell.

Something was different about her, though. I just knew God had brought her into my life at the right time and in the right place. We talked about our lives, families, backgrounds, our challenges, passions, favorite inside jokes, and most importantly, faith. She was authentic and true to who she was.

When the flames of Christian romance begin to sizzle, it's a spectacle to behold. When your identity is so closely tied to Christ, there's nothing better than to meet someone who shares your Christ-based morals and values.

After our date, Rachel reached out again, wanting to know even more about me. Suddenly, almost out of nowhere, things were beginning to come together. Rachel and I were starting something built upon the cross.

But if this was going to work, I had to keep reminding myself, *This time, I will praise the Lord.*

EVERY SAINT HAS A PAST, AND EVERY SINNER HAS A FUTURE

THE FIRST HEAVY METAL CHURCH OF CHRIST • DAYTON, OHIO

I f the Devil had tempted Jesus into setting up a Match.com profile, His dates would have made an episode of *The Bachelor* look like a five-year-old's Chuck E. Cheese birthday party.

On paper, Jesus should have been a Holy Don Juan. He had the power to be a walking one-man winery who could turn tap water into Romanée-Conti, wow a party of 5,000 by taking full advantage of Olive Garden's unlimited bread sticks, and then clap-on a chorus of angels to set the mood for a romantic candlelit dinner while having an intelligent conversation about every prophet from Aaron to Zephaniah.

A bevy of Bethlehem beauties would have lined up at His sandy feet, mesmerized by His brown tousled hair, the sporty sash hung casually cross His chest, and His God-given golden Coppertone skin. Looking for long walks on the beach? Please, that's soooooo B.C. He could have waltzed the girls along the top of the Sea of Galilee. Off in the horizon, a *Simpsons* blue sky would dim into a picturesque sunset. He'd turn to His lady with a heavenly glimmer in His eye and nonchalantly say, "You see that sun? My dad made that on the first day. It was good."

And He would have been good. If only He had been bad.

Looking at the miracles Jesus performed, you'd think that fathers would have been launching their daughters at Him. Women should have howled for His love. He could have ignored a girl and not texted her back, giving the age-old excuse that He had died, but rose again just to see her pearly white smile, and He *still* would have gotten her. But you know what? He never did that.

Instead, Jesus was rich with meekness and lowliness. He carpooled into Jerusalem on a donkey. If someone slapped Him, He turned the other cheek. He even took time away from His hectic travel schedule to give His full attention to Mary Magdalene's tell-all about the losers in her life, perfectly content to remain in the friend zone. At the end of the day, Jesus was and will always be a "nice guy."

When I was dating in my 20's, I often scratched my head every time I heard women say they wanted a nice guy, only to turn salty, cast the nice guy into the Mediterranean, and cannonball themselves into the lap of a bad boy. Logically, I assumed that nice guys gave women exactly what they want: to be showered with gifts, glorified with attention, and given an immediate response to every call or text message. Bad boys, on the other hand, would create mystery and riot the female heart through their unshakable confidence, giving women so much space, they could binge all the alien documentaries on Netflix they'd want.

While the Bible doesn't say anything about dating, it does talk about nice guys and bad boys.

Pontius Pilate knows what I'm talking about. After all, he was the short straw that had to free Barabbas, the biggest, baddest bad boy your momma warned you about. He was a rebel, the renegade leader of an insurrection, and the type of guy that Taylor Swift would date, dump, and then write break-up songs about that eventually win Grammys.

Back in those days, it was Passover tradition to release one prisoner from death's row, based on popular vote. To cater to his wife's concern for Jesus, Pilate served up the nicest guy on the planet against the Bible's Big Bad. The Roman guards paraded Barabbas out, as the *Cops* theme song "Bad Boys" played in the background. He assumed that, obviously, the crowd would do the right thing and give the one "Get Out of Jail Free" card to Jesus. Right? *Right?!?*

Pilate appeared before the crowd and said something along the lines of, "Which one of these two men do you want me to release to you? The murderous and barbaric Barabbas? Or Jesus Christ, who's very polite in small-to-medium-sized groups and an all-around swell guy?"

"Give us Barabbas!" they answered.

Pilate was befuddled. "Seriously?!? But Jesus hasn't done anything wrong. What do you want me to do with this nice guy?"

The crowd shouted, "Crucify him!"

. . .

The First Heavy Metal Church of Christ in Dayton, Ohio
August 16, 2015 – 12:00 P.M. Worship Service

I was pushing the pedal to the metal on I-74. My personal "Highway to Hell" hit a detour as I burned rubber on my way to an outlaw biker church. I felt "Bad to the Bone": music blaring, sunroof open, and a fresh pack of allergy pills in the glove compartment (okay, so maybe I wasn't as tough-and-gruff as I thought).

Since our church date, Rachel was going Goo Goo Dolls over me, and our connection was quickly revving up as the dates continued. She was barraging me with text messages, begging to know what I had planned next for my church tours. She didn't see me as a "nice guy," but rather a Christian road warrior with an edge. I was waving goodbye to my past, which was now firmly in the rearview mirror. For church number 42, I was ready to embrace my inner Christian bad boy and stand shoulder-to-shoulder with my wayward brothers-in-faith at The First Heavy Metal Church of Christ (FHMCC). I hoped no one would notice my lack of a neck tattoo.

When I arrived, I was greeted by a sign that read, "Loving the hell out of you every Sunday at noon." I pulled in next to a line of Harleys, and off in the distance by a nearby graveyard, I spotted a long black hearse that looked like it had been plucked straight out of a Mad Max movie. It was customized with a "Paint It, Black" exterior, hand-painted flames, and mirror-tinted windows that were pictured with images of the Skull Dollz, named after the church's women's face-painting ministry. The hearse's interior contained a black, spray-painted wooden pew as the front seat, and of course, such a vehicle wouldn't be complete without a casket in the back.

At this time, FHMCC gathered every Sunday at noon inside a former elementary school. Services were held in the gym on a stage flanked by a medieval suit of armor on the left and a six-foot-tall metal cross on the right.

Hoping to avoid sticking out like Alice Cooper in a L'Oréal commercial, I had traded in my usual Sunday best for a faded black shirt, black baseball cap, and ripped jeans. I fit right in.

The gym was hotter than a Red Hot Chili Peppers concert in the Sahara during the Summer Solstice, so I hit up the concessions stand to get some bottled water. Unlike most churches, where coffee is the beverage of choice, I noticed that many congregants were equipped with cans of Monster Energy drink for their extra Sunday-morning kick.

Rooster, the harmonica-wielding lead singer of God's Dirt, jump-started service by shouting, "Come on, someone bring the Holy Spirit in here! Come on, I wanna hear you shout! Come on, shout! Shout the name of Jesus! Shout His name!" Mixing bluegrass and rock, this week's guest band soon had the congregation raising their arms and making the sign of the

213

horns with their hands.

All throughout the service, I saw that FHMCC had some interesting alternative ways to connect with the congregation. From leading off the announcements with everyone shouting, "Unleash the Kraken," to the pastor spraying the congregation with a Super Soaker, this church wasn't afraid to pave a new road to spread its message.

FHMCC was the brainchild of Pastor Brian Smith, a heavy metal musician who became disillusioned with what he called "Country Club Christianity." He didn't feel welcomed at traditional churches due to his rocker look, so he rebelled against the religious establishment by forming his own church to reach those who frequented strip clubs, bars, and biker clubs.

Pastor Brian didn't want to spit fire and brimstone; he wanted to cast fishing nets to the lost and the damned who would have felt uncomfortable in a traditional religious setting. And he just happened to use heavy metal music as a lure. It didn't matter what you did or who you were. All were welcomed: bikers, drug addicts, prostitutes, gang members, convicted felons, and even writers who need all-day allergy relief. While many Christians look at Pastor Brian's outreach efforts as poisonous, the fact is that he reaches out to a forgotten target audience, preaching "To Hell with the Devil."

On this particular Sunday, Pastor Brian delivered a unique sermon, mixing rock ethos with Biblical canon. He referenced Hebrews 12:28–29, describing God's power as an all-consuming fire. If someone thinks they can contain God, to quote Judas Priest, "You've Got Another Thing Comin'."

"We're all gonna have to "Ride the Lightning"—ooh, Metallica reference," Smith said. "We're all gonna have to make that jump. Someday, you and me are gonna be layin' on a hospital bed. When we're layin' there, as our life is getting to leave us and we're about to take the Great Vacation, I don't want my last thoughts to be coulda, shoulda, woulda. The time is now. Livin' your last moments in regret, Satan will have a field day with your mind."

When the service was over, I decided to get another look at that hearse. Upon closer inspection, I saw that song lyrics were stamped all over it, but the one that stuck out to me was the Iron Maiden reference on the windshield: "Live After Death."

When it's time for us to be buried and we're taking our final ride in a long black cadillac, we'll either be hearing "Hell's Bells" or "Knockin' on Heaven's Door." He punched our ticket out of hell to sell out that Big Concert Hall in the Sky. We can't beat death after we've died; we can only beat death during the life God has given us through a relationship with Jesus Christ.

The Bible tells us that God continually works with and gives grace to people who don't deserve it, don't even seek it, and don't appreciate it once they get it. Barabbas was one of the most undeserving and worst sinners of them all, yet, he was the one who was freed over a nice guy like Jesus.

In a way, we're all bad boys. We're all lost and condemned sinners. We're all Barabbas. And yet, because Christ took our place on the cross, we have been saved. All we have to do is believe and let God transform our lives.

I guess it's true: nice guys really do finish last. Christ finished last so that He could put us first.

CHURCH 43:
"TAKE ME TO YOUR LADDER, I'LL SEE YOUR LEADER LATER"
CHURCH OF SCIENTOLOGY • ST. PAUL, MINNESOTA

I had come in peace.

My latest church odyssey had me trekking across the religious cosmos, landing in the unknown world of Scientology. Founded by sci-fi writer L. Ron Hubbard, many critics consider Scientology to be nothing more than a celebrity-filled cult based in the outer reaches of the spiritual Milky Way.

Who knows? Maybe I watched too many UFO episodes of *Unsolved Mysteries* as a kid. As I was going to churches that no one had gone before, I had to know what a Scientology Sunday service was like. With previous church explorations, I often had conspiracy theories that were proved wrong after setting foot in a new place of worship. If there was any church that had been abducted by HBO documentaries and national news headlines, it was the Church of Scientology. Could I give a fair shake to such a controversial religion—taking one small step for curiosity, one giant leap for understanding?

This was one of the questions orbiting my mind when I met the Scientology chaplain. He walked up to me and introduced himself with this icebreaker: "So there was an astronaut who landed on an alien planet inhabited by a race of beautiful women. When he climbed out of his spaceship, the women approached, and he saw that they were all some 20 feet taller than he was. One came up to him and asked, 'I suppose you want to see our leader?' The astronaut looked up at her and replied, 'Take me to your ladder. I'll see your leader later.'"

My eyes lit up like the Millennium Falcon with its brights on. I wasn't sure how to react. Ignoring my lack of reaction, the chaplain shook my hand and laughed at his own joke. His smile expanded into a wide grin that was the size of the Hubble Space Telescope.

I thought to myself, *What have I gotten myself into this week?*

. . .

Church of Scientology in St. Paul, Minnesota
August 23, 2015 – 10:30 A.M. Sunday Service

To be honest, I was more nervous than a kitten in an episode of *Alf.* I knew very little about Scientology, other than that Tom Cruise was a member and Rachel told me she knew a friend in Scientology who had to eat a placenta. I didn't believe her, there was no way that could be true.

The night before my visit, I had visions of being lowered into the church by a series of wires, dangling just centimeters above the floor in a reenactment of that scene in *Mission: Impossible*. I wasn't sure how the Church of Scientology would welcome newcomers or even *if* they would welcome outsiders. By this point, I had been to over 40 churches, most of which were aligned with my Christian beliefs. I wanted to remain neutral in my judgments, but I was honestly worried that my visit would turn into some kind of religious *War of the Worlds*.

Flying solo, I opened the front door and right walked in. Easy-peasy; no delicate acrobatics required or alien lights to suck me up. Two ladies sitting behind a desk greeted me. They were both dressed like hotel valets, with black pants, white dress shirts, and golden ties and vests. I asked to attend the morning service, and they in turn asked me to fill out a form with my contact information. *Great, that's not so hard*, I thought.

When I was done, one of the attendants led me to a state-of-the-art dining room and gave me the tiniest water bottle I'd ever seen. She invited me to take a seat and asked me to wait. So I waited. And waited. And waited some more with my miniature water bottle as my only companion.

After waiting for a while, questions started to probe my brain: *Why am I waiting here by myself? Where is the church service located? What are they gonna do with my contact information? Are they preparing a placenta breakfast for me to eat as a newcomer initiation ritual?*

As the questions mounted, I realized that the service was supposed to have started ten minutes ago. Being an outsider, I got antsy and walked back to the front desk. Before I could ask the receptionist what the Dalek was going on, the chaplain walked up to me and introduced himself with his weird alien joke. I wanted to "E.T. phone home." But it was too late to turn back now.

The chaplain was dressed in black preacher's garb that was accented with a clerical collar. He sat down with me in the dining room smelling like he had just finished a Marlboro. We sat and chatted about his own expedition into Scientology and oak furniture. The conversation reduced my anxiety somewhat, but like the Alien Queen embryo growing inside Ripley in *Alien 3*, the thought had impregnated my mind and was ready to burst out: *If the chaplain is with me, where is everyone else?*

"Well, I guess it's just us today," he said, answering my thoughts and making me wonder if he was telepathic. He explained that the church had five regulars, but several of them must have had to work that day.

Instead of taking me straight to the worship area, he gave me the full tour. I learned that The Church of Scientology in St. Paul used to be a science museum, and it has several interactive displays with click-and-play videos that explain several key concepts and the core fundamentals of Scientology. While I was extremely cautious about its content, I had to admit that their presentation was quite visually appealing.

One of the principles these videos taught was the idea of Dianetics, which Hubbard developed as a kind of self-help psychology. It's a large part of what propelled Scientology into popularity as a new religion. The chaplain explained that our minds are essentially recording every sight, sound, taste, smell, emotion, and touch in our life. These recordings are called the "time track," a consecutive record of all the experiences we accumulate throughout our existence. Our minds use this accumulated information to make decisions and solve problems.

Most of this data is intellectual and stored in the analytical part of our mind, which thinks, remembers, and calculates. The other part of the mind is more emotional and reactive, and it throws bad experiences back at us in an irrational attempt to keep painful things—like getting shot at, going through a major break-up, or re-watching the movie adaption of Hubbard's *Battlefield Earth*—from happening again. Thus, our painful past experiences are the cause of our fears, insecurities, and irrational behavior.

Dianetics explains how these negative responses are stored and how we can free ourselves from them. To help, Scientology employs trained auditors to take an individual through a series of questions that are aimed to free oneself from barriers. During the audit, the auditee holds two giant silver cans, while the auditor reads findings on a gold-plated device known as the Mark Ultra VIII E-meter.

The chaplain and I eventually made our way up a twisting spiral staircase to the second floor. The "Take me to your ladder, I'll see your leader later" joke became increasingly appropriate as we ascended. The chapel was hidden within a constellation of offices where more church employees were located, each wearing the same attire as the ladies downstairs.

We finally reached what looked like a gigantic lecture hall. It was impressive, with more than 200 cushioned seats, a gigantic IMAX screen, and a pristine black grand piano on the side. At the center of it all was a podium with the Scientology symbol attached to the front.

Since I was the only congregant that morning, the chaplain explained that he had a lecture planned, but I was free to chime in and ask questions. With that, he began the service with the Creed of Scientology, which he himself interrupted at various points to inform me of random facts about Scientology.

After the Creed, he went right into his sermon, titled, "You Can Be Right." I would like to write more about it—and he certainly did his best—but most of it was way over my head. There was something about how killing a mosquito would harm the animal kingdom and would be considered wrong, but if you had a number of people in the room, and the mosquito had malaria, then you had to smash the mosquito. If you don't stop a malaria-carrying mosquito from biting someone, the guilt would lie on you. Talk about your dangerous hypothetical situations!

After a ten-minute lecture on what's right and what's wrong, he moved on to talk about arguments within a relationship and how I should always find out why my girlfriend is right. For example, if she's always burning dinner and it leads to several big arguments, I need to wipe out her wrongness by asking, "What would be right about burning my dinner?"

As he explained, "This can evoke a raging tirade, but if one flattens the question, which by continuing to ask it until it no longer produces a reaction, she will happily cease to burn dinner. This can happen with your girlfriend," he paused, then continued in a spirit of political correctness, "or boyfriend."

Whatever floats your boat. As for me, my mental boat had sailed a long time ago.

When the day was done, my exploration of Scientology felt a lot like a first date.

The visit wasn't as bad as I had feared it would be. No one asked me to take a personality test by holding the Ultra Mark VIII or offered me a complimentary placenta for breakfast. Not once did Jerry Maguire come out and shout "Show me the money!" for an offering, though one of the pamphlets the chaplain gave me did advertise advanced lectures for as little as $11,000. The chaplain himself was friendly, and the church was on its best behavior, but deep down, I knew it would never work. It's not you, it's me. I had to go see other churches. I had to end the spiritual courtship.

Fortunately, I discovered a silver lining in this visit: It definitely helped me understand how others may view my Christian faith. The way many people think about Scientology is probably similar to how non-believers view Christian churches. We pray. We praise. We eat and drink the symbolic body and blood of our risen Savior. When you're a Christian your entire life, it's easy to forget how alien it might sound to a non-believer. Using Scientology's idea of Dianetics, this experience helped me "time track" such a perspective in my analytical mind as I recorded every sensation of this strange visit.

But if someone ever uses another alien joke as an icebreaker, my reactive mind may just grab the nearest tin-foil hat.

CHURCH 44:
SERMON FROM THE MOUND
ST. FRANCIS XAVIER BASILICA • DYERSVILLE, IOWA

Dad took me to the Field of Dreams after I turned nine. It was his idea of a father-son bonding experience after we had seen the movie a handful of times. It starred Kevin Costner as an Iowa farmer trying to make ends meet. One night, he's strolling through his crops when out of left field—which, coincidentally, would become left field—he heard a voice say, "If you build it, he will come."

This wasn't like the voice you hear in the McDonald's drive-thru speaker. No, this was a whisper that spoke with God-like confidence. When the voice repeated itself, Costner had a vision of his land transformed into a baseball field.

He doesn't know why this is happening. He doesn't know who "he" is. Nothing about this makes any sense. "Until I heard the voice, I'd never done a crazy thing in my whole life," he says. Yet he pursues his vision and risks everything to build the ballpark.

Throughout the movie, his brother-in-law tries to pick off his faith with doubts. Costner mulls things over, but chooses to go with his gut. Eventually, he's redeemed when the baseball field becomes a portal for the ghosts of America's favorite pastime. "Shoeless" Joe Jackson appears—a man who had been unjustly excommunicated from the sport—and recruits more ghostly ballplayers from the cornfields. The players mistake the ballpark for heaven and are given the opportunity to have one more chance at-bat. Among those watching in the stands, the believers see them. The non-believers don't.

The film has a number of themes, but to me, it's a modern-day version of the Parable of the Sower.

Never was this better explained than by my old church's associate pastor. He had come from a small-town Nebraska church with all the necessary tools to make sermons worth the price of collection. He was brilliant at making use of sports metaphors in his sermons, and I always found my attention span going into extra innings when he used an example from baseball. One time, when he preached about the Parable of the Sower, he carried in a towering, eight-foot-tall cornstalk that could have been plucked from the Field of Dreams outfield. He used it as a prop to help explain the difference between the harvest and the weeds—the faith of believers and non-believers. For the first time in a long time, I looked forward to church every week.

But then there was a changeup.

Maybe it's just that I was now paying closer attention, but over time, I noticed that our "One True Church" was putting itself in *A League of Their Own*.

The errors of sinners—the source of everything wrong in the world— were covered as though they were SportsCenter highlights. The church lost its command, carelessly throwing Scripture like wild pitches. Eventually, the strike zone expanded when sermons painted the corners by critiquing opposing churches that welcomed outcast sinners and those that employed female clergy.

In the midst of all this, I couldn't get rid of the memory of visitors being banned from the communion table. You'd have to pay your dues in an adult confirmation class or stay benched on the pews.

Then my brother, who had stopped attending himself, was cut by the church—given a pink slip in the form of an excommunication letter. To quote Bob Uecker, everything that was happening felt "Juuuuust a bit outside."

I really wanted to root, root, root for my home church. After all, I had grown up wearing its colors. I didn't want to become a fair-weather worshiper and jump on the bandwagon of another church when the going got tough. Maybe this was just a slump. But my loyalty no longer felt right. We had moved the Green Monster from Fenway Park into our hearts and minds, walling off any viewpoints that weren't exactly within our purist foul lines.

I always thought the Christian message was that Christ loves us, not that we're right and everyone else is wrong. But it seemed like fewer and fewer people in my church agreed.

To maintain my church membership, I joined the church's fast-pitch team. Baseball became my spiritual outlet, combining my love of the sport with some semblance of Christian fellowship. My sermon was on the mound. The crack of a bat echoed like a hymn. I'd trot to the outfield, surrounded by God's green creation, as a way to connect with something sacred. I could get away from the religious hecklers at the pulpit and instead be in a place where I could chat strategy with the Great Manager in the Sky.

Like faith—and like much of life—baseball requires a lot of patience. You wait and wait and wait for something to happen. Then, when you least expect it, a fly ball comes your way.

"Can o' corn," shouted my associate pastor from center field.

I was playing right field in a game we had to win if we were to have any shot at making the championships. As Murphy's Law brought the ball straight towards me, all eyes turned to me, counting on me to make the easy catch. That's when my confidence sank like Peter in the Sea of Galilee. I horribly misplayed it, the ball bonking off my head. I don't remember what happened to the ball, but I do remember the sighs, the stares, and the shame.

When the inning ended, I sensed my team's disappointment in me. I had failed my teammates, and I still felt like my church was failing me. I spiked my glove and hat in disgust as my teammates and the church members in the stands looked on in silence. It was the only time in my life when I've made such a scene in public.

We lost by a run.

After the game, I was heading to my car when the associate pastor ran up to me with an ultimatum. I guess he didn't like my reaction earlier. "Dave," he said, "you need to come back to church if you want to keep playing for us. No church, no ball."

He repeated himself, hurling another verbal sinker to strike out my membership as I was caught looking before he jogged away. "No church. No ball."

We lost more than the game that day. My church lost me that day, too.

. . .

St. Francis Xavier Basilica in Dyersville, Iowa
September 24, 2015 – 6:30 A.M. Mass

You never know when a rally will spark. Who knows where the trigger will come from? Whenever it does happen though, you don the rally cap, decide that enough is enough, and make a life-changing decision to make a comeback.

"No church, no ball," was the phrase that kicked off my rally back to Christ.

At first, my faith was in a rain delay. I had no idea where to go. Ever since I was baptized when I was a mere 21 days old, I had gone to the same house of worship.

My 8th grade confirmation verse was from Acts 4:12: "Salvation is found in no one else, for there is no other name, given to men, by which we must be saved." Now, I found myself caught in a pickle between my God and my church. If I couldn't find my salvation in anyone else, why did it feel like the man-made religion I had always followed was telling me that it was the only way to Him?

Maybe it was God, and maybe it was me, but somehow, the idea of visiting 52 different churches in a year was planted in my mind. "If you build it, He will come." Just like in *Field of Dreams*, sometimes the craziest ideas start with a whisper.

By visit 44, it had been a little over a year since I felt that I had been waived from my church. Now I was rounding third to complete *52 Churches in 52 Weeks*. Everything in my life had changed for the better after I dove headfirst into my faith. Now I felt like a cross between Kevin Costner in *Field of Dreams* and Charlie Sheen in *Major League*. I had never done a crazy thing in my entire life, and now, this spiritual joyride had become the "Wild Thing" that made my heart sing. I was #winning, and as I entered the seventh-inning stretch, I was making plans to go on a cross-country road trip. My batting line-up showed nine churches on the scoreboard within a three-week span. Leading off would be St. Francis Xavier Basilica in Dyersville, Iowa.

Despite being located in a small town with a population of 4,000, the St. Francis Xavier Basilica is a towering landmark overlooking the surrounding cornfields.

While I had come to better respect the Catholic faith and understand its rituals, visiting a Catholic church still made me feel like a member of the away team. Due to this, I always sat in the back to avoid those dreadful stares from church members coming back to their pew from the members-only communion. Mass felt like it was quicker than a double play that morning. The service lasted less than 30 minutes, with a brief sermon mentioning that Pope Francis was visiting the U.S. later in the week.

Still, while I had officially come for the church, it was the Field of Dreams that spoke to me in an unmistakable voice that I hadn't heard since James Earl Jones was voicing Sith lords from the Galactic Empire.

That weekend, Dyersville was hosting a "Team of Dreams" charity softball game. The event recruited Hall of Fame baseball players to play in an exhibition game at the Field of Dreams movie site. This year, the game featured some of the all-time greats: Reggie Jackson, Brooks Robinson, Wade Boggs, Carlton Fisk, Robin Yount, Andre Dawson, and Rollie Fingers.

And then there were Jose Canseco and Bill Buckner. In the first inning, Canseco hit a line drive single to left field and made it safely to first base, where he stood next Buckner. It was odd: Canseco and Buckner were ballplayers notorious for their human errors, and now they stood side-by-side.

Despite all his power feats, Canseco made baseball's all-time blooper reel when he misjudged an easy fly ball. I could relate, the ball bounced off his head and over the wall, making it a home run. As ridiculous as it looked, at least it was during a regular season game. Buckner, on the other hand, is infamous for his blunder in Game Six of the 1986 World Series. The Boston Red Sox were putting the finishing touches on the New York Mets to win their first World Series championship since 1918. The Mets had a runner on second base, and a slow roller bounced to Buckner at first base. He rushed the ball, but instead of scooping it up for an easy out, he fumbled the ball, and it rolled between his legs into right field.

The Mets won the game and went on to win the World Series. Buckner was the scapegoat, his mistake having occurred in front of 20,000 fans, while millions watched from home. Now, when people talk about Buckner, no one leads off with his impressive 20-year major league career, his 2,700 lifetime base hits, or even the wild pitch that got the winning run in scoring position just a few pitches earlier in that very 1986 game. Instead, everyone remembers the error. The failure. The screw-up.

During the "Team of Dreams" game, a local radio personality was doing the play-by-play over the P.A. The guy joked that the other team should hit the ball toward Buckner. When Robin Yount came up to bat, he drilled Mike Boddicker's underhand pitch straight at Buckner. The ball whizzed past Buckner's outstretched glove, his 65-year-old body stuck to the ground as the ball rolled into right field. "Classic Buckner," the talking head observed, before launching into a number of jokes that tore into Buckner even 30 years after his error.

Later that day, I went back to the Field of Dreams. No one else was there. The crowds had long gone, and trash was still strewn around, waiting to be picked up. I was alone in the outfield. It was quiet and peaceful.

In a way, there's a relationship between baseball and faith. We are all searching for meaning in life, and we take different actions to find a spiritual framework within our everyday lives. Most find this at church, but I've found that Scripture is actually all around us. For me, the romanticism of baseball evokes a spiritual experience. It's my idea of heaven.

I couldn't stop thinking about the jabs thrown at Buckner. We all make errors and commit sins in life. We strike out, we're caught looking, and we get called out. When things don't go our way, we wonder if God is watching us. What's His scouting report on us? Sometimes, we lean too far off the first base of God's Word, and the Devil tries to pick us off.

When Jesus came into the game, His team of disciples had donned their rally caps. They were expecting Him to bat clean up—like Babe Ruth calling

His shot—and knock the Devil's sin-laden knuckleball straight out of the ballpark. Evil Empires would crumble, Christianity would prevail on earth, and ticker tape would fall from heaven to the tune of Queen's "We Are the Champions."

But it didn't exactly happen that way.

Instead, Jesus came in as a lowly pinch hitter. He wasn't making the big bucks. He was there to make up for our errors and sins, taking the boos and jeers intended for us as He came up to bat. Sometimes in baseball, manufacturing runs is just as efficient as playing long ball. When He got to the plate and the Devil was scheming to tag us out, He served as an example that any baseball fan would appreciate. When Christ picked up the lumber and lay down the ultimate sacrifice play, He took the out so we could slide safely into our heavenly home.

CHURCH 45:
BIG DECISIONS IN THEIR LITTLE WORLD
CROSS ISLAND CHAPEL • ONEIDA, NEW YORK

When you start dating someone you really like, it's a lot like watching Bob Ross paint.

You come in with a palette of fresh paint, having taken the necessary clockwork to coat-over any smudges from your past, and get a do-over with a blank canvas. You have an idea—a fantasy, of how this Big Picture is supposed to look. The problem is that you don't know—in fact, you're not supposed to know exactly how it will turn out. You hope it doesn't get messed up like last time. Paralyzed by perfectionism, you stare at the possibilities of the future with the same intensity as Uma Thurman in *Kill Bill* when she's staring at her big toe. But you know what? You're not a paralyzed Uma Thurman in *Kill Bill*.

You're you.

Your little piggies are just fine, you probably have no clue where to find a cadmium-yellow tracksuit, and the nearby thrift store doesn't sell ninja swords. No, you have a paintbrush. The nothingness of this new canvas bothers you, and eventually, you simply need to move that paintbrush to start filling in the storyboard of your life. So you wash the brush in an odorless paint thinner, beat the devil out of it, and start adding color to your dreams.

Rachel had two little ones: Tony, who had just turned nine, and Elle, who was five. Because of the kids, I advised that we take things slower than a tortoise with arthritis trudging through the Boston Marathon in peanut butter.

On our second date, I took her to a painting class after church. I hoped that it would give her a chance to relax and have a few hours away from the "mommy-mommy-mommy-mommy-mommy" lifestyle of being a single mom.

We were tasked with creating an underwater turtle scene. I had no clue what I was doing. Growing up, the only experience I'd had with painting was watching Bob Ross on PBS after episodes of *Mister Rogers' Neighborhood*, *Lamb Chop's Play-Along*, and *Barney & Friends*.

Our instructor advised us to simply start applying small brush strokes and take it a little bit at a time. After all, it's not like da Vinci painted the Mona Lisa during his lunch break. Painting—like dating——takes time and patience until something worthwhile emerges.

Over the course of the next two months, Rachel and I spent more and more time together. We shared qualities that we were drawn to: a sense of humor, an endearing personality, and Christian morals to ground everything. She invited me into the lives of her family. Backed by the cross as our easel, we were mixing color into each other's lives, blending rich and vibrant memories with broad, circular brush strokes to create the picture that was our future.

But not everything can be sunshine and rainbows. As the picture progresses, you eventually need to add some darkness. Traces of the past will try to creep in. It had only been two years since Rachel had escaped from an emotionally abusive marriage. She had been painted into a corner, and a war hero that she didn't truly know had vandalized her heart. Her ex's addictions to drugs and gambling were hidden in shadows. War changes people; marriage changes people. Now, after the matrimonial discharge, she was raising Tony and Elle by herself. With her faith, she was starting over to achieve something better.

"You absolutely have to have dark in order to have light," Bob Ross once said. "You gotta have opposites: dark and light, light and dark, continually in painting. It's like in life: you gotta have a little sadness once in awhile so you know when the good times come."

As our paintings became clearer, something much deeper began to emerge. Colorful coral and plant life began growing from the black depths. Our sea turtles had risen and were now surfacing toward the light—toward something better.

Before we called it a day and signed our initials, the art instructor gave us all one last recommendation: "In your painting, you can draw as many turtles as you'd like to your family."

Rachel had painted her family with three turtles.

If the good times had indeed finally come, my family had room for four.

. . .

"The World's Smallest Church" Cross Island Chapel in Oneida, New York
September 26, 2015 – 4:18 P.M. Prayer

The scene looked like Bob Ross had dropped in from the heavens to paint one last piece on a standard 18" x 20" canvas. The sun was just hanging above the pond, along with some happy little clouds. Nature had taken its trusty fan brush, loaded it with sap green and a touch of van dyke brown and blended them together into a big ol' tree. He needed a friend, so another was placed next to him, and soon enough, there was a deep woods filled with all kinds of trees and little rascals—squirrels, geese, bees, who knows? It's your world. Make a decision.

In the middle of the pond was Cross Island Chapel, a titanium white church built on a low platform next to a wooden cross. A small billboard near the road told you everything you needed to know about it: "Built in 1989. Floor area, 51" x 81" (28.68 sq. ft.). Seats two people. Non-denominational and open to the public upon request. Cross Island Chapel is dedicated as a witness to God."

Rumor has it that the chapel was built for a small wedding in the late '80s. It only had room for the minister, bride, and groom atop the platform, and the rest of the wedding party had to anchor nearby in small boats. All the guests witnessed the vows from ashore. The chapel had remained there ever since.

No church services were held here, unless you'd count a congregation of geese who—as the bottom of my shoes had to avoid—didn't make mistakes, just made some "happy little accidents."

So instead of seeking out a service, I had come to the world's tiniest church to pray. It's the little things that matter, and this visit was to help me see what was emerging in my life's Big Picture. Rachel and I had been dating for two months, and everything was lining up for the next stage of our courtship. But with kids involved, I knew it wouldn't be easy.

I had grown to admire Rachel's character. Sure, she wasn't perfect, but a person's faults are largely what makes them so darn likable. As a single mom, her day consisted of paying near-constant attention to her kids. She tirelessly got them out of bed in the morning and back into bed at night. She fed, bathed, and dressed them. She brushed their hair, kept them safe, refereed them, and answered their cries, questions, and tantrums.

I had learned that, for her, a vacation often meant a quick solo trip into Dollar Tree to pick up paper towels while I supervised the kids with YouTube videos. She was constantly having to stay one step ahead of two kids to keep them from getting too tired, too bored, or too cranky, any of which could result in kicking and screaming at the expense of the downstairs apartment neighbors' hearing aids.

Hers was a life of constant monitoring, constant touch, and constant use of her vocal chords, where one minute she could sound like Mary Poppins, and the next, Batman. She faced constant scrutiny and second-guessing from her ex-in-laws. And she was doing this all by herself, teaching them everything: manners, safety, respect, resourcefulness, discipline, curiosity, creativity, empathy, and, most importantly, that Jesus loved them.

"Are you sure you're ready for this?" she texted me one night after our phone conversation had ended early due to a nighttime tantrum.

The question was a test of my bravery, but I already knew the answer. I was ready to make some big decisions and be a part of their little world.

I had learned that even as you're teaching kids all kinds of things—how to read, how to sit still at the kitchen table, how to build a LEGO set—yet they're teaching you about simplicity in their own little ways. With the kids, I would forget about the stresses of spreadsheets, deadlines, and due dates. They make you realize how much you're rushing through life, as kids are artists of living in the moment. They teach you how to use your imagination and make any moment a masterpiece. In all the complexities of life, our search for the best things often leads us to those things that are simple enough for a child to understand.

In life, you have to actively ask yourself what you want to be. You have to dream and then be willing to go for your dreams. You have to pursue something that adds color to your heart and soul. For me, this was something worth living for, and now, I was wondering whether I had found the Big Picture God had been leading me to throughout my spiritual adventure.

I could see myself as a part of Rachel's picture. I could see myself being a huge influence in Tony and Elle's lives. They wanted—no, needed—someone to be present in their little world who wouldn't let them down. That's more important than any Spider-Man or Elsa toy I could ever buy them. They would copy what I did and what I'd say. The way I saw it, the best gift I could give them was an amazing Christian, faith-based relationship with their mother.

So that was my prayer that day. My vow to God was to make the lives of Rachel and the kids better than they had been when I entered their picture. Then I stopped praying and, instead, decided to be the answer to their prayers.

Your actions are the paintbrush on the canvas of your life. Make your painting interesting.

Before I called it a day, I turned around to look at the other side of the pond. I hadn't even noticed what was over there before. I had to squint to see what was in the distance, but when I did, I saw something sitting on a wooden log. It had risen from the pond's murky depths to bask in the sunshine.

It was a family.

A family of turtles.

CHURCH 46:
MONKS THAT MAKE BEER
ST. JOSEPH'S ABBEY • SPENCER, MASSACHUSETTS

One night, Jesus was bustin' a move on the dance floor, doing the Chicken Dance with His mom at a wedding in Cana. He flapped His chicken wings, wiggled His tail feather, and clapped four times to the beat. But then, Mary looked down at her empty cup and observed, "They have no more wine."

"Woman, why do you involve me?" Jesus replied. "My time has not come."

But Mary was really thirsty and begged her son to do something, forcing Jesus to remember that whole "honor thy mother" thing, which evidently included performing a miracle to give her some liquid courage for the Macarena later. Jesus agreed, and Mary ordered the servants to do whatever her son said. He instructed them to fill several jars with water.

Right on cue, the Hokey Pokey started. Jesus put His right hand in, took His right hand out, put His right hand in, and shook it all about. He did the Hokey Pokey and turned the water into wine. That's what it's all about.

And then there was plenty of red, red wine—really good wine. Wine so fine, the banquet's host commented that, normally, the choice wine was served first and the cheap stuff came after everyone couldn't tell the difference, but now, the best had been saved for last.

So before anyone could say, "You're drunk. Go home," and find their designated camel drivers, the wedding guests decided to party hardy late into the night—even the Apostles, who likely attempted some fad dance

235

that was popular at the time. Probably the Floss.

And just like that, Our Lord JC was In Da House. He was hip. Cool. The new Savior on the block that everyone was talking about. Mark it on the Julian calendar: this was the date when the world came to know The Fresh Prince of Contemplative Prayer. He had come down from heaven for the people, and His first trick was transfiguring beverages to get this party started. Word to His mother.

It took several years for me to get into my head the fact that Jesus' very first miracle was turning water into wine. Even the Bible itself sneaks it into the Gospel of John and quickly moves on, as though it's slightly embarrassed by this. Growing up in Wisconsin, where there's a bar for every church, my bubble-wrapped Christian upbringing forbade the very idea of alcohol consumption. Never once did I witness my parents partaking. My church preached that drinking beer was a sin and that wine was reserved for the Communion table. Never in all my years of sermon-listening, parochial-school instruction, or Bible-study discussions was the transformation of water into wine discussed as the miraculous act that launched Christ's ministry.

Then, one morning when I was in high school, the phone rang at 6:00 A.M. You know it's never good news when you receive a call that early. A drunk driver had killed my grandma. She had been in the passenger seat going to a farmer's market with a friend. Her body was left mangled into a pile of blood, gasoline, and glass. We later learned that the drunk driver was 17 years old, which was a dagger to my heart, as I was the same age.

I had to wonder why, out of all the miracles Jesus had at His fingertips to heal a needy world from sin—from curing the sick, to raising the dead, to feeding the hungry—why did he start with helping people get tipsy?

If Jesus' first miracle was transfiguring water into wine, at what point does consuming alcohol in the age of drunk driving and binge drinking become a sin? How much is too much? When is it okay to drink? What happens when sin seemingly becomes subjective? Why was the first miracle linked to alcohol?

. . .

St. Joseph's Abbey in Spencer, Massachusetts
September 26, 2015 – 6:25 A.M. Mass

I've been hungover with these questions for years. I tried to conceal them in the brown paper bag of my mind; after all, no one should question God. Yet, here I am with a heavy set of questions.

My whole life, I had sworn off alcohol in the name of God. During my high school and college years, I skipped out on beer pong and keg parties. When friends asked why I wouldn't drink, I cited my grandmother's death, serving as a major buzzkill. I always left events that involved alcohol when things got crazy. I tried to do the "right thing" by seeking "Christian" friendships, but those always left an extra-special bitter taste in my mouth.

On the night of my 24th birthday, I found myself with no plans and few friends. When Patrick offered to hang out and buy me a Rolling Rock, I thought *Why not?* My High Life as a stout Christian had left me dry. So we went out and saw a live band, and I ended my lifelong personal Prohibition by downing a beer that tasted like tree bark. The odd thing was, I also tapped into some fun that night. I met people, made new friends—many of whom had cats—began socializing, met these new friends' cats, and found a new life.

Fast-forward nearly a decade later, and I had become a craft beer connoisseur, taste-testing everything from India pale ales to Russian imperial stouts to Belgian quads. Out of nowhere, craft beer suddenly held a special place in my heart...and my liver.

Eventually, this led to an interesting discovery: some of the best breweries in the world are operated by monks. The centuries-old Roman Catholic Monastic Order of Cistercians of the Strict Observance (say that five times fast) are not only known for quiet contemplation and devotion to God, they're also known for their ability to make a good beer.

At first, monastic breweries seemed countercultural to my mind. How can one worship God and also produce a beverage that, in our culture, is almost synonymous with addiction? But apparently, Trappist breweries started out brewing beer to serve their communities. After all, in the days before water purification systems, beer was safer to drink than water.

Nowadays, there are 11 monasteries in the world with onsite breweries: six in Belgium, two in the Netherlands, and one each in Austria, Italy, and, most recently, St. Joseph's Abbey in Spencer, Massachusetts.

In order to support the rising costs of healthcare and maintaining the abbey, the cash-strapped monks at St. Joseph's Abbey became interested in brewing beer. After returning from a tour of Belgium, several monks honed a recipe for their Spencer Trappist Ale and soon began distributing it. In December 2013, Spencer Brewery was certified as the first Trappist brewery in the United States and the first outside of Europe.

When I first approached the bell tower high above the abbey church for visit number 46, I didn't know what to expect. When I entered, a sign greeted me with a bold concoction of upper- and lower-case letters: "PLEASE OBSERVE SILENCE IN THE CHAPEL OUT OF REVERENCE FOR THE BLESSED SACRAMENT, especially before and after the Liturgies. Thank you! —the monks." I guess this was their passive-aggressive way of saying, "Shhhhhhhh."

Inside the chapel, the interior felt medieval with all the stone. A few stained-glass windows got a little bit of light in, but overall it was starkly dark. There were only two small sections for visitors. Each one only had a few short pews, and even though it was 6:25 on a Saturday morning, there was only one vacant spot.

When the church bells rang, the monks marched in to conduct morning mass, and everyone around me knelt on the cold stone floor—there were no comfy, padded kneelers here. Everyone contorted their bodies so their praying hands could rest on the pew behind them. A four-foot-tall wall separating the visitors and the monks largely blocked my view of what was going on. All I could see were a few monks preparing the Sacrament, while the others chanted. Some older women around me chanted in unison with the monks, though I didn't know what they were saying.

At one point, two rows of people behind me exited. Thinking the service was over, I followed them, only to realize they were a visiting group and had decided to go outside and pray by themselves. I thought about going back inside, but feared opening the door would only further interrupt the monks and visitors who were focusing their attention to God.

Given that the whole service was only 15 minutes long from what I observed, I didn't find any answers to my questions. I was left to continue grappling with the connection between Christ and booze.

In thinking these matters over, I often felt like a bad Christian, since I couldn't distill why the first miracle was so trivial. And you know what? Maybe that's okay. It's allowed. You can ask questions. You don't have to know it, see it, or "get it". Forget Dos Equis; The Most Interesting Man in History came to conquer death, not become a brewmaster.

When the host said, "Everyone brings out the choice wine first and then the cheaper wine after the guests have had too much to drink, but you have saved the best 'til now," maybe that was the point all along. Maybe Christ intentionally chose that moment to show that He was going to shake things up. Maybe it was a statement that He was saving the best for last.

A few hours after mass ended, I visited the abbey's gift shop and asked a monk at the cash register where I could purchase their beer (which in retrospect, is a really strange question when talking to a monk for the first time in your life). He said they didn't sell it near the abbey, but I could purchase a 4-pack at a liquor store that was a ten-minute drive away. As for the beer: questionable nose. Opaque amber. Malty caramel. Sensation of cleansed sin in the aftertaste.

EMPIRE STATE OF SKEPTICISM

REDEEMER PRESBYTERIAN CHURCH • NEW YORK CITY

The worms. That's what I remember most about the night my faith was squirming.

What started with one soon became over two-dozen. Writhing. Slithering. Wiggling beneath the moonlight. Up and down, left to right, they stretched their floppy stomachs to inch forward in the dirt, shortening and widening, twisting and turning. They were putting my P90X Ab Ripper X workouts to shame. In the freshly sprayed soil, they surfaced from below the ground to munch on decayed roots, dying leaves, and my plans to order an appetizer.

"When are you going to give up this make-believe, fairytale Jesus bullshit?" Patrick asked, snapping my attention away from the lively garden beside us.

"We're not doing this tonight," I replied, refusing to take the bait. I was in no mood for yet another theological tug-of-war with my best friend. I just wanted to hang out and have fun at Madison's best outdoor dining venue, a literal Biergarten of Eden if I've ever seen one, complete with a brick patio, ivy-leaf decor, and a spectacular view of the high-rise apartments towering over us.

Patrick shook his head and looked away. I stared down at my beer. We weren't seeing eye to eye. Despite our friendship, there was always a rift between us: the rift between faith and reason, God and science, Creationism and the Big Bang.

For a long time, I thought I could be a fisher, not of men, but of my best friend. I hoped that by winsomely and courageously displaying my inspirational faith, I could reel Patrick in and bring him back to everlasting safe shores. But somewhere along the way, I accepted his atheism for what it was. He debated for the sheer joy of debating, while building a mental dam around his ever evolving, Theory of Everything, scientific mind that was fortified by an increasingly secular worldview. Nothing I could say would sway his opinions, and everything God-related would be struck down. After awhile, I grew frustrated with even trying. If he wanted to find every possible way to deny the existence of God, then what could I possibly say to change his thinking?

Despite this, even though he could be a jerk at times, Patrick frequently demonstrated that he genuinely cared for me, which is more than can be said for the majority of Christians who've come and gone in my life faster than cars in a fast food drive-thru. He wanted me to be happy, and he couldn't understand my inherited logic for why I restricted myself to live according to 2,000-year-old texts from parts of the world I've never visited.

What I really appreciated about our skirmishes though was how Patrick really forced me to think. In a twisted way, he cared enough to point out that, even in my late-20's, my spirituality was still infant-like. I had no rhyme or reason for why I believed. I just believed.

But not that night. A group of Patrick's friends also made an appearance at the biergarten. They were all freethinkers, like him. Most were ex-Christians, and some even volunteered for a local anti-religion foundation. We moved our table closer to theirs. Away from the worms. Now I would be the one squirming.

"Hey, everyone! This is my friend Dave. He's a Christian," Patrick introduced me with enough snark in his voice to communicate that he'd already had one too many drinks.

You know how, when you place a worm on a fishhook, it dangles helplessly before you cast it into the water? That's how I felt in that moment: like live bait in a conversation with stout atheists. I hit the water and immediately knew I was in too deep. The discussion quickly and aggressively turned to how religion wasn't just wrong, but even respect for religion was wrong. They talked about atheist thinkers like Richard Dawkins, Sam Harris, and Christopher Hitchens, who had dug tunnels through Christianity's claims and placed God's Word on equal footing with nursery rhymes. It wasn't just a feeding frenzy on my beliefs: they dragged me through endless rounds of scientific discourse and buried me with their philosophical arguments. They had no problem crushing my rationales for my faith.

Being outnumbered six to one and with little wiggle room, I felt like a spineless invertebrate in my convictions, with no backbone to help me speak up for what and why I believed. In true introverted fashion, I buried myself in my thoughts and looked up at the high-rise apartments towering over us.

That was the moment when I realized the Rod Flanders-like bubble I had been living had just burst wide open. We lived in a progressive, postmodern Tower of Babel. We may have all been speaking English, but we weren't speaking the same language.

The problem was much more profound and rooted much deeper than any worm could crawl to. Atheism isn't the problem; the problem is ex-Christians who have a distorted, know-it-all understanding of the Bible. We live in a culture where the mission field is increasingly made up of ex-Christians.

I realized that if I truly wanted my best friend to bite on Christianity, the Bible—even with its timeless wisdom—was the wrong bait if I wanted to hook, line, and sink a freethinker. If there were any chance of netting my best friend, I would have to become a bookworm and do some digging myself.

While unearthing a variety of new spiritual content during *52 Churches in 52 Weeks*, I had started to listening to a number of audio sermons from Tim Keller. As my dating life paralleled with my spiritual side, Keller provided deep insights that was miles ahead of the typical Christian dating advice out there for young Christians. In fact, it was his sermon on love that I listened to before my very first church date with Rachel.

In addition to addressing the very questions that many single young adult Christians have, Keller was also able to articulate the problems we face in an age and culture of skepticism. Having been raised in a church where questions were swept away, I found his confidence and intellectual spin on the Bible to be infinitely refreshing. Through his sermons, he was able to clearly articulate exactly what it means to be a Christian in today's progressive world was.

Keller wasn't like other megachurch pastors I'd heard who enjoyed the Southern comforts of the Christian cocktail in the Bible Belt, where even the cats and dogs seem to be Charismatic. No, Keller had planted a church in the epicenter of New York City to welcome a melting pot of believers and skeptics alike. He drew from both esteemed Biblical scholars and secular academic resources for his sermons, taking on heavy-hitting objections to faith by explaining the Bible and its lessons through intellectual reasoning, wisdom, and even humor.

He also wasn't afraid to demonstrate his faith by appearing in Q&A sessions with some of New York's most intense interrogators. One such interview that stood out for me was with Martin Bashir, who had recently annihilated megachurch pastor Rob Bell for his controversial views on heaven and hell. He made the pastor gulp so much, not since the Fall of

Man had the world seen an Adam's apple drop so low. Bashir wasn't afraid to put pressure on Keller, grilling him with some of life's hardest questions: "With all the suffering in the world, how could there be God?" "With the reprehensible behavior of Christians over the centuries, isn't the Christian Church the best proof against God?" "What am I supposed to make of Old Testament texts about murder and concubines, and this bizarre Book of Revelation?"

Having willingly put himself in the hot seat, Keller articulated a defense of the Christian faith that appealed to reason. Were all of his answers perfect? No. But instead of dodging, he stood up as an example for what he believed.

During one such talk, he asked a very simply question of his own that was aimed at skeptics: "Why would you not want Christianity to be true?"

. . .

Redeemer Presbyterian Church (East Side) at Hunter College in New York City
September 26, 2015 – 10:30 A.M. Classical Worship Service

This was a big day for me. My plan was to go to the core of the Big Apple, driving through New York traffic to see Tim Keller preach. Then, after the service, I would head to Philadelphia to join what was expected to be a two-million-person crowd for Pope Francis's first papal visit to the United States. Two of the most popular heads of their respective denominations in one day. It was almost too much to fathom.

There was just one problem: with Redeemer Presbyterian Church, I was taking a gamble as to whether I would see Keller preach. Redeemer had no regular church home, so it rented space in three different locations in the city, and the pastors would alternate between them. So which location would Keller be speaking at this morning? I didn't know.

When it comes to renowned churches, it can sometimes be difficult to find out ahead of time if a specific popular preacher will be presiding at a specific service, particularly if the church has multiple locations. At one megachurch in Georgia, I called to ask where their celebrity pastor would be preaching that Sunday, and the receptionist immediately became defensive and wouldn't give me an iota of information. Then, when I called another megachurch in Southern California, they were more than willing to help, even transferring me to the pastor's personal secretary. I figured that when it came to Keller, Redeemer wouldn't give me a New York minute if I tried to find out ahead of time. After all, Keller had specifically stated in interviews that his first obligation was to be a pastor of a church. Becoming a tourist attraction for Christians was not what he wanted.

Still, I felt certain that for this project to be a success, I'd have to see both Keller and Francis preach in person. I would simply have to have faith that God would lead me to the right place.

Dreading dealing with traffic in a city of six million people, I drove into The City That Never Sleeps early in the morning in the hopes that at least a few would be asleep. I found a rare free parking space a few blocks from Central Park, then strolled along 69th Street before coming across Redeemer's "R" logo taped to the glass doors of Hunter College.

I had arrived about an hour and a half early, so after I passed through the building's metal detector, I asked the security guard outside the locked auditorium if I could take some pictures before the service started.

Bad idea.

This apparently concerned the guard enough that he left his post and returned with one of New York's Finest. I had raised their suspicions, and now I had to explain the 52 Churches in 52 Weeks project and why I had arrived so early to the female officer. After realizing I was no threat, the officer escorted me to the building's third floor to a room where Redeemer served refreshments before and after service. During our walk, the officer hinted that after 9/11, law enforcement could never be too careful. Given the size of the crowd that Redeemer pulls in every week, there was a police presence on every floor.

An hour later, the doors opened. Each Redeemer service offers a different musical theme that varies between contemporary, classical, and jazz. For this gathering, the auditorium was filled with the sounds of violins playing classical music as parishioners drifted in. In a unique twist on most worship service arrangements, the ushers were located at the very front of the auditorium, forcing service-goers to walk toward the stage if they wanted a bulletin.

When I looked in the bulletin, I was extremely disappointed to see that Keller's name was not listed as presiding at this service. I had come so far to see him, and for a moment, I seriously contemplated exiting the church and trying my luck at one of the other two locations. But I reminded myself that seeing Keller shouldn't be the point. I forcibly shut my mind up and re-centered my thinking on Christ's message, no matter who was preaching about it.

Toward the middle of the service, a younger pastor came out to give the sermon. He was of Asian descent and dressed to the nines in a *Men In Black*—esque suit and Bill Gates-style rimmed glasses. His public speaking was highly polished, even more so than his varnished shoes.

The sermon focused on the Bible's finality, with Christ's death finalizing prophecy as the final sacrifice to purify us of our sins. The young pastor stated that Christianity is different from other religions, in that other faiths require believers to climb to God, whereas Christianity is about a God who came down to us.

He then transitioned to talking about the implications of Adam and Eve residing naked and unashamed in the Garden of Eden. For a time, they were perfectly comfortable with who they were and did not seek more. Yet the moment they turned from God through the bite heard 'round the world, they decided for themselves what was right and what was wrong. His point was that our contemporary mindset encourages us to believe that there is a rational explanation for everything. In the modern secular world, we've kicked God out of our gardens, and yet we still realize that something is missing. Something within us says that we are not accepted by the world, making us feel naked and ashamed. We see this with how traditional values seem to be at fault. The modern Western world has embraced the narrative that we have to express our individual selves and embrace our personal dreams in order to succeed. If we don't do this, we're somehow seen as incomplete people. The pastor hypothesized that's why so many people come to New York: to pursue their dreams and make it on Wall Street, Broadway, or Madison Square Garden. There is a sense that the Big Apple will eat you up and spit you back out if you don't fulfill your dreams.

Despite everything the pastor said, I left the service feeling that I had been spit out. Instead of immediately jumping in my car to weave through millions of people just to see the pope—adding a big-name Christian celebrity to my project—I settled in at a bar a few blocks down the street. I wanted to just stop for a bit. I had to silence my mind, re-center my thinking, and remind myself that this day should never have been about Tim Keller or Pope Francis. It should have been about Christ's message, no matter who was onstage speaking about it.

I couldn't stop thinking about the last time Patrick had visited my place. We had been in my backyard, and he was picking apples from my apple tree. Looking back on it now, it was a symbolic moment. The apples still attached to the tree looked fine, while those that had fallen were turning black with mold and decay. Patrick had picked one from the tree that looked perfect, but when he bit into it, he immediately spit it out. We looked inside and saw worm trail had infected it, starting the decay from the inside out. He dropped it to the ground, alongside the other spoiling apples.

I was haunted by the image of the apple—not just the one Patrick had bit into that day, but also the forbidden fruit that Adam and Eve had first tasted. What had happened to that apple? Adam and Eve had probably discarded it, and it spiraled downward—like our sinful natures—to the ground below. When sin wormed its way into the world, letting us fall prey to the maggots and worms, did that fruit become the first thing to die? If so, did it also plant the first seeds, so that one day something new would arise?

THE PRI¢E OF THE PRO$PERITY GO$PEL
"INDEPENDENT" PENTECOSTAL CHURCH • CENTRAL ARKANSAS

At a young age, I witnessed the Yodely Guy plunge off a cliff.
This was quite a traumatic sight for a young child watching *The Price Is Right* every weekday morning. Luckily, the 2D-scrolling cartoon mountain climber didn't meet his demise to a soundtrack of yodeling music every day, but as I aged, it seemed to happen more frequently. Contestants would incorrectly guess the price of random kitchen appliances, forcing him to reach a 25-step peak, topple over, and then fall to a soundtrack of breaking glass and audience sighs. The contestants would droop their heads and walk away, knowing they had caused Yodely Guy to cross over into the Great Swiss Mountain in the Sky, all because they were miles off regarding the price of a Swiffer.

While the New Testament never mentioned Rod Roddy asking the Son of God to "Come on down" and be the next contestant on *The Price Is Right*, all four gospels describe the time Christ went up against the merchants of His day.

When Jesus entered the temple and took a look behind Door Number One, He found the moneychangers had turned God's house of prayer into a bunch of pricing games. That's when the Anger Danger of Our Lord and Savior went over the edge like a game of *Cliff Hangers*. He played *Punch-a-Bunch* with the merchant stands, went *Bonkers* by overturning the tables, and "making a whip of cords, drove them all out of the temple with the sheep and oxen." If Bob Barker had been there, he would have ended the episode with that classic line, "Help control the pet population. Have your animal sacrifices spayed or neutered."

While the moneychangers get a bad rap for being greedy, it's possible they didn't intentionally set out to deceive people. After all, you have to remember the number one rule of real estate is location, location, location. Back then, travelers were obliged to purchase local animals for sacrifice, as it would have been too hard to bring them from home. Having a stall located in or around the temple would have made business as *Easy as 1–2–3*. But somewhere along the way, the commercial activity snowballed out of control. Jesus set things straight that day, but after seeing His reaction to commerce occurring at a place of worship, one has to wonder why any church would even consider going down such a *Golden Road*.

Unfortunately, this happens more often than you'd think.

While on my quest to visit a variety of churches throughout the country, I found that the vast majority of megachurches, basilicas, and cathedrals— all of which I enjoyed visiting and considered Biblically sound in their doctrine—had a gift shop or bookstore just a few steps away from the worship area. One renowned church actually required worshipers to walk through its gift shop in order to reach the sanctuary and attend its services. I saw church logos plastered across souvenir pins, spoons, magnets, mugs, coasters, pens, pencils, books, bookmarks, postcards, calendars, toys, DVDs, and oils, just to name a few products readily available for purchase before even opening a hymnal. One in-church bookstore even featured a variety of overpriced images depicting Christ's crucifixion, all with price tags strung around His nailed hands. It was shocking to see the neighboring Penitent and Impenitent Thieves had been replaced by signs for Visa and MasterCard as acceptable forms of payment.

Jesus dying on the cross for your sins: $0. The eleven-inch crucifix depicting His death at the church bookstore: $149.95. The intellectual juxtaposition of a church selling Christ merchandise, despite His opposing commercialization in the temple: Priceless.

And then there was the prosperity gospel. After visiting the largest megachurch in the U.S., I found that despite my initial concerns, I actually enjoyed the experience. I didn't have any problems with a megapastor owning a big house after penning dozens of *The New York Times* best sellers. Such megapastors were successful,they were doing something with their lives, and they'd earned it. So what if they enjoyed the material success that went with it? Wouldn't you? I was sure they were also contributing millions to charities and outreach programs without pompously gloating about their philanthropy. I ignored the criticism, since I had experienced, firsthand, how uplifting messages of hope were more encouraging than the fire-and-brimstone sermons of my youth. These megapastors' mega-watt smiles could provide a beacon of hope for people when they were in a spiritual fog.

Yet every time I walked out of such megachurches with their spinning golden globes, light shows, and cloudy fog machines, I left with a markdown on my inner peace. In-church bookstores were front-and-center at the main entrances, with stacks upon stacks of Christian books ready to be plucked from the bargain bin. Church lobbies featured posters of their smiling preacher's pearly whites, promoting the latest book just outside the cross-less worship areas. Communion, which is supposed to symbolize the body and blood of Christ, was handed out in mass-produced pre-filled cups that looked like they had been bulk ordered from the nearest warehouse store. During services, associate pastors would rattle off Bible passages during mini-sermons on how tithing could lead to greater blessings. Ushers would pass out giant gray buckets for the collection, and every time I saw them, I couldn't help but think back to the moment at one megachurch, when I witnessed the sweet older woman seated next to me morph into Bruce Lee as she karate-chopped her husband's wrist the moment he moved to grab his wallet during the offering. They were enjoying the show, but there was no way they would contribute to our contemporary idolatrous worship of the golden calf—or, as we know it, the greenback cash cow.

I assumed these churches hadn't intentionally set out to deceive anyone. They were simply preaching a message that speaks to the peaks of Christianity by helping people in their darkest valleys. But deep down, I sensed that things were fishier than the aquariums in the church bookstores.

After visits to such churches—which generally asked for my contact information in exchange for a free swag bag—I often received letters thanking me for coming. I started to add this to my test-within-a-test, hoping to see how different churches followed up with visitors. But a few months after visiting one specific rich and famous prosperity gospel church, I got a rather unique letter. It came in an envelope bearing images of its preacher's familiar smiling face. In an enlarged italic font, it said, *"INSIDE: Experience God's blessings in your life today!"*

When I opened it, an enclosure with big bold letters greeted me with: "God wants to bless you **MORE THAN YOU KNOW!**" Below were checkboxes next to amounts of $25, $50, $100, and a blank $_____ fill in.

The accompanying letter doubled down on the use of bold letters, proclaiming, **"God's Word tells us in Psalm 35:27, 'Let them continually say, 'Great is the LORD, Who delights in blessing His servant'... Look at what this verse says—God wants you to say that He delights in blessing you. Isn't that amazing?"** The letter continued, now with the words underlined: "He wants you to continually remind yourself that it's His pleasure to bless you."

I looked through the material a few times, trying to understand what the catch was. Where was the money going? Other than a vague mention of sharing "The message of HOPE around the world," there was nothing.

With this, my attitude toward the prosperity gospel began to change. Everything about it seemed to be promoting the selfish idea of "What's in it for me *right now*? What do I get back for believing in God? Is there anything more substantial than that whole wishy-washy thing about eternal salvation?"

"I'll take 'Slippery Slope' for 500, Alex."

How would Christ react to churches that capitalize off His message, turning hope for everlasting life into hope for His Midas Touch? How far will churches push Almighty God to the side in favor of the Almighty Dollar? How often do churches put a dollar sign in front of someone's $oul?

My yodeling tune began to change.

I started to suspect that such churches were encouraging believers to climb to the top of the prosperity gospel summit, only to topple off its slippery slope when the dreams they fed off of couldn't be fulfilled.

And I was about to see the worst of it.

. . .

"Independent" Pentecostal Church in Central Arkansas
September 29, 2015 – 7:30 P.M. Worship Service

I wasn't looking for the prosperity gospel. The prosperity gospel found me.

While driving along the interstate in Arkansas, I came across the most extravagant-looking church I had seen during all my travels. It was a gargantuan worship building, so imposing, so rich, I had to pull off and take a closer look. I couldn't even take a picture of the entire thing, due to its sheer size.

The steeple was proudly perched nearly 200 feet above ground. A clock tower loomed, supported by eight giant Corinthian columns. The church's name was elaborately written in gold on an ornate sign in front of landscaped scrubs in the shape of the church's initials. When I wandered past the connected school, I came upon a massive LED billboard that could have been mistaken for a NASDAQ stock ticker. The screen informed me that Tuesday night services would begin at 7:30—just an hour away. It seemed I would be making an impromptu church visit.

"I'm going to church tonight," I texted Rachel. "You'll never guess what denomination it is."

"What?" she replied.

"Pentecostal," I said, attaching a picture of the massive church before me.

"What!? You're not!"

Rachel had been Pentecostal for a time. After falling head over heels in love and saying "I do," she moved to Texas and converted to her then-husband's Pentecostal faith. Talk about a culture shock: they spoke in tongues, fainted at the pastor's very touch, and placed a great deal of emphasis on the Holy Spirit. She was never able to comprehend it, despite living the lifestyle for years.

And it was indeed a lifestyle.

Per the denomination's literal interpretation of 1 Timothy 2:9–10, which says, "Women [are] to dress modestly, with decency and propriety, adorning themselves, not with elaborate hairstyles...but with good deeds, appropriate for women who profess to worship God," Pentecostal women are discouraged from wearing makeup or jewelry. They cannot cut their hair and must wear it in a bun. And all women are required to wear full-length skirts that fall below the knee at all times.

When I looked at Facebook photos from Rachel's past, she looked like a happy housewife from *Little House on the Prairie*. But in reality, her life was far from happy. Her husband's insecurities led him to use religion as an authoritative measure to make her obey him, both in appearance and in action. She felt enslaved and like she was living a lie. After three strikes of emotional abuse, manipulation, and physical confrontations, she had enough of their *Family Feud* and made an escape for it with the kids.

Now two years later, I was in for the steal, looking to win the jackpot into her heart. If I was going to be the number one answer for her and the kids, relating to her Pentecostal experience was something that I didn't need to ask a survey of 100 people to do.

"You have no idea what you're in for," she warned.

She was right.

I aimed to remain objective and unbiased throughout the experience. After 47 church visits, I felt that I had done quite well in remaining rational and reserving judgment on unfamiliar churches or denominations. After all, a one-time visit could never help me accurately judge an entire community.

However, during this visit, remaining unbiased and fair-minded proved to be almost impossible for me.

The setting was more like a gala for wealthy VIPs than a traditional church service. The ushers were dressed in elaborate high-class tuxedos, giving white-glove service to valet park any dignitary's vehicle who pulled up to the porte-cochère. The men were all dressed in suits and ties; the women, in modest skirts with their hair in a bun.

I had never before felt such a sense of shame for what I was wearing. Not having planned on visiting a church on a Tuesday night, I came in unshaven and wearing a striped sweatshirt and jeans with holes in the knees.

Given how underdressed I was, I received some odd glances. Since I didn't have an engraved invitation, I decided to sneak in and quickly take a seat in the back in order to avoid suspicion. I was a little worried that someone would kick me out for not looking the part.

The sanctuary was enormous. As I later learned on their website, the marble floors were made of "Biblical stone" from Jerusalem. A giant statue of Gabriel, trumpet in-hand, stood at the front of the church, with four colossal Corinthian columns bookending the sides.

When the service began, I initially appreciated all the movement around me. People were fired up to be there and had no problem shouting their excitement. As drums beat and people sang hymns, some individuals randomly jumped out of their seats and ran down the aisles like contestants on *The Price Is Right,* running around the church for no other apparent reason but to show excitement.

But things took a detour for me when a man gave testimony about a $2,000 medical bill he hadn't been able to afford. He prayed really hard, and when he called the hospital, hoping to convince them to knock off a $100 or so, he was told that his bills had been paid in full.

The congregation responded by hooting and hollering in excitement. People rose to their feet and shouted, "Hallelujah!" and "Amen!" Several men in front of me exited their pews and ran victory laps around the church.

The man kept shouting, "If He'll do it for me, He'll do it for you! If He'll do it for me, He'll do it for you! If He'll do it for me, He'll do it for you!"

Throughout all the hoopla, I quietly sat back in my seat, bothered, thinking, *What kind of message is this sending, especially to those who end up needing to pay their medical bills in full? "Am I not praying hard enough? Am I lesser Christian?"*

After the man's testimony, approximately 50 children came up to sing, while 15 of the tuxedo-clad ushers lined up with collection plates. Although there was no formal arm-twisting for money, all the pomp and circumstance certainly felt like it was heart-twisting you to put something in the bucket.

Then came the sermon. The pastor was built like a barn and bellowed his thoughts in a deep-bellied accent. What was particularly interesting about this sermon though was how disjointed it was. The preacher prefaced his remarks by praying that whatever was in his heart would be what he preached.

He initially focused on the idea that all Scripture was inspired by God, and that it was intended to make us profitable and to provide correction. Then he threw up a PowerPoint slide, bearing the bold and underlined question, "**What Could God CORRECT in My Life Today That Would Carry Me to GREATER BLESSINGS?**"

I assumed he meant beyond correcting his inappropriate use and abuse of capital letters. He continued with that thought, saying that as we journey through life, we must submit to God in the hope that He would make our load lighter. The more we pray to God, the more blessings and victories we'll receive, whether they be financial, medical, or personal.

Then he spiraled over to Paul, took a Y-turn with Timothy, and detoured over to what's wrong with churches that invite parishioners to "Come as you are, leave as you came." After all, "If you go to a church where you get your ear tickled, you're in the wrong church!" Apparently, I was going to the wrong church with Rachel, because First Free Church's motto was "Come as you are." The pastor followed this up with a story about the extremely religious King Hezekiah, boasting that God rewarded him by making him the richest man in Jerusalem.

At this point, the decibel level within the church was at a low point, so to fire up the masses again, the preacher changed the subject and started shouting about how the gates of hell shall not prevail against the truth:

"We know the direction this country is going. It is very possible they will take away tax exemption for churches that will not open their doors and arms to all people, regardless of what they believe. It's amazing to see Muslims having more freedom and rights than Christians do. It's a sad day we're in. Somebody said, "How can they ever take our churches away from us?" I'll tell you how they can take them away real fast. All they would have to do is for you to say not to open your doors to all public, and then we're gonna tax you. Anybody ever hear of taxes? Anybody ever hear of property tax? Can anyone imagine the property tax on this church? If you think about how this building that God has given us would be taxed, you'll see how close we are to losing it. Well, I got news for ya. We're not worshiping a building!"

There was so much here to unpack. First of all, I'm not even going to touch on the Muslim reference, which is an entirely different subject for a different book. But even beyond that, I was rather disturbed by this rant about tax exemption, since it seemed so out of place.

Later, I did a brief Google search on the church, and two local articles came up that were both related to taxes. In one, the head pastor was quoted as saying that he was just a church employee who received a W-2 and paid taxes just like any other preacher. Then, six years after that first interview, the local media reported that the local government had reversed a rare tax exemption for him and eight other local preachers when it was discovered they were not actually paying property taxes on their homes. So what's going on here?

I agree that churches should be tax exempt, as having to pay taxes could destroy an actual, legitimate church that relies on offerings (rather than the commercial activities like those I mentioned earlier). But when a pastor isn't even properly disclosing his own income to local tax officials and then rattling up a congregation to side with him in his personal tax battles, you have to wonder: what is he really preaching?

To close out the sermon, the pastor lifted his nose and asked the congregation, "Why do you dress the way you dress? Can we be more consistent with our walk with God? Can God correct our course? Thank God for holiness. Thank God for clean-shaven men and holy-dressed women. Thank God for the holy anointing of the Holy Spirit. Thank God we still believe the Bible that teaches women to wear long hair. Thank God for the truth!"

Then the preacher called for all the men to come forward for an altar call. I stayed in the back, too perturbed at this point to want to have anything to do with what was going on around me. As I sat in my pew, surrounded by women in their bobby-pinned hairdos and beneath-the-knee dresses, the preacher thundered, "It takes a real man of God to be up here!" I rolled my eyes, more interested in looking for a camel that could fit through the eye of a needle.

Any attempts at remaining unbiased had come crashing down a long time ago. I wasn't so much upset at Pentecostalism, since this church was independent from national Pentecostal organizations—and thus could keep its income statements confidential. I was more upset about the influence of a prosperity gospel that treats prayers like Plinko chips, where one could hope they'd land in a $2,000 slot. The emphasis was on money, tax exemptions, and "GREATER BLESSINGS." Forget Galilee. It felt like Jesus had walked atop a Sea of Liquid Assets.

Maybe I'm treading in dangerous waters. All throughout *52 Churches in 52 Weeks*, nothing really upset me when it came to other churches. But this was different. Like Christ showed us at the cleansing of the temple, actions speak louder than words when it comes greed and corruption within His Father's house, and He wasn't afraid to ruffle some feathers to expel it.

So yeah. This church got me pretty riled up. I don't have any feel-good Jesus-y comments to wrap up this chapter with and leave you feeling comforted with warm fuzzies. Maybe I could jot something down about how He paid the full price of our salvation, all so that we can have a down payment on an eternal home. I could put a positive spin on this whole encounter.

But the truth is, I'm still mad about it, which is why I'm still ripping into a church that insulted me and blinded its members with promises of gold. If this church wants to play dice with God's Word—the same book that coined the phrase "Money is the root of all evil"—you better hope you don't roll snake eyes. Eve can tell you what happened when she came face-to-face with those two pips.

So here I am, just another Yodely Guy wandering through life. I've been dropped face-first on the ground and left broken and shattered in the bottommost pits of sin, as the losing horn blasts in my mind. I don't have all the right answers, but I do know that I don't need a brand-new car to in order to believe in God. I just keep going. I keep persevering. I keep marching to the drum of my one God.

And that's why I need God more than ever.

CHURCH 49:
HELLO FROM THE OTHER SIDE OF THE POND

SADDLEBACK CHURCH • LAKE FOREST, CALIFORNIA

When you drive over 26,000 miles—450 hours in the driver's seat—all by yourself, you have some time to look under the hood of life and overthink. You also find plenty of time to listen to Adele and blurt out your own made-up song lyrics to her melodies: "Hello God, it's me. I was driving to California dreaming of who I used to be, zigzagging across the country, younger and free. Listening to one particular song on auto-repeat."

When you're doing some serious soul searching and looking for answers to life's greatest questions, you tend to flood the engine of your mind with your own personal game of 20 Questions. Why am I here? Why am I traveling so much? What am I learning from this? Is spending this much time and money just to go to church really worth it? What am I doing with my small, ordinary, non-famous life? Would it have been better if I had tried something else, like learning to speak with a British accent and becoming a lovable late-night comedian who sings carpool karaoke with Adele?

At some point in our lives, most of us hit a fork in the road, with no sense of direction for where we're going in life. With no GPS signal, we simply engage cruise control and make our way through the predictability of our daily routines, driving the same streets to work, where we interact with the same coworkers, eat the same thing for lunch every day, and look forward to the same mythical weekend where all hopes for fun, excitement, or relaxation reside.

"Jesus, Take the Wheel" we pray in our best Carrie Underwood inner voice, hoping that our lives will just magically have some meaning. But when we don't contribute, nothing changes, and we go about our lives like a car flag just flapping in the wind.

It often seems like heaven is a million miles away. Does God really hear us from the other side? When we cling to Model-T past thinking, our dreams and potential fly by in the passing lane. It's no secret that both of us—you reading and me writing—are running out of time.

When you're traveling from Point A to Point B while seeing places and things you've never seen before, something changes within you. Whereas the Magi had the Star of Bethlehem, I had Google Maps pointing me in the direction of my next weekly visit as I sought something higher in life— some kind purpose.

My journey involved a lot of driving, and after passing the umpteen-millionth minivan with those stick-figure family decals on the back window, it got a little repetitive. But inside, I felt like I had been given a green light to do something more with my life. I no longer felt like there was an 18-wheeler of spiritual freight on top of me that would have required semitruck shoulders to carry. Instead, I was leaving my skid mark on the world, hoping to inspire others by leaving something behind. My senses were heightened in a way they had never been before. Like a new car, everything felt shiny and smelled fresh again. I was a wide-eyed wanderer, more aware of spiritual blind spots, and I was finally on the home stretch in my adventure in faith.

Somewhere along the way, I realized that God wasn't done with me yet. We're not brought into this world to wake up, go to work, and die. Adventure nurtures the soul, and in my case, I finally felt healthy and whole for the first time in years.

For too long, I had been tire-kicking what I could be. I was past due for a spiritual tune-up, needing to shift out of neutral and head toward something worthwhile. I was looking for a purpose-driven life, and I was now heading to just the place to help me find it.

. . .

Saddleback Church in Lake Forest, California
October 3, 2015 – 7:00 P.M. Worship Service

Having driven from the hustle and bustle of New York City all the way to the sandy beaches of Orange County, I was now saying hello to the other side of the country. I rolled into the parking lot of Saddleback Church after a 48-hour cross-country drive—and like 20 different McDonald's drive-thrus along the way.

Considering how *52 Churches in 52 Weeks* was recycling the scrap from my past and refurbishing the interior of my faith, I was hoping to hear Saddleback's senior pastor, Rick Warren, preach this Saturday night. Warren had gained global fame for penning A Purpose Driven Life in 2005, a book that sold over 30 million copies and was on *The New York Times* Best Seller list for 90 weeks. The book takes readers on a 40-day spiritual joyride and could be best described as a road map for Christian living in the 21st century. It's considered one of the most influential Christian books of all-time, due to its popularity among ministers, and it propelled Saddleback into the limelight, making it one of the biggest megachurches in the world, with weekly attendance regularly topping 20,000. The church gained so much prominence, it opened campuses all throughout California and even ventured across international borders with locations in the Philippines, Hong Kong, Argentina, and Germany.

Unfortunately, on my drive over, I learned that Warren wouldn't be preaching the weekend I'd be visiting, but I was still curious what Saddleback was all about. The church was in the middle of a series of sermons by several highly respected speakers, apologists, and social critics it had invited. Saddleback was promoting the sermon series with the hashtag #GreatestQuestions.

Walking around, it looked like a sun-drenched, church paradise. Middle schoolers were practicing skateboard tricks in the parking lot, splashing waterfalls and water features set one at ease, and the cross played peekaboo through rows of towering palm trees.

As wonderful as the setting was, the staff was even better. I've said this before, but it bears repeating: most megachurches know how to welcome people. At least four different greeters took a moment to say hello before I even walked through the front doors. All the volunteers seemed to be accepting and appreciative. They made it a goal to put a smile on your face. You could tell this was a church community that expressed a desire to bring people into the Kingdom of Heaven.

With Warren away, this day's speaker was Dr. Os Guinness, an English social critic and world-renowned author. Interestingly, he is also the great-great-great grandson of the famous Dublin brewer, Arthur Guinness, who was a strong evangelical Christian. His faith and beliefs were what gave the Guinness business its principles of generosity and social responsibility.

Yet even with this impressive pedigree, Os was born to medical missionaries in China during World War II. He was sent back to England for school, where he developed a passion for theology by reading what he called "An odyssey of books." He explored the arguments of freethinkers such as Friedrich Nietzsche, Jean-Paul Sartre, and Albert Camus, as well as those of Christian authors like C.S. Lewis, G.K. Chesterton, and Blaise

Pascal. Through his intellectual approach and way of thinking, Os eventually came to the conclusion that Christian doctrine was true.

Unlike most Christian apologists who preach to win arguments, Os Guinness prefers to win the hearts and minds of his listeners by staying true to the gospel message. With his charming British accent and frequent scholarly references, I felt the urge to pick up a cup of tea.

Guinness's talk this day was on the subject of "What is my purpose?" As he put it, there is a great deal of emphasis on the philosophy of YOLO— short for "You only live once." He explained that this is essentially a bastardization of Solomon's injection in Ecclesiastes 8 to "Eat, drink, and be merry," where people are living without a sense of meaning.

Guinness was adamant that we need to get away from the sloppy idea of thinking that all religions are the same, and he instead broke down the world's major faiths, worldviews, and philosophies into three "families," all which give very different answers to the question "What is my purpose?"

First there are the Eastern religions, such as Hinduism and Buddhism, as well as various New Age faiths. Their answer to the question of purpose could be summarized in two words: "Forget it." The world, time, and our lives are all bound up in a giant wheel. The problem isn't what happens when you die; the problem is what happens when you come back around again. The goal is to escape the wheel. As a result, freedom isn't about the pursuit of individuality, but rather gaining freedom from individuality.

The second "family" comprises the secularist worldview, which sees purpose as a do-it-yourself project. Like Atlas, the whole world is upon our shoulders. This view holds that we're the product of pure chance, and while the world may be our oyster, it is also much more demanding and often leads to a cruel, bleak future.

Then there is the Biblical view of the Abrahamic religions (Christianity, Judaism, and Islam), which find life's purpose through creation and calling. Because we are created in God's image, we are called to be who we ought to be. We change, grow, live dynamically, and are shaped by God's word— and, in the case of Christians specifically, the good news of Jesus Christ.

Guinness unpacked the notion of a calling, using the Parable of the Talents, which appears in Matthew 24 and Luke 19. In the story, a master puts his servants in charge of his goods while he's away on vacation. When he returns, the master evaluates his servants' stewardship based on how wisely they invested the talents he had given them. The master rewards the servant who invested and profited from his share, but harshly judges the servant who played it safe.

When it comes to serving God through one's calling, Os called it nonsense to think that everyone needs to become a minister, monk, or nun. We are all born with gifts and acquire skills. Our gifts may be in hospitality, business management, or even having a great British accent or singing voice. God won't give everyone the same exact vision, but we are all still called to use the talents we've been given to reach people in ways that the institutionalized church may not. In that regard, you can take your talents and multiple them by five, by ten, or 100. One's calling can be very practical in everyday life. By doing so, it gives one a sense of purpose.

In the grand scheme of things, we're only here for the blink of an eye. One day, the Lord will return and ask, "What have you done with the talents that I've given you?"

What will be your answer?

CHURCH 50:
SHE LOVES ME, SHE LOVES ME NOT
WAYFARERS CHAPEL • RANCHO PALOS VERDES, CALIFORNIA

My first crush was Tricia. She was "The One" in first grade: Slimer-green eyes, Barbie-blonde hair, and still had all of her baby teeth intact. She was super cute with a smile that could Lite-Brite up my world and mush my heart into Play-Doh. I loved her, cooties and all. I also loved Hi-C Ecto Cooler, so that should tell you a lot about my emotional maturity at that stage of my life.

Between daydreams of becoming the fifth Ghostbuster and starring in a Tonka truck commercial, I prayed that God would send down the fluffy pink Love-A-Lot Bear so that she could use her double-hearted belly badge to Care Bear Stare Tricia into magically falling in love with me. I had faith that God, in His infinite matchmaking wisdom and connections with the Care Bears, would set us up and we'd eventually get married in a really fancy church.

I figured my chances had improved when, the following school year, my mom bought me Mr. Sketch scented markers. As long as I played my markers right, I was sure that just one whiff of my blueberry-scented marker would impress Tricia, and then it'd only be a matter of time before we'd be sitting in a tree, K-I-S-S-I-N-G. First comes love, then comes marriage, then comes a baby in a baby carriage. Specifically, there would be four babies, all boys, which I'd name after the Ghostbusters. I had it all figured out.

But Tricia didn't fall head over heels in love with me at the lingering scent of my markers, Egon Spengler didn't become the name of my third offspring (yet), and my childhood dream of matrimony with Tricia blew up more than the Stay Puft Marshmallow Man if he had starred in a Michael Bay movie.

Now, before I go any further, I'd like to add a sidebar to the men reading this: when you're courting a woman, it is the man's job to make the love story unfold. The experience of being courted is what engages the woman's emotions—not scented markers (surprising, I know). Part of that experience is the anticipation, the wonder, the curiosity of what's going to happen next. It's all about having a positive effect on a lady's emotions. You want them to feel that they've been swept off their feet, figuratively—or, in the case of Tarzan's Jane, literally. Having six-pack Tarzan abs also helps.

But when I was a wimpy seven-year-old with no game and regularly wiped my boogers underneath my desk, I didn't know this. Or have abs. Or have a firm grasp on how to tie my shoes. Or that I should just find a Kleenex for my boogers. But one thing I did have going for me was my ability to be bookish shy.

When our school sponsored a roller-skating night at the local roller rink, all I could think was, Finally. Since I didn't want to man up and approach Tricia directly, I was sure that God would act as my wingman by divinely orchestrating a situation where I could talk to Tricia.

In the View-Master of my imagination, I pictured her wiping out and God arranging for me to swoop in at the last minute, like a knight in shining He-Man underwear, rescuing her from the perils of a bruised butt. In my fantasy, Tricia would be eternally grateful and would go over to the DJ, where, for the small fee of a dollar, she would procure and then gift me the ultimate token of grade-school adoration: a tissue-paper flower.

Ah, yes. With its green chenille stem wrapped around a wrinkled piece of pink tissue paper, nothing better symbolized eternal love for those hopeless romantics who hadn't yet hit puberty. The boys were supposed to give the fake flowers to the girls, but for the popular boys, it was the girls who would give the flowers to the boys. Instead of risking embarrassment to the public perception of classmates thinking I had the hots for a girl, God could work His magic where the DJ would announce, "I have a flower to give away... To: Dave, From: Tricia," and the entire school would go, "oooOOOoooh!"

But as the night progressed, Tricia still hadn't arrived at the skating rink. I started mentally plucking at the petals in my head: *She loves me, she loves me not. She loves me, she loves me not.* I tried to distract myself by skating to the hip-hop beats of MC Hammer and Kris Kross while falling down more times than I could count. I kept glancing at the front door all night, waiting for the moment when Tricia would skate in so she could wipe out and I could catch her in the nick of time.

So I kept waiting.

And waiting.

And waiting.

After an hour and a half, the realization began to set in that she wasn't coming—probably because she couldn't afford it. After all, she hadn't lost any of her baby teeth yet, so the Tooth Fairy hadn't visited her to give her money. It seemed like a logical explanation.

The night ended without anything happening. A few weeks later, Tricia announced that her family was moving to Texas. I experienced heartbreak for the first time in my life and wallowed in my Frosted Flakes about the unfairness of life. After she moved away, I never saw her again.

I never did get that flower.

. . .

Wayfarers Chapel in Rancho Palos Verdes, California
October 4, 2015 – 10:00 A.M. Worship Service

Things never worked out with Tricia, but now, 25 years later, I had a new crush—three, in fact. As I stood outside of Wayfarers Chapel, the world's most romantic wedding destination, I couldn't help but think about what might soon unfold in the next chapter of my life.

Rachel was an addiction counselor, but even she couldn't cure me from the withdrawal symptoms I was experiencing—I missed her and the kids desperately. Before leaving for the final stretch of *52 Churches in 52 Weeks*, several of her friends and family members had started dropping hints that they considered us "official." Her friends were trying to convince me to move closer, her mom had started introducing us to friends as a couple, and a lifelong family friend took me aside one day and said, "I've seen this family for a long time, and you're exactly what they've been needing."

But it was the kids, Tony and Elle, who really made it clear that they wanted me to be a permanent fixture in their lives. A few days before I arrived at Wayfarers Chapel, Rachel had texted a picture from Tony's birthday celebration featuring all three of them waving to me. Despite visiting some of the world's most awe-inspiring churches, it was that picture that really captured my attention. It reminded me of something Tony had said before I left. Rachel and I were tucking him into bed, and as his head touched his Spider-Man pillow, he told me what he really wanted for his birthday: "Dave, I hope one day you're gonna marry Mom, and you'll be my dad!"

When a child says something like that, your entire universe shifts. You remember what it's like to dream again, because suddenly, you're someone else's dream. I knew then that I had to take the next step.

When the service began, I saw that Wayfarers Chapel's minister was wearing quite the unique wardrobe. Instead of the traditional all-black preacher's garb, he was decked out in a fashionable fuchsia clerical shirt, complete with tab collar. His stole was tye-dyed and contained so many colors, it could have caused Joseph's brothers to go colorblind.

Behind him was a stone alter with the words, "Our Father, Who Art in Heaven" carved into it. The church itself was all glass and was surrounded by towering redwood trees and soaring sea gulls. To the right was a panoramic view of the Pacific Ocean. You could look out the various windows and just know you're exactly where you need to be. There's a beautiful power and sacred feeling when the environment you're around uses God's creation as the framework for a worship place.

The liturgy was associated with the Swedenborgian Church, as Wayfarers Chapel is a national memorial to its founder, Emanuel Swedenborg. The chapel was built by Lloyd Wright, son of the famed architect Frank Lloyd Wright—who had constructed other churches I had visited—who aimed to emphasize the harmony between God's natural world and the inner world of the mind and spirit when he built this church.

At one point, the minister gave the congregation a minute to be still and reconnect with nature, "listening to the small voice that speaks to each of us from the wilderness," as he put it. A quiet trickling fountain located near the altar was the only source of sound in the chapel, and it created a tingling sense of relaxation that shivered down the spine. Even the later musical selections were calming, featuring a West Coast jazz vibe paired with relaxed tempos and light melodic tones.

For his sermon, the minister talked about the balance between our physical and spiritual natures. He quoted from Matthew: "The eye is the lamp of the body. If your vision is clear, your whole body will be full of light. But if your vision is poor, your whole body will be full of darkness. If then the light within you is darkness, how great is that darkness." As he explained, we humans process the world almost entirely through our eyes. However, the minister talked about ophthalmology, the study of the eye, in almost mystical terms, using it as a metaphor to shine a light on what's behind the scenes spiritually.

"If the eye is the lamp of your body, the eyes are windows to the soul."

After the service, my eyes were looking out over the seemingly endless ocean and infinite sky. I was surrounded by the chapel's gardens, which featured numerous plants and flowers, many of which were planted because they were mentioned in the Bible. As I considered all the botanical growth around me, I almost couldn't believe the spiritual growth spurts I had experienced over the past year.

That's the mysterious thing about growth: you can never actually see it happening. Growth is invisible in the moment and can only be measured over a period of time. It feels so gradual, like a bunch of caterpillars running in a 100-meter sprint and then get stuck in mud. But after some time and a whole lot of patience, you sprout from the dirt and bloom as something new, reaching heights you never could have dreamed of when you were a seed buried in darkness, yearning to see the light.

That's what the Christian change within me felt like that day. I felt wiser. Stronger. Smarter. Through this continuous, deep, and personal spiritual experience, I had been given a chance to see a whole new world. I now understood that the true essence of who I am is not restricted to my physical being. It can't be touched, smelled, or measured. There's an untapped strength that's growing stronger than ever before.

Like our Savior who died physically, but whose spiritual transcendence lives on, we can all positively impact those we encounter. Like a child picking dandelions and giving them away with a generous and considerate heart, Christ saw Himself as love and put it out into the world, giving it away freely.

The weekend before my big trip, Tony yelled "DAAAAAAVE!" when I pulled into the apartment complex where Rachel lived. He had stopped what he was doing and jumped out of the grass, sprinting toward me for a hug. Elle wasn't far behind him, excitedly rushing toward me on her miniature legs and with a fistful of dandelions in one hand. When I put Tony down from our hug, I pulled Elle in next, holding her and asking how she had been.

"Here you go," she exclaimed with a proud smile and outstretched arm. I took one of the oversized limp yellow flowers she offered and realized I had finally gotten my flower.

As we walked toward the apartment to see Rachel, Elle turned around and looked up at me like she had just watched one too many episodes of Full House featuring the Olsen twins. "Dude," she said before pausing with a puzzled look in her eyes, "you're supposed to give those to mom."

CHURCH 51:
THE PROMISED LAND OF MILK AND HUNNY
CHAPEL OF THE HOLY CROSS • SEDONA, ARIZONA

Despite what Charlton Heston may have led you to believe, Moses was never good with words. He even pointed this out to God back when He was still bad at picking disguises.

I read somewhere that there are two different types of people in the world: those who plan their Halloween costumes months in advance and those who put on some cat ears at the last minute. Apparently, God started out in the cat ears category.

When Moses fled to Mount Horeb to live under a rock, God decided to recruit him. But He knew that all His divine glory might freak out a mere human being like Moses, so God took a look at what was around Him and decided to appear before Moses as a talking burning bush. Now, this was no doubt impressive, and it was definitely a step up from that time He lay the cosmic smackdown on Jacob when He dressed up as a professional wrestler.

But this is God we're talking about, the omnipotent ruler of heavens and Earth. Surely He could whip up something better than a fern or *Nacho Libre?*

So God consulted the angels to help amp up the celestial effects the next time He spoke to Moses. When it was time to sign His John Hancock on the Ten Commandments, He went full out, going as a rumbling, quaking mountain that was consumed by smoke and fire as thunder rumbled and

267

lighting crashed around it.

This was waaaaaaaay better.

But as the Old Testament progressed, God got a little carried away with Himself and vowed to be the Omega of all future Halloween costume contests. He appeared to Ezekiel as some kind of giant chariot hurricane that mutated into a monstrous man/lion/ox/eagle creature with multiple heads rotating like a Macy's Thanksgiving Parade float set upon monster truck wheels. Oh yeah, and it was covered by eyes that shot rainbow beams. Look it up. After that one, I think the angels convinced God to tone it down a notch or two.

So back at Mount Horeb, God—disguised as a burning bush—didn't beat around the bush to tell Moses that he was His Main Man, would deliver the Children of Israel from slavery, and would lead them to the Promised Land of milk and honey.

But Moses pointed out that he was slow of speech and probably wasn't the right guy for the job. After all, how was a tongue-tied guy supposed to majestically tell Pharaoh, "Let my people go," when he had a fear of public speaking and three-syllable words?

So God asked him, "What's that in your hand?"

"It's a stick," replied Moses.

"Use that."

And so Moses used the stick and became the miracle worker of the day, delivering his people from enslavement. Through God's power, Moses' staff could transform into a snake, command the Red Sea to stand at attention, and even win wars when he raised it above his head, much to the chagrin of those closest to him whose noses had to do battle against his 40-year armpit perspiration.

But the real test for Moses wasn't the lack of Old Spice; it was the adversity of the wilderness. The Children of Israel whined, hungered, and thirsted. After everything they had seen, even after doing the Egyptian as the Red Sea drowned their pursuing enslavers, they still wanted to kill Moses. He cried out to God, "What do you want me to do for all these people? There's no water, no rivers, no Dasani vending machines—despite having exact change—and they're all dying of thirst. These people are ready to stone me!"

And again, God asked, "What's that in your hand?"

"A stick," Moses replied.

"Use it to hit that rock over there."

You don't need to be as dumb as a rock to know that rocks don't produce water. But Moses obeyed God's command and did it anyway. He got into a batting stance, took a home run-winning crack at it, and lo and behold, God decided to show-off. Sparkling water came gushing out, creating a spring so plentiful, it quenched the thirst of all.

Despite being slow of speech and literally stuck between a rock and a hard place, Moses trusted in God's plan and taught us all a lesson that could only be learned in the desert.

Actions certainly do speak louder than words.

. . .

Chapel of the Holy Cross in Sedona, Arizona
October 5, 2015 – 6:00 P.M. Taizé Prayer Service

During the first few months of *52 Churches*, when I started getting bored of churches within a close drive of my place, visiting Chapel of the Holy Cross became a pipedream for me. With time, it seemed inevitable that I'd eventually swing by.

When I finally drove into Sedona, the sky was clearly feeling under the weather. The clouds hovering above the local Walgreens seemed to be in desperate need of some Prozac. But clouds don't have wallets and lack the zen-like patience needed to wait in line for over-the-counter medication, so instead, they got emotional and cried showers, giving the dry, cracked ground some much-needed rainfall.

Then, almost on a dime, the weather had a mood swing, and the clouds parted, revealing endless blue skies and radiant white clouds. The sun beamed down on the red rock, giving off a brilliant orange glow that was brighter than a pumpkin wearing Donald Trump's TV makeup.

I parked in a valley and looked up the hill at a towering cross that appeared to have been driven into the bedrock like a giant Excalibur. The chapel was a powerful statement, a fortress of God that had been built right into the cliff. When I got out of my car, another patch of black clouds opened up, and the rain started to pour again. I made a dash for it, hiking up the steep incline to get shelter inside the chapel.

You can't climb a mountain without encountering some thorns along the way, and the ascent to the chapel included various forms of cacti, thorns, and shrubbery (no talking, burning bushes though). It was an interesting metaphor for life: living in sunshine all the time doesn't tell us much about ourselves, but a good storm will always demonstrate the stability of our foundations.

The chapel was buzzing with tourists who were also escaping the storm. Many were as awestruck as I was, talking in hushed voices about the marvelous structure and the various sculptures and tapestries. The sanctuary was surprisingly quaint, with the altar containing a sculpture of Jesus's face created by the chapel's founder, Marguerite Brunswig Staude. Behind the altar were wide glass windows that provided a panoramic view of Sedona's landscape. But in the middle of the nave—oddly, yet evidently on purpose—was a crucifix laid down on the floor.

The chapel was Catholic in faith, but according to Diocesan policy, they could not conduct liturgies at the chapel (liturgies could only be performed at a nearby parish church). Instead, the staff held Taizé prayer services every Monday night.

As my bulletin explained, the Taizé style of chant uses a sung prayer to quiet the mind and help the worshipper get lost in devotional energy. By frequently repeating the same refrains, it allows the silence of the heart to meet God in contemplative prayer. It's a style of prayer that comes from a monastic community in France that devotes itself to a life of prayer and simplicity.

The service was short, with a few gathering songs, Psalms, and a brief word from one of the staff members to prepare everyone for the Taizé chant, which would conclude the service. During the chant, we were instructed to take time for prayer, give gratitude, and place a candle before the crucifix laying on the ground. "There's so much in this world to pray for," she said. "So much."

The congregation sang the Taizé chant of "Oh Lord, hear my prayer" as, one-by-one, the congregants lined up near the back of the room and were handed a small tealight candle in a red glass cup. Many people were crying and using the time to reflect on loved ones. When I received my candle and held it in my hand, I felt a rush come over my body.

This was my burning bush moment. When this whole crazy quest started, I was at rock bottom in the lowest of valleys. My wish back then was to meet an amazing Christian woman, someone who could be my soul mate and laugh at my lame jokes. Now, as I walked to the cross, the flame flickering in my palm, I realized it was the first time I had manifested a prayer into an action. The candle was an illustrative sermon for what I had to become for the next step in my life. The hearts of Rachel and her children were in my hands, and I had to be careful to take such a responsibility seriously.

When I placed my candle next to the cross, I prayed to God, feeling grateful for His hand on the lessons I needed to help me get through my own personal desert, for meeting Rachel, and for His giving me a chance to be a Christian role model for Tony and Elle. They came into my life as I was finding my way out of my personal wilderness. Now, if all went right, I could complete their family. I could take this entire *52 Churches in 52 Weeks* experience and what I had learned from it and—like Christ had become for me—I could be their rock.

Salvation can be found in some strange places—places that you'd least expect. For Moses and for everyone in that chapel, we found it in a rock. All the candles were shining beacons to illuminate everyone's story in that chapel. Who knows what kind of stories were behind each of those candles. All I know is that whatever burdens may have been in those prayers, they'd been laid thanks to Christ laying Himself for us so He too could do the impossible and break out of the rock of an empty tomb. As the candles shone brightly and the sun set into the horizon, I couldn't help but think about what a beautiful ride it had been. I was humbled in a way that words can't do justice to. It was beautiful. Absolutely beautiful.

A few days later, and after two weeks of being apart, I reached Rachel's apartment, the Promised Land full of milk and my hunny. When I arrived, Rachel folded herself into my outstretched arms and laid her head on my shoulder, and I passionately kissed her on the lips. That night, she gave me the feeling that people write novels about. We made our relationship official, boyfriend and girlfriend, with dreams of marriage in the future.

I had the girl. I had the family. And most importantly, I had found the Christ-centered relationship that I had always dreamed about.

Without valleys, we can never reach the peaks.

CHURCH 52:
THERE'S NO PLACE LIKE CHURCH
THE "ONE TRUE CHURCH" • CENTRAL WISCONSIN

I was born and raised as an ultra-traditional Lutheran, which basically meant I spent my formative years seeing things in black and white. It was all good versus evil, heaven versus hell. There was no in-between gray area. As a result, people fit into one of two camps: right or wrong.

This wasn't taught directly; it was just something I picked up from my parents and pastors during my cable-deprived childhood. Fortunately, since I went to—as my pastor liked to call it—the "One True Church," I was spoon-fed the idea that all I needed to do was "Just *believe!*" while wiggling my little spirit fingers like a member of the Lullaby League. I was sure it'd only be a matter of time before Glinda the Good Witch would whisk me away to heaven in her magic bubble, where I'd tap dance through heaven's pearly gates with the Lollipop Guild in a pair of checkered lederhosen.

But then there was the rest of humanity, poor souls who'd see the grains of sand in their hourglasses run out. The Wicked Witch of the West would command her flying monkeys to pick off pretty much everyone else and their little dogs, too. Victims would be dropped into the fiery pits of hell, where there'd be lost of gnashing of teeth and cackling laughter. *Good thing I go to the right church*, I'd remind myself whenever such thoughts loomed and then go back to watching cartoons.

But as I grew older and started to notice the corruption within my church, thoughts started to swirl within my mind like the twister that carried Dorothy away from Kansas. A blown-in window knocked me out, and I awoke in the eye of the storm, with images of my past spinning around me. There was my senior pastor denying communion to upset visitors. There was the cover-up regarding our Tom Cruise-lookalike associate pastor who was married with four kids and who left amid a scandal, accused of hitting on a 13-year-old girl in my class. And then there was me, pedaling a bicycle that transformed into a broomstick—the very broomstick that had been used to beat me over the head with sermons filled with religious persecution of gays, lesbians, and female clergy.

All these rules, all this persecution, all the hypocrisy—it felt like organized religion had cast a spell over what Jesus was really all about. Believing that God exists and following what He stands for became two very different things. Why were we drawing lines in the sand to keep people out when we should have been crossing over them to reach others? Church was supposed to be the sanctuary that welcomed everyone, the shining Emerald City that showed us how to treat others.

If I'd only had the brain, the heart, the nerve, I could have sung a swell musical number to my pastor about how I still believed in God... I just didn't *feel* God.

Intellectually, I still identified as a Christian, but by showing up to church just for the sake of showing up, I felt like the Scarecrow: propped up with a pole up my back, my head being stuffed full of straw and emergency Bible verses. Inside, my heart felt Tin Man-hollow, made of little mettle like an empty kettle, full of rust and in need of some DW-40. I would be cowardly lyin' to say I had the courage to tell the church, "Put 'em up, put 'em up," and challenge the status quo. Instead, I stayed within the lines of the church's Yellow Brick Road, all because, because, because, because, BECAAAAAAAAAAAAUUUSSSSSEEEE! Because I didn't want anyone to question my belief. *Insert catchy run of fairy notes here*

I could have said something to the pastors in private, but I didn't want to play mental gymnastics with my soul and risk the embarrassment of others knowing that I'm a lesser Christian than the next guy. Faith was presented as a black-and-white, yes-or-no question: you either believed, or you didn't. How dare ye question the Great and Powerful God?

I had questions—questions that would have brought my faith into question if I had asked them. I was afraid that I'd have to work through some kind of Good Christian Daily To-Do checklist to find the root of my spiritual dryness, plagued by questions like: "Are you praying enough?" "Are you reading the Bible every day?" "Are you going to church every week?" "Are you repenting for all your sins?" "Are you doing this?" "Are you doing that?"

Oh, and then I'd be sure to hear the requisite "I'll be praying for you."

No thanks.

I knew I had to do something different with my spiritual life; I just didn't know what. But after 33 years of a church membership, I had become disillusioned. I was getting nothing out of worship, so why keep going?

The day I walked through those doors for the final time, I was dropping off my softball uniform.

A few weeks earlier, after playing for the church's softball team—the last semblance of Christian fellowship I had at the time—my associate pastor gave me an ultimatum regarding my lack of attendance: "No church, no ball," he said before turning his back and walking away. It was the kick in the rear that I needed to cut the strings.

The church secretary took my uniform and handed me a sign-off sheet. "I just need you to sign your name here, Mark," she said.

I stood there stunned.

Did she just call me Mark?

She stared at me in annoyance as she waited for an answer. "It's Mark, right?"

"No," I replied, "it's Dave. My name is Dave."

. . .

The "One True Church" in Central Wisconsin
October 11, 2015 – 10:30 A.M. Traditional Worship Service

G.K. Chesterton once wrote, "There are two ways of getting home. One of them is to stay there. The other is to walk round the whole world till we come back to the same place."

Now I know what he meant.

When my confidence in Christians dropped harder than a house on the Wicked Witch of the East, I gave up on the only church I'd ever known and became a wayfaring stranger. Maybe I'd find a new church in town, maybe I wouldn't. But the more I saw, the more I had to seek. It turned into a spiritual adventure across the country to see how different churches were inspiring others through the Word of God.

And now, for the 52nd church in the 52nd week, I was going back to where it all started.

The October leaves were changing, lighting up the trees with a splash of color. The fall landscape wasn't the only thing that had changed. I had changed. It occurred to me that maybe it wasn't the church that needed to change; maybe it had been me all along. The biggest question was, after all this, after all my travels and seeing a who's who of preachers and visiting spiritual go-to destinations, could I forgive the mighty fortress that was my old church?

I had to forgive. I needed to forgive. If I was following Christ's example, what kind of Christian would I be if I didn't forgive?

275

So I walked in, took my bulletin from an usher at the very spot where I'd served for years, and looked up at the altar where I used to light candles as an acolyte. Some of the people in attendance I knew; some I didn't.

The service opened as it always did—by ringing the church bell 40 times—and then the pastor welcomed the congregation to the "One True Church" where we served the "One True God." The organ blasted the hymns, I followed the regular sit-stand-sit-stand-sit-stand pattern, and the congregation intoned the weekly Lord's Prayer with the same rhythmic excitement of the Wicked Witch's guards singing "O-eee-ooh! Eooooh-ooh!"

Not much had changed.

Then, a pastor from another church came up to the pulpit to deliver the sermon. I was familiar with him, as he'd preach two or three times a year whenever one of the pastors needed a vacation or to attend a conference. He started by rambling a bit about how we were approaching the end of the church year and there wasn't anything specific to celebrate in Christ's life. Eventually, he came to the topic of "Who is the Lord we worship?" and how he would compare the Holy Trinity to the gods of other religions, describing them as "false idols" and talking about them in oversimplified terms, using the Tin Man, the Cowardly Lion, and the Scarecrow for his lesson.

He pointed to the troubles of the heartless Tin Man, who was so rusted, he couldn't move until Dorothy squirted him with oil. Likewise, the heartless gods of other religions can do nothing for the people who worship them, as the idols require people to maintain them—to squirt them with oil—whereas God the Father is our creator and breathed life into us.

Then he moved on to the Cowardly Lion, who was worthless and helpless in his pursuit of becoming the King of the Forest. But Jesus is the King of Kings, the Lord of Lords, the Lion of Judah who rules in our hearts.

Finally, he said God is not like the Scarecrow—a bundle of hay in a melon patch that is sewn together and cannot speak. Instead, the Holy Spirit speaks to us, delivering God's messages.

He never related this to the false idols of other religions that he mentioned earlier, instead wrapping things up by proclaiming: "There is no comparison between the idols of this world and the Triune God. For the idols are breathless and heartless, they're helpless and hopeless, they're brainless and speechless. But our God is the breath-giver of life, our God is the helper of the helpless, our God is the ultimate teacher of spiritual truths of salvation."

I knew what was coming next. I had occasionally glanced at the Communion table throughout the sermon, where a white cloth covered the bread and wine that represent the body and blood of Christ. A feeling had been mounting. After seeing the church deny visiting believers in the past, I pictured Toto pulling back the curtains to expose the fraud pulling the levers behind-the-scenes, left with nothing but smoke, mirrors, and disappointment.

What am I doing here? I thought.

I picked up the friendship register in my pew, which is essentially a form used to track members' attendance and Communion habits, and looked at the two checkbox options next the lines where you'd fill in your name: 'Members' and 'Visitors.' I wanted to forgive, but I knew this wasn't where I was supposed to be anymore. I didn't belong to this exclusive club. I marked down 'Visitor.'

When it came time for the Sacrament to be distributed, I closed my eyes and tapped my mental ruby slippers together three times to convince myself, *There's no place like church, there's no place like church, there's no place like church*, as one by one, members trudged down the aisle in a line toward the Lord's table. An usher came to my pew and gave me the green light to go up, but I couldn't go up. I remained hunched in my seat, head bowed, and prayed. I wanted to know if my actions were right to even write about my old church. I wanted things to end happily and to be able to forgive the past.

And I realized that it wasn't the church I needed to forgive. I needed to forgive myself.

When I started using my brain, I found that Christ had been in my heart all along. I'd never lost Him. I just needed to take that one extra step to find the courage within myself to rediscover my faith. The Scarecrow, the Tin Man, and the Cowardly Lion already possessed what they sought. The paper diploma, the heart-shaped clock, medal of courage—they were all just material filler. The best gifts are the God-given talents we were already born with. Often, our limitations are of our own doing. We just have to learn it for ourselves.

In the end, Glinda the Good Witch tells Dorothy that she could have gone home at any time simply by clicking the heels of her ruby slippers, but she had to learn that for herself. At that, the Scarecrow asks Dorothy what exactly she learned. She replies, "Well... if I ever go looking for my heart's desire again, I won't look any farther than my own backyard, because if it isn't there, I never really lost it to begin with."

Anything truly important is worth overcoming obstacles to achieve. We go searching for things we think we want, but in the end, we all travel through some dark forests and discover something new within ourselves.

When I walked out of those church doors for the last time, I left the past behind. It was time to go home.

. . .

I had been planning the moment for the last two months.

When we first met at First Free Church, Rachel was looking for a Godly man who could love her and her little munchkins as his own. She wanted someone who could look beyond her past and lead her closer to Christ, a spiritual man who wasn't dating just for fun, but who was humble, honest, and could accept her coffee addiction. Love can be easy in the early romantic stages of a relationship, but she desired a man whose behavior and intentions would be loving in all kinds of circumstances. I was exactly what she was looking for, and she was exactly what I was looking for.

After *52 Churches in 52 Weeks* had ended, we continued our church dates at First Free Church, listening to Pastor Shane's bad jokes and motormouth sermons. It was everything I had ever wanted. I'd gotten a life—a rich one that I could never have ordered with an Amazon Prime membership—a life where I had the opportunity to date the Proverbs 31 woman I'd been searching for. Her children were a bonus. They were excited to have me in their lives, and I wanted to be in theirs. I was set: I had the perfect girl, the perfect family, and even the perfect church. I know it sounds cliché, but it was true. If I had never gone searching for my faith, I never would have intrigued her or attracted her. It was all only, purely, because of God.

When Christmas rolled around, I knew just what to get her. It was the first gift I'd ever considered giving to a girl, but never did. But Rachel was special. She might be The One. I wanted to keep Christ at the center of our relationship, as did she. She opened the box, revealing a sterling-silver necklace with a diamond-encrusted cross pendant. Wrapped around the cross was a 14-karat-gold heart.

"You're my happy ending," I whispered to her. "Like we said at the start, we'll keep things Christ-centered."

We kissed, my hands around her waist and our eyes locked together before we wished each other a good night. After all the rejection, the past relationship mistakes, and my trying to figure out who I really was in this world, everything had ended up coming together. I owed it all to God.

She never spoke to me again.

EPILOGUE:
52 WEEKS LATER

This is where the Happily Ever After was supposed to go.

After falling down the rabbit hole of spiritual self-discovery, I thought this lovely and rich tale about rediscovering my faith would lead to a fairytale ending—one that poured the literary sugar into a swirling teapot of True Love. It would inspire even raving Mad Hatters, March Hares, and Red Queens to believe that dreams really can come true when you put Christ first in your heart.

I was convinced that going great lengths to seek God—after all, He's gone great lengths for us—would solve all my personal puzzles and unanswerable riddles. Everything would magically fall in place so that I could become the best possible Christian man. Along the way, a lucky lady would come along, and Cupid's arrow would hit a bullseye in our hearts. We'd get married at a 53rd church—a church the size of Cinderella's Castle, where friends, family, and little animated forest creatures would witness our vows. Rachel would waltz down the aisle in a white gown with her kids as the flower girl and ring bearer. We'd say "I do" and seal our vows with a kiss so passionate, it would have made the Frog Prince blush. The scene would end with Tinker Bell setting off fireworks with her magic wand and us riding off in a horse-drawn pumpkin carriage, complete with a sign in back that read, "Just Married." Then we'd honeymoon in Never-Never Land, because what happens in Never-Never Land stays in Never-Never Land.

At the end of *52 Churches in 52 Weeks*, everything felt so real and so right. It was like stepping into a dream you've had for as long as you can remember and finding out that the dream is more real than your actual life. Having been God's faithful servant, I would now be rewarded.

But the script had some last-minute rewrites.

Three days after I gifted the cross necklace to the Christian girl of my dreams, she sent me a text: "How do you explain a heart that does not feel? I am not happy, I feel burdened, and my heart is not in this relationship. After many nights of praying, I'm at peace with knowing that I am content being a single mother of two beautiful children. I want nothing more in life than that right now... I hope to talk to you about this, but I can't mutter the words right now."

Remember when Humpty Dumpty sat on a wall? And then Humpty Dumpty had a great fall? And all the king's horses and all the king's men couldn't put Humpty Dumpty together again?

Now place Humpty Dumpty atop the Magic Beanstalk. Then blindside Humpty Dumpty by shoving him off the edge. Then watch Humpty Dumpty fall thousands upon thousands of feet and land egghead-first in the frying pan of the witch who tried to cook Hansel and Gretel. Now Humpty Dumpty is shell-shattered, yolk-splattered, insides-spilled, and broken into a million itty-bitty pieces. And now turn the burner on to max heat. Soon enough, Humpty Dumpty is scrambled and dished onto the plate of someone with an egg allergy. Disgusted, the diner scrapes Humpty Dumpty into the dirt, and all the king's horses and all the king's men couldn't tell who Humpty Dumpty was and trampled all over him without a second thought.

That's how it felt.

I had put all my eggs in one basket and was left broken and shattered, my guts spilling out, my heart cracking open, my words staining this paper.

Texting on eggshells, I messaged Rachel back, telling her to reach out when she was ready to talk. She just needs some time to clear her head, I rationalized. So I waited, refusing to believe what she had texted me, while the Hickory Dickory Dock in my head went tick-tock, tick-tock, tick-tock.

But Rachel never wanted to talk. She never reached out. I never saw her or the kids again. A few days later, pictures of her on vacation—a vacation we'd been planning together for months—popped up on my Facebook feed. She was already flirting in the comments with another guy. To every relative and friend who commented, she threw out "I love you"'s like she'd been hoarding one-cent Tootsie Rolls for too long and had to get rid of them a day before the expiration date. I came to the Grimm realization that she had moved on emotionally long ago. Now she was free! Liberated! The spell of our relationship was broken, and she could put whatever attraction she had for me to sleep. She was ready for the next Prince Charming to come along on the internet.

To use some fancy-schmancy theological terminology, it fucking sucked. After months of dating, the girl who had come into my world during the most life-changing, transcendent year of my life had gone from love, to like, to disdain, to disgust in almost no time flat. She hadn't even given me the courtesy of a phone call. I found myself once again picking up the broken pieces and trying to put myself back together again.

I didn't get it. From what all the celebrity pastors said about Christian dating, I was doing everything right. I was the perfect Christian boyfriend: kind, gentle, meek, humble, didn't rock the boat, treated her like a Disney princess, and kept Christ as the bookmark in our little storybook. I hadn't made any glaring mistakes, so why did the (what I thought was a) pure-hearted Beauty feel compelled to cut and run from me like some hideous Beast?

They say hindsight is 20/20, and in this case, that's certainly true. Looking back, even the Three Blind Mice could have seen the warning signs. I had stopped raising the bar and reverted back to who I was before, conforming to everything a good Christian man should be.

Rachel had been trying to subtly communicate her feelings about her dying attraction. She was never straightforward, instead wishing upon a star that I'd figure it out and be the knight in shining armor she'd originally seen me as. She threw out so many red flags, you could have mistaken them for Little Red Riding Hood's laundry. She began testing me, pulling back, forgetting dates, and I ignored what she was trying to communicate, never caring to translate the messages. I had adopted a Goldilocks philosophy: infatuated when the highs were too hot, content when the lows were too cold, and lying to myself that everything would be juuuuuuuuuuuuuuuuuuuust right.

Oh, grandmother, what big dreams I had.

All the better to see them fall apart, my dear.

Without answers and without closure, I tried following the breadcrumbs through the Magical Enchanted WTF Happened Forest, searching the very core of my being to understand why I was going through another breakup.

Breakups weren't anything new for me, but this one cut deep. Kids were involved—kids who looked up to me and believed that I might be, not just their stepdad, but their dad. I had failed Tony, I had failed Elle, and I had failed Rachel.

I'd thought things would be different with Rachel. When we first started dating, there were no intentions beyond just spending some time together. We started as friends, planting a magic bean in each other's lives, which grew with time. We tended our friendship, nourishing it with verbal sunshine, and it grew to be something more. Much more. Then that "something more" became too much. And that was The End. A person whom I thought I knew fully and completely had suddenly chopped down what we started, becoming another footnote in my life's storybook.

I wanted this tale to be a blessing for others. How could I do that when I couldn't even inspire my own girlfriend to stick around?

Three months passed. Even though things hadn't worked out, I wanted to wish her the best. Plus, I still needed to pick up my belongings from her place. I texted her and asked if I could come by to retrieve the items and say goodbye properly. She replied that everything would be ready.

When I arrived, the lights were off and no one was home. I looked up at her second-floor apartment window like it was Rapunzel's tower, and she wouldn't let down her golden hair. My stuff sat in plastic bags on her doormat, treated with the same reverence you reserve for your weekly garbage collector. "Thank You! Thank You! Thank You For Your Patronage," the print on the grocery bags said. It was the closest thing to a goodbye that she was going to give.

When I got home, my mind in a heated argument with my heart about how I felt about her, I unpacked my stuff. At the bottom of the pile was the cross necklace. It was the final nail in the coffin—or, more fittingly—the final nail in the cross.

It's humbling to know that you can devote an entire year of your life to spiritual transformation—sincerely putting the desire to have a renewed relationship with Christ into action—and yet, after praying, living, writing, and breathing His essence into every fiber of your being, someone on the same side of the Christian fence can look at your worth, think "Meh," and discard you like a piece of trash.

That night, a part of me died.

. . .

The next day, I was still trying to Rumpelstiltskin the heartbreak, still trying to spin straw into gold. This wasn't going to be the happy ending I wanted, but I knew it was the ending that needed to happen. Weaknesses are revealed through heartbreak, and I knew the breakup would be a blessing that would help me discover the man I must become for the girl that will show me why all the others had failed. Maybe she's reading this right now. All I know is that as much as I wish I had met her earlier, the timing wouldn't have been right. I needed to go through all this. I needed to be humbled. I wouldn't have been the right person for her, and she wouldn't have been the right person for me. We both needed to go through the ups and downs, turns and spins, bumps and bruises before we could become two totally imperfect people road-tripping through life together while sorting out our own histories, mistakes, and issues.

That morning, I just needed to drive, to clear my head, to get away from it all. I needed to be able to tell the forest from the trees. And then, I came across an actual forest with trees. An exit sign promoting the Cross in the Woods appeared. I didn't think anything of it and drove right on past it, but something inside kept telling me that I had to go back. After all, some of my most memorable church visits were completely spontaneous.

When I arrived, fresh powdered snow decorated the pines, the sky was clear, and the morning sun played peek-a-boo with the handful of visible clouds. No one else was there. It was just the cross and me. It was peaceful. Silent. Still. Scripture wasn't just written in the Bible that day; it was all around me, in the trees, the air, everything. I was living it, breathing it, seeing it.

I realized that I had been trying so hard to mix my own fairytale with Christianity that I had misplaced what Scripture is all about: finding yourself in Christ.

During that drive, I was listening to a Tim Keller sermon. At the end, he referenced a poem written by George Herbert in 1633 called "The Temple." The best lines come from the middle: "O all ye who passe by, behold and see; Man stole the fruit, but I must climbe the tree; The tree of life to all, but onely me."

Maybe it was poetic: the Fall of Man began at a tree, and it ultimately came to an end on a tree. Everything in the Biblical narrative—from Genesis, to the prophets, to the gospels, to the epistles—leads to it. In every Christian church I visited, I saw it. Even in the final remnants of my failed relationship, it was there: the cross. The only thing that tied all of my personal experiences on this whole spiritual adventure together was the cross.

Any religion I encountered during my quest that was devoid of the symbol felt fraudulent to me. The cross gave me purpose, strength, hope, and both earthly and eternal life. Most see the cross as just being about Christ dying to atone for our sins or embodying God's love for mankind. That's certainly true, but it only scratches the surface. It's a symbol that overflows with richness, beauty, and amazement.

Historically, the cross was a devilish device designed to cause excruciating torture, perpetual agony, and public shame to terrorize its witnesses into not perpetrating sin. It represented suffering in its cruelest form. And yet, that's also where the cross gets its power. Suffering and loss are a part of life. We can flog our minds with 40 lashes and shoulder burdens in our own personal Calvary. We can pray and pray and pray and still fail and fail and fail. After awhile, we can feel forsaken to the point of wanting to stay trapped in that empty tomb.

But nothing is over until you say it's over. You can't grow if you don't lose. Christ's story is one in which He planted His spirit like a seed and it grew. Sure, it wasn't the tale of victory that most had envisioned. His followers had thought Christ would bring glory and material victory.

Instead, it turned into a tragedy of failure, defeat, and embarrassment. The crucifixion represented the humiliating loss of Jesus, but ultimately, His death would completely transfigure the cross to represent something new, something more: a new beginning full of unimaginable grace, repentance, and the power to bring us closer to Him. Being one with Christ, we don't have the power to shush storms, originate the game of Simon Says by commanding Simon Peter to walk on water, or cure blindness with supernatural spit mixed with mud, but we can be resurrected in a frail, yet perhaps more lasting and real form. Through Christ's example, we can break free from our mental tombs, cross that line in the sand, and have a second chance.

The Christian life is one of death and resurrection. When a part of you dies, you can rise to live again. We can take what Jesus was all about, ascend to greater heights, and aspire to be a blessing to others. Do more. Share more. Create more. Give more. Be more. When we do that, we let His message breathe into our own personal spirits so that they can become lights that will tear through the darkness and brighten the world.

A WORD FROM THE AUTHOR

Thank you for reading *52 Churches in 52 Weeks*. I hope you enjoyed the book, and more importantly, that you found some kind of spiritual nugget that will enhance your walk with Christ. If you enjoyed the story, I hope you'll consider leaving a review on Amazon or Goodreads. Reviews, good or bad, play a big part for a new writer's career. I would be extremely thankful and appreciative if you'd consider writing one for me.

Building relationships with readers has been one of the most rewarding experiences that has come with writing. Feel free to message me at the "52 Churches in 52 Weeks" Facebook page, or feel free to leave a comment on my YouTube page, "52 Churches in 52 Weeks • David Boice." I've posted numerous videos detailing church visits, church takeaways, and must see churches. You can also follow me on any of the social media links below.

Until then, thank you for reading!

David Boice
YouTube: 52 Churches in 52 Weeks • David Boice
Facebook: 52 Churches in 52 Weeks
Medium: 52 Churches in 52 Weeks / @Wayfaring_Stranger
Instagram: daveboice
Twitter: @52_Churches

ACKNOWLEDGMENTS

All glory to God for what He has showed throughout this journey. Thanks to Dave Provolo for his help with cover design and Elisabeth Chretien as the copy editor. And lastly, I wouldn't have been able to complete the project without the fierce support and prayers of readers like you.

Made in United States
North Haven, CT
14 September 2024

57416637R00178